Unwind: 10 ways to manage stress and improve your wellbeing

Unwind: 10 Ways to Manage Your Stress &
Improve Your Wellbeing
Author: Robert Burns
Publisher: Allen & Unwin
Dist. by Independent Publishers Group
Publication Date: January 2004
257 pages, 5¼ x 8, paper
Paper, $14.95 (CAN $22.95) ISBN: 174114101X
Publicity contact: Sara Hoerdeman
(312) 337-0747; sara@ipgbook.com

UNWIND:
10 ways to manage stress and improve your wellbeing

2ND EDITION

Robert B. Burns PhD, FBPsS

ALLEN&UNWIN

First published in 1992

This edition first published in 2003

Allen & Unwin
83 Alexander Street
Crows Nest NSW 2065
Australia
Phone: (61 2) 8425 0100
Fax: (61 2) 9906 2218
Email: info@allenandunwin.com
Web: www.allenandunwin.com

National Library of Australia
Cataloguing-in-Publication entry:

Burns, Robert, 1939- .
   Unwind : 10 ways to manage stress and improve your
   wellbeing.

   Bibliography.
   ISBN 1 74114 101 X.

   1. Stress management. 2. Job stress. 3. Stress
   (Psychology). I. Burns, Robert, 1939- 10 skills for
   working with stress. II. Title.

Set in 11/12.5 pt Caslon 540 by Bookhouse, Sydney
Printed by Griffin Press, South Australia

10 9 8 7 6 5 4 3 2 1

Contents

Preface

The aim of this book is to help you learn how to cope with stress, primarily in the workplace but also in your personal life. The need to manage stress both at work and at home is vital if you are to achieve your goals and objectives, whether they be work related or more personal. As an employee, a self-employed person, an employer or home worker you will find the stress management skills taught in this book valuable for the betterment of your health and psychological wellbeing.

The approach taken in the book is participatory. As you read about a number of different stress management skills and techniques, you are asked to complete various activities. There are over 80 activities aimed at helping you achieve effective management of stress.

The 10 skills for managing stress offered in this book are:

1. **Understanding what stress is and how it affects you** By understanding the process and effects of stress you will be able to identify your major sources of stress, anticipate stressful periods and plan for them, and find your optimum stress levels in all areas of life. You can then be honest about what you can really cope with.

2. **Improving your decision making** Decision making skills can be greatly improved by learning to divide a problem into manageable components, and gathering sufficient information about the problem to put it into perspective. You will discover

your range of decision-making styles and learn which is most appropriate for a particular decision.

3. **Mastering the benefits of relaxation** There are a variety of simple and easy to master relaxation techniques that are very effective in reducing and managing stress.

4. **Maintaining good health** Eat a balanced diet, have regular meals and always begin the day with an adequate breakfast. Maintain your recommended weight, exercise appropriately and get sufficient sleep. Research has consistently demonstrated that the fitter you are the less likely you are to develop either physical or mental illnesses. If you are fit, you have more energy to confront daily problems and more resilience when things do not work out well.

5. **Enhancing your self-concept** An improved self-concept will help you feel more confident and able to cope.

6. **Being positive** By adopting a positive attitude, rather than allowing your life to be dominated by negative thoughts, you will find you can achieve more and no longer withdraw from or avoid situations which stress you.

7. **Building relationships** Having someone to turn to, talk to and even rely on, has been shown to be a most significant factor in helping people to minimise the occurrence and impact of stressors on their lives and health.

8. **Learning to communicate assertively** Develop the skills of asking for what you want, stating your preferences and saying 'no' to those who demand too much.

9. **Managing your time effectively** Determine your priorities, distinguish between what must be done and what it would be nice to do. Most of us end up doing too much too quickly and inefficiently. Training yourself to think in terms of objectives is a crucial skill. This does not just refer to major life decisions but also to all aspects of life. Until you know what is important for you, you will find it difficult to set objectives for yourself.

10. **Being prepared for future shock and even disaster** The changes that are bound to come in your lifestyle and career must be anticipated as global economic, political, techno-logical and social forces sweep the world. Added to this is the recent upsurge in natural and man-made disasters that impose trauma on innocent passers-by and on rescue/emergency service workers.

In addition to helping you learn the 10 skills of stress management, this book also reinforces the following key points about stress:

- Stress is a constant part of everyone's life
- Stress can be experienced both positively and negatively, as a source of both energy and discomfort
- Stress affects your health status
- Your perception of events plays a key role in determining their stressfulness
- You need to identify the sources of your stress
- You need to be able to recognise signals from your body and your behaviour which tell you that you are failing to manage your stress
- You need to change unhealthy reactions to stress
- You can help others to cope with stress.

Please note that the activities and stress management skills presented in this book have been written assuming that you will be working on them by yourself. However, they can easily be adapted for groups working with a leader and, where necessary, indications of the way in which they may be adapted to suit a group context have been provided. The activities and skills have been designed for the greatest possible relevance but if you find one or two that do not suit your particular needs, please skip them and read on. While this book will help most of you, a few readers may have such serious problems that they cannot cope alone. In such cases, professional help should be sought from a doctor or psychologist if physical and/or psychological health is deteriorating badly. There are also a number of private organisations which are there to help people cope with sudden crises and emergencies. Their phone numbers are usually prominently displayed in newspapers and Yellow Pages. Use them—they are there to help you.

I hope that this book will bring you great benefits, and help you to lead a happier, more productive life as you bring your stress under control.

R. Burns
Buderim, Queensland, 2003

Introduction

The key
sources of stress

What is stress?

The dashboard clock reads 8:55 am and you're trapped in traffic, miles from your office. Despite leaving earlier than usual, there is absolutely no chance you'll arrive on time for that important 9 am meeting, and in the afternoon you have to take a faulty electric kettle back to the shop where you bought it yesterday and argue for a replacement or your money back.

In addition to coping with the everyday annoyances of our busy lives, 50 per cent of us will experience a much more serious stressor—such as a car accident, being made redundant without warning, a home break-in or an act of personal violence. In all these instances, our brain snaps to attention, preparing the rest of the body for the potential consequences of the insult. Blood pressure climbs. The heart pumps more blood, chock-full of surging stress hormones. The so-called 'fight or flight' response has commenced. And while such compensatory mechanisms help us cope with an immediate crisis, doctors are discovering that longer term perturbations also occur in the brain and elsewhere throughout the body following a stressful and/or traumatic event. What's more, individuals may be significantly and inherently different in the ways they deal with stress, and may even be differentially vulnerable to its effects.

Stress is different things to different people. To a Olympic marathon runner it is the challenge of pushing physical resources to the limit. To the homeward-bound motorist it can be the hassles of heavy traffic and obnoxious exhaust fumes. To the student it can be exam pressure. To the employee it can be dealing with a boss who is never satisfied. To the line manager it is employees who don't seem to appreciate the requirement to meet targets. To the spouse it is juggling personal needs to meet the needs of the partner and other family members. The strident sound of 'heavy metal' music excites some but disturbs others. Crowding makes many people feel agitated, yet loneliness can be equally difficult to cope with. Individual perceptions and interpretations of events and situations strongly influence the ways we react to events and the stress they connote (see Skill 1, p. 37 and pp. 75–9).

ACTIVITY I.0

Take a piece of paper and write the word STRESS at the top. Now write down all the words and images that come to your mind as you think about this word.

Most people respond to the word 'stress' in negative ways. They see it as a destructive, debilitating force. Were your words mainly negative too?

Some stress is good for you

We tend to talk about stress as if it's all bad. It's not. Some stress is good for you, and even necessary. I have to get my stress response to a certain optimal level so I can perform in front of an audience when I give a talk. Otherwise, I may come across as lethargic and listless. The word *eustress* has been coined to describe positive stress. Eustress results from exhilarating experiences. It is the type of stress you are likely to experience when you inherit a large amount of money or receive an unexpected promotion or reward. Eustress is the stress of winning and achieving. But while some stress is good, too much is not good. Negative stress, of course, is *distress*. It is the stress of losing, failing, overworking, being criticised, not coping. Distress affects people in a negative, usually harmful manner. Unfortunately, we all experience distress from time to time. If you're too stressed, your performance falls off. The key is to learn to move yourself to that optimal peak point, so that you're not under-performing but you're also not so stressed that you're unable to perform (see Figure I.1). How much we're able to do—that is the challenge. Your goal should be to try to learn to control your stress to make it work for you for your advantage. We must always allow ourselves enough essential challenges to make life fulfilling and interesting—but an overload produces exhaustion and ill-health. Moderate amounts of stress or stimulation are necessary for healthy functioning.

There are many definitions of stress, but generally they focus on the fact that stress is a personally construed perception, made by an individual who sees himself or herself as unable to cope with a situation. Lazarus' (1966) definition is perhaps the best, when he states: 'Stress arises when individuals perceive that they cannot adequately cope with the demands being made on them or with threats to their well being.' Succinctly then, *stress is an imbalance between perceived demands and personal resources.* It is a natural, unavoidable and essential part of living and growing. We cannot avoid it even if we want to.

Figure I.1   Performance breaks down with increasing demand

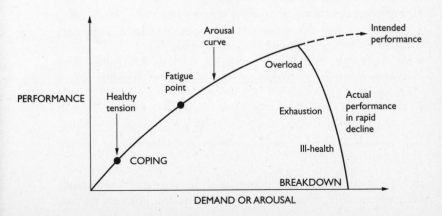

The different kinds of stress

Stress management can become complicated and confusing because there are different types or levels of stress—acute stress, episodic acute stress, and chronic stress—each with its own characteristics, symptoms, duration, and treatment approaches.

Acute stress

Acute stress is the most common form of stress. It stems from demands and pressures of the recent past and anticipated demands and pressures of the near future. Acute stress is thrilling and exciting in small doses, but too much is exhausting. A fast run down a challenging ski slope, for example, is exhilarating early in the day. That same ski run late in the day is taxing and wearing. Skiing beyond your limits can lead to falls and broken bones. Overdoing on short-term stress can lead to psychological distress, tension headaches, upset stomach and other symptoms. Fortunately, the symptoms of acute stress are recognised by most people. They're a laundry list of what has gone awry in our lives: the car accident that crumpled the car bumper, the loss of an important contract, a deadline that's almost on us, our child's occasional problem at school, and so on. Because it is short term, acute stress doesn't have enough time to do the extensive damage associated with long-term stress.

The most common symptoms of acute stress are:

- emotional distress, involving some combination of anger or irritability, anxiety, and depression;
- muscular problems, including tension headache, back pain, jaw pain, and the muscular tensions that lead to pulled muscles and tendon and ligament problems;
- stomach, gut and bowel problems, such as heartburn, acid stomach, flatulence, diarrhea, constipation and irritable bowel syndrome; and
- transient over-arousal, leading to elevation in blood pressure, rapid heartbeat, sweaty palms, heart palpitations, dizziness, migraine headaches, cold hands or feet, shortness of breath and chest pain.

Acute stress can crop up in anyone's life. It is highly treatable and manageable, often because the situation goes away, and stress management skills such as relaxation and positive thinking are quite effective for it.

Episodic acute stress

There are those, however, who suffer acute stress frequently, whose lives are so disordered that they are regularly in crisis. They're always in a rush, but always late. If something can go wrong, it does. They take on too much, have too many irons in the fire, and can't organise the plethora of self-inflicted demands and pressures clamouring for their attention. They seem perpetually in the clutches of acute stress.

It is common for people with acute stress reactions constantly to be over-aroused, short-tempered, irritable, anxious and tense. Often they describe themselves as having 'a lot of nervous energy'. Always in a hurry, they tend to be abrupt, and sometimes their irritability comes across as hostility. Interpersonal relationships deteriorate rapidly when others respond with real hostility. The workplace becomes a very stressful place for them. They are often the Type A individuals discussed later (page 62).

Another form of episodic acute stress comes from ceaseless worry. 'Worry-warts' see disaster around every corner, and pessimistically forecast catastrophe in every situation. The world is a dangerous, unrewarding, punitive place where something awful is always about to happen. These 'awfulisers' also tend to be over-aroused and tense, but are more anxious and depressed than angry and hostile. Their anxiety can extend into a panic state. The symptoms of episodic acute stress are the symptoms of extended over-arousal: persistent tension headaches, migraines, hypertension, chest pain and heart disease.

Chronic stress

Chronic stress is the grinding stress that wears people away, day after day, year after year. It destroys bodies, minds and lives. It wreaks havoc through long-term attrition. It's the stress of unrelieved poverty, of dysfunctional families, of being trapped in an unhappy marriage or in a despised job or career. It's the stress that the never-ending 'troubles' have brought to many people of Northern Ireland, the Middle East, Eastern Europe and the former Soviet Union. It is the stress of the refugee and the displaced person, who may not know where the next meal or shelter is coming from. Chronic stress comes when a person can never see a way out of a miserable situation. It's the stress of unrelenting demands and pressures for seemingly interminable periods of time. With no hope, the individual gives up searching for solutions. Chronic stress kills through suicide, violence, heart attack, stroke and, perhaps, even cancer. People wear down to a final, fatal breakdown. Because physical and mental resources are depleted through long-term attrition, symptoms of chronic stress are difficult to treat and may require extended medical as well as behavioural treatment and stress management.

Increasing stress levels in the twenty-first century

It is apparent that stress levels are rising, as measured in surveys of employees and the general public. Two reasons amongst others stand out. Firstly, as Alvin Toffler (1980) predicted, a combination of rapid economic, technological, political and social change, with an increasingly bewildering variety and choice in our lifestyles, organisations and institutions, produces the syndrome he called 'future shock'—a pathological condition that increasingly afflicts people who cannot cope in an age of escalating change. Things become more and more temporary, lifestyles and work patterns more diverse; the old stability has gone. Totally new concepts in science and technology reduce many of us to the status of naïve visitors in a world we understand less and less.

Secondly, allied with these changes are the global disasters that are being increasingly experienced not only first-hand, but also second-hand, by millions of people in vivid and realistic ways through modern satellite TV transmissions. The immediacy and tension of major floods, earthquakes, bushfires, 'legal' warfare and terrorist activities are 'in our faces' most days, even if we are many thousands of miles away. We experience, as witnesses, their terror, danger, damage and death, with consequent stress responses. In Skill 10 we will be discussing these modern sources of stress, particularly post traumatic stress syndrome, in more detail.

Although most of the activities in this book address issues of individual and interpersonal stress, others help to expand your awareness of the impact that global issues can have. One goal of this book is to demonstrate that passive acceptance of negative conditions is not a solution. Frequently, individuals and communities do have the ability to do something about threats posed by stressors in the environment, and to create a context of living in which people feel more at ease. In that way, the inevitable change to which many of us feel hostage can be a stimulus for growth and health, at work, in the home and in the community.

Stress at work

What are the causes of job stress?

Most of us have to work—we are not rich enough not to. We often have to work at jobs and in conditions that we would not choose if we had the choice. A range of reports and studies from around the world echo the same message—that stress from the work context is increasing, and forms the major source of stress for many people.

In a 1996 British Trades Union Council (TUC) survey of safety representatives, 68 per cent identified stress as one of the top five health and safety concerns of their work colleagues, a much higher rating than for the next most mentioned hazard, with the public sector having higher levels of stress than the private sector. Voluntary organisations, education and banking/finance had the highest stress ratings. The TUC survey identified 'new management techniques', such as quality circles and performance-related pay, as the main causes of stress (48 per cent). Other causes of stress identified by safety reps included bullying (35 per cent) and long hours (31 per cent). (Note: percentages do not total 100 per cent because more than one answer could be given.) A repeat of the survey in 2000 again showed stress to be the major cause for concern for 66 per cent of safety reps, with workloads and cuts in staff the main causes of stress.

A MORI poll (2001) indicated that 60 per cent of UK working adults had suffered from stress at work over the last three years, and over 40 per cent said the stress level had worsened; another UK survey (VAR International) for National Stress Awareness Day, November 2001, revealed 53 per cent of people were suffering from stress, with long hours and deadlines cited as major factors. Fifty seven per cent of those said stress had increased over last 12 months. Work in a 24-hour society, workers felt, was reducing job satisfaction and their productivity. The Bristol Stress and Health at Work Study (Health and Safety Executive, 2000) revealed that 20 per cent of workers (over 5 million nationally) reported feeling extremely stressed at work, with overwork and lack of managerial support the culprits. A poll of National Health Service nurses in 1999 found that 90 per cent felt their stress levels had increased due to workload.

In a survey by the national Tertiary Education Union, in July 2002, 8000 academics in Australia at 17 universities rated stress as their major problem. Half the academics working in Australia's universities are apparently at risk of psychological illness from unhealthy stress levels, with higher than average levels of stress-related medical conditions such as migraine, hypertension and coronary heart disease. An Australian Government survey in 1995 found 50 per cent of employees experienced increased stress in their jobs, while 26 per cent had taken time off the previous year for stress reasons.

Job stress is one of the most common work-related problems in the EU, as the 1996 European Survey of Working Conditions showed, with 28 per cent of workers claiming stress from work. A national survey of German employees between 1998 and 1999 showed nearly half complained of increasing stress at work. In Japan, 63 per cent claimed stress at work in 1997, according to the National Institute of Industrial Health Japan.

The main messages are clear. Occupational stress is a major health concern for working people around the world—across all sectors and in all sizes of enterprise, accruing huge costs to business and to employees, sick leave payments and lost earnings. New management techniques, bullying and long hours are reported as the major factors causing people concern about stress. The too-lean organisation may be becoming the too-mean organisation. No wonder the EU choose Work Related Stress as the theme for the European Week for Safety and Health at Work 2002.

Nearly everyone agrees that job stress results from the interaction of the worker and the conditions of work. Views differ, however, on the importance of worker characteristics versus working conditions as the primary cause of job stress. These differing viewpoints are important because they suggest two possible ways to reduce stress at work. Many psychologists believe that differences in individual characteristics such as personality, assertiveness skills, decision-making skills and coping style are most important in predicting whether certain job conditions will result in stress. In other words, what is stressful for one person may not be a problem for someone else. This viewpoint leads to prevention strategies that focus on workers and ways to help them cope with demanding job conditions. Although the importance of individual differences cannot be ignored, the other approach suggests that certain working conditions are stressful to most people. Evidence for this point of view argues for a greater emphasis on working conditions as the key source of job stress, and for job redesign and organisational management change as primary prevention strategies. Figure I.2 summarises the interaction of these two major sources of stress, work conditions and individual predispositions, and some of the effects wrought in terms of symptoms of individual ill-health.

Poor physical working conditions

Stress at work can be made worse by inadequate physical working conditions such as excessive noise or heat, air pollution, cramped working space or inadequate lighting. Taking nuclear power plant operators as an example, it is known that the design of the control room itself is important in terms of worker stress, and that control room designs need to be updated, requiring more sophisticated ergonomic designs. Furthermore, one study (Otway and Misenta, 1980) highlighted an important stress factor—in the accident that occurred at a nuclear power station on Three Mile Island in the USA—as being the distraction caused by excessive emergency alarms.

In a study carried out by Kelly and Cooper (1981) on the stressors associated with casting in a steel manufacturing plant, poor physical working conditions were found to be a major stressor. Many of the stressors were concentrated in the physical aspects of noise, fumes and, to a lesser extent, heat, plus the social and psychological consequences of isolation and interpersonal tension.

A further possible source of stress was seen to be in the lack of job satisfaction, particularly arising from the stressors above, and partially also in the nature of casting liquid steel in a continuous process lasting some 70 minutes. For 75 per cent of this time the casters were exposed to—and, by the nature of their task, unable to move away from—very high levels of noise (up

Figure 1.2 A model of stress at work

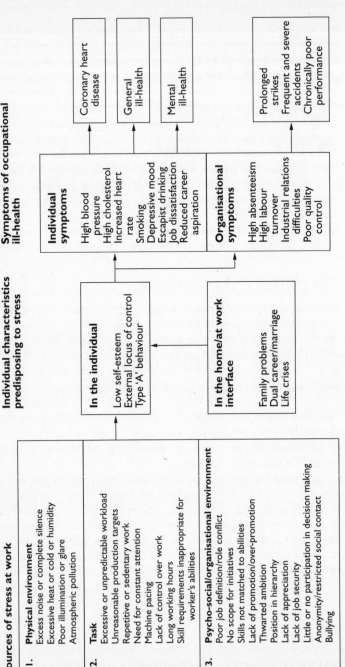

Sources of stress at work

1. Physical environment
Excess noise or complete silence
Excessive heat or cold or humidity
Poor illumination or glare
Atmospheric pollution

2. Task
Excessive or unpredictable workload
Unreasonable production targets
Repetitive or sedentary work
Need for constant attention
Machine pacing
Lack of control over work
Long working hours
Skill requirements inappropriate for worker's abilities

3. Psycho-social/organisational environment
Poor job definition/role conflict
No scope for initiatives
Skills not matched to abilities
Lack of promotion/over-promotion
Thwarted ambition
Position in hierarchy
Lack of appreciation
Lack of job security
Little or no participation in decision making
Anonymity/restricted social contact
Bullying

Individual characteristics predisposing to stress

In the individual
Low self-esteem
External locus of control
Type 'A' behaviour

In the home/at work interface
Family problems
Dual career/marriage
Life crises

Symptoms of occupational ill-health

Individual symptoms
High blood pressure
High cholesterol
Increased heart rate
Smoking
Depressive mood
Escapist drinking
Job dissatisfaction
Reduced career aspiration

Organisational symptoms
High absenteeism
High labour turnover
Industrial relations difficulties
Poor quality control

Coronary heart disease

General ill-health

Mental ill-health

Prolonged strikes
Frequent and severe accidents
Chronically poor performance

SOURCE: Based on C. Cooper, 'Job Distress', *Bull. Br. Psych.*, 1986, 39, pp. 325–31.

to 110 decibels for much of the time), as well as periodic and unpleasant air pollution caused by the activities of other workers and machines close by.

These conditions necessitated the wearing of ear protection in the form of earmuffs or cotton wool swabs, which isolated the wearers from those around them.

Shift work

Numerous occupational studies have found that shift work is a common occupational stressor, affecting blood temperature, metabolic rate, blood sugar levels, mental efficiency and work motivation, which may ultimately result in stress-related disease.

A study involving air traffic controllers (Kelly and Cooper, 1973), for example, found four times more hypertension, as well as more diabetes and peptic ulcers, among these subjects than in a control group of pilots. Although these studies identified other job stressors as also playing a part, shift work was isolated as a significant problem.

Shift work may be associated with increased ill-health, at least partly because it can disrupt circadian (daily) rhythms as well as normal social behaviour.

Changes in the work environment

Changes in the work environment (e.g. to a different line of work or a different level of responsibility) have been associated with significantly higher rates of heart attack in the year following such changes.

Increased health problems have also been shown to arise from the extremes of job demand—for example, those who are engaged in boring, repetitive work suffer more frequently from depression, sleep difficulties and stomach disorders. Correspondingly, individuals judged to hold responsible jobs with high levels of demand and pressure are also found to have a significantly higher risk of certain physical disorders, including high blood pressure and ulcers.

Unemployment

Unemployment is also associated with increased levels of physical and psychological complaints. This is a major life change involving the loss of self-esteem, and serves to illustrate that work meets not only the financial, but also the social and psychological, needs of the individual.

Failure to meet these needs, whether through unsatisfactory or non-existent employment, can carry a high personal cost in terms of mental and physical well-being.

Job overload

Work overload can be either quantitative (i.e. having too much to do) or qualitative (i.e. the work being too difficult), and certain behavioural malfunctions have been associated with job overload. For example, in a study of air traffic controllers, by Crump et al (1981), it was found that one of the primary short-term but uncontrollable stressors was 'being overloaded'.

In an investigation of stress among British police officers (Cooper et al, 1982), work overload was found to be a major stressor among the lower ranks, particularly police sergeants. Sergeants who scored high on depression tended to be older operational officers, who believed that they were overloaded, and who saw a number of bureaucratic and outside obstacles as standing in the way of effective police functioning. They complained about the long hours and heavy workload, as well as the increased paperwork, lack of resources and the failure of the courts to prosecute offenders.

Job underload

Job underload, associated with repetitive, routine, boring and understimulating work, has been linked with ill-health. Moreover, in certain jobs, such as those of airline pilots and air traffic controllers, periods of boredom have to be accepted, along with the possibility that there may be a sudden disruption due to an emergency situation. This can give a sudden jolt to the physical and mental state of the employee, and have a subsequent detrimental effect on health. Furthermore, boredom and lack of interest in the job may reduce the effectiveness of the employee's response to emergency situations.

Physical danger

There are certain occupations that are regarded as being high risk in terms of potential danger—for example, police, mine-workers, airline pilots, soldiers and fire-fighters. However, stress induced by the uncertainty of physically dangerous events is often substantially relieved if the employee feels adequately trained and equipped to cope with emergency situations.

Poor person/environment fit

Some work environments have physical conditions that place the employee out of their comfort zone. Temperature, noise, air pollution, humidity, chemicals harmful to the skin and fatiguing positions for performing work can all contribute to a poor person/environment fit (Russell, 1978).

The comfort zone for humans in temperature is rather narrow—from about 15–28 degrees Celsius. Similarly, absolute silence can be as deafening as high noise levels. Of course, employers under health and safety laws must ensure that their workers use safety and other equipment such as ear muffs, hard hats and outside clothing, and are provided with a safe environment in which to work. But even wearing safety items can be uncomfortable.

The use of word-processors has brought repetitive strain injury to the fore in the last decade. Improved ergonomic office furniture has been introduced to combat this. The introduction of more technology into the workplace has led to machine-paced work where the assembly line worker has to keep pace with a machine over which they have little control on repetitive, monotonous work. This imposes high muscular workloads and/or high sensory demands.

Job satisfaction

Job satisfaction may stem from a variety of sources. Job status, task variety, a sense of accomplishment, challenge, autonomy, supportive colleagues/employers and opportunities for career development are among the major sources of job satisfaction.

Money is not always a major source of job satisfaction. White-collar workers tend to stress the achievement, autonomy, career prospects and status elements more than blue-collar workers.

Stress and burnout often appear as a progressive loss of energy, purpose and concern for the job, as there is a lack of pay-off in terms of accomplishment, recognition or appreciation. Workers with low job satisfaction tend to report more physical health problems and greater levels of stress (O'Brien and Kebanoff, 1978).

Role ambiguity and conflict

These can result in stress-related illnesses, particularly for administrative, clerical, managerial and professional people where conflicting or uncertain job expectations, too much responsibility, too many 'hats to wear', are common. Such issues do not often impact on more manual or lower grade jobs where routine activities are involved.

The relationship between role conflict/ambiguity and components of job satisfaction tends to be strong. However, personality differences are important in determining how an individual reacts to role conflict—for example, greater job-related tension occurs in introverts than in extroverts, and rigid people show greater job-related tension under conditions of conflict than do flexible individuals.

The degree to which an individual is responsible for people and their safety also appears to be a significant occupational stressor. For example, this type of responsibility is a potential stressor for police, although not to the extent that it is for air traffic controllers. This has been shown in a study of occupational stress in air traffic controllers, which isolated responsibility for people's safety and lives as a major long-term stressor (Crump et al, 1981).

The problems that role conflicts can generate have been amply demonstrated by Cooper, Mallinger and Kahn (1978) in their investigation into dentists. It was found that the factors that led to abnormally high blood pressure levels amongst dentists were related to the role of the dentist—that dentists consider themselves to be 'inflictors of pain' rather than 'healers'; that they have to carry out non-clinical tasks such as administrative duties, and building and sustaining a practice; and that their professional role interferes with their personal life, primarily in terms of time commitments.

Career 'blockages'

The next group of work-related stressors is related to career development, which has been found to be a fundamental stressor at work. Stressors tend to be found in the areas of job security and thwarted ambition.

Erickson, Fugh and Gunderson (1972), studying a large sample of Navy employees, found that an individual's military effectiveness tended to be directly related to the degree of job advancement (including pay advancement) and suitable status, and that psychiatric problems were frequently the result of inadequacies in these areas. However, in terms of pay, Otway and Misenta (1980) have suggested that large increases in workers' pay would not necessarily mean simultaneous increases in job satisfaction, and might even result in personnel remaining in jobs that no longer give them satisfaction.

Career development blockages have been found to be most notable among female managers, according to a study by Davidson and Cooper (1983). In this investigation, the authors collected data from over 700 female managers and 250 male managers at all levels of the organisational hierarchy and from among several hundred companies. It was found that women suffered significantly more than men across a wide range of organisational stressors, but that the most damaging to their health and job satisfaction were the ones associated with career development and allied stressors (e.g. sex discrimination in promotion, inadequate training, male colleagues treated more favourably and not enough delegation to women).

Poor relationships at work

Relationships at work—which includes the nature of those relationships as well as social support from colleagues, the boss and subordinates—have also been related to job stress.

Poor relationships with other members of an organisation may be caused by an individual's role ambiguity in the organisation, which in turn may produce psychological strain in the form of low job satisfaction. Moreover, it has been found that strong social support from peers relieves job strain, and also serves to reduce the effects of job stress on cortisone levels, blood pressure, glucose levels and the number of cigarettes smoked.

Where male executives had problems, these were generally associated with relationships, as Cooper and Melhuish (1980) discovered in their study of 196 very senior male executives. It was found that a male executive's predisposition (e.g. outgoing, tough-minded, etc.) and his relationships at work tended to be central to his increased risk of high blood pressure. Top male executives were particularly vulnerable to the stresses of poor relationships with subordinates and colleagues, to lack of personal support at home and work, and to the conflicts between their own values and those of the organisation.

Organisational structure and climate

Another potential source of stress is related to organisational structure and climate, which includes such factors as office politics, lack of effective consultation, lack of participation in decision-making processes, poor communication and lack of family-friendly policies. Many studies reveal that greater participation leads to higher productivity, improved performance, lower staff turnover, and lower levels of physical and psychological ill health such as escapist drinking, heavy smoking, absenteeism— all symptoms of developing stress.

High demand for performance

Unrealistic expectations, especially in this time of corporate reorganisations which sometimes put unhealthy and unreasonable pressures on the employee, can be a tremendous source of stress and suffering. Increased workload, extremely long work hours and intense pressure to perform at peak levels all the time for the same pay, can actually leave employees physically and emotionally drained. Excessive travel and too much time away from family also contribute to employees' stressors. A recent study in Britain by the Department of Trade and Industry found that 1 in 6 workers worked over 60 hours per week compared to 1 in 8 two years ago, and 1 in 8 women now work more than 60 hours each week, double that of two years ago.

Technology

The expansion of technology—computers, pagers, cell phones, fax machines and the Internet—has resulted in heightened expectations for productivity, speed and efficiency, and increasing pressure on the individual worker to constantly operate at peak performance levels. There is also the constant pressure to keep up with technological breakthroughs and improvisations, forcing employees to learn new software all the time.

Job stress and women

Women suffer from mental and physical harassment in the workplace. Apart from the common job stress, sexual harassment in the workplace has been a major source of worry for women. This creates a very hostile work environment, replete with essentially offensive or intimidating behaviour, often consisting of unwelcome verbal or physical conduct, all a constant source of tension. Subtle discriminations in the workplace, family pressure and societal demands add to these stress factors.

Dual careers

Changes in the role of women in the workforce, in the structuring of the workforce towards more part-time work, combined with economic conditions that require two incomes, mean that many households have to cope with dual careers. The problems that this creates can be enormous, influencing the enaction of essential household roles, the quality of marital relationships, and the mental and physical health of every family member. In the UK, a survey of 5000 working mothers in June 2001 revealed that 93 per cent frequently felt under stress through trying to balance work with raising a family. Both members of a partnership may find promotional prospects depend on availability and willingness to transfer to other parts of the country or even abroad.

No longer can we behave as if there was no connection between home and work, that workers have no families. There is emerging consensus that conditions of work impact on family relationships beyond the effects of wages and benefits. This is true for both men and women. It is feasible to ask an employer to be flexible as to which hours are worked while keeping to the total per week. If they say it is too difficult, show them how you could get around the barriers and still do the job you are being paid for. Given the flexibility offered by modern computer technology, quite a number of jobs could be worked more flexibly than they are.

But—in trying to overcome the problems associated with dual careers:

- Don't try to emulate what others do, but find the right balance for you and your family.
- Take up time management.
- Don't feel guilty. Both employers and families have insatiable appetites which you will never satisfy.
- Make sure you support each other and have quality time together.
- Learn to be positive about the successful parts of your lives.
- Keep a sense of proportion. It is not the end of the world if the children are late for school on the rare occasion, or you have to ask for another day in which to finish a report.
- Accept you will never have a perfect solution to the work–life dilemma. Children's needs change as they grow older, as do those of ageing parents, so there may be requirements to change the balance over the years.

Bullying

Bullying is unfortunately endemic in the workplace. A study by Manchester University Institute of Science and Technology in 2000 found that 1 in 6 respondents had been bullied at work in the previous six months. The European Survey of Working Conditions (2000) found 9 per cent of workers subject to bullying that year. A British TUC survey in 2000 revealed that bullying was a significant source of stress, ranking second just behind 'long hours'. It was particularly prevalent in the public service, education, health and voluntary sectors.

If there was any industry safe from bullies, one would imagine it would be in the health, education and voluntary sectors, but unfortunately this is not the case. Bullying is rampant in these service sectors, even though they are fields where their pro-social missions would apply to employees as well. Teachers, helpers and healers should, one would hope, be the least likely to abuse their power over their subordinates, for such behviour flies in the face of the motivations which would have led them into these professions in the first place.

Other types of workplace where bullying is more likely to occur are those with an extremely competitive environment, where there is a fear of redundancy or a fear for one's position. Some organisations may inadvertently encourage a culture of promotion through putting colleagues down. An authoritarian style of management, organisational change and excessive workloads are also contributory factors. We must distinguish between unreasonable deadlines, excessive workloads and other conditions that make the job unbearable, and bullying that is primarily person-related such as insults, gossip, rumour, humiliation, offensive/suggestive comments, ganging up and exclusion. Bullying can in part be institutionalised where authoritarian management practices hold sway, in that research studies reveal that much bullying is by a superior. Some managers are under so much stress themselves that they use bullying as a management tool.

Training managers in conflict management seems to be necessary to provide support and guidance for both victims and perpetrators, as is a critical look at what kind of leadership styles are nurtured within an organisation.

Personal or family problems

Problems outside work can contribute to stress, such as relationship problems, financial problems, bereavement, divorce, moving house, long distance commuting, schooling problems, and problems caused by both partners working. Such non-work stress simply adds to work stress, as employees tend to carry their worries and anxieties to the workplace. When a person is in a depressed mood, unfocused attention or lack of motivation affects their ability to carry out job responsibilities.

It must be noted that these work-related stressors do not inevitably cause stress. Some people cope adequately with adverse or demanding environments. However, a significant higher incidence of physical and psychological ill-health associated with certain occupations must be seen as a reflection of the reaction of many individuals to negative aspects of their work environments. Activity I.1. asks you to examine how you are coping in your work environment.

ACTIVITY 1.1

Work activity analysis questionnaire

Complete this questionnaire as it relates to your daily work.

For each activity listed below, indicate the frequency of occurrence by placing an X in the appropriate box. It is important to respond candidly to each question, in order to obtain an accurate profile of yourself.

	Rarely or never	Occasion-ally	Fairly often	Usually, if not always
Planning				
1. I set myself daily goals/ objectives.	☐	☐	☐	☐
2. My objective includes target times and deadlines.	☐	☐	☐	☐
3. I rank these according to their importance.	☐	☐	☐	☐
4. I have to drop what I'm doing to deal with other problems.	☐	☐	☐	☐
5. I measure my progress against my objectives.	☐	☐	☐	☐
6. I deal with my most challenging activities during my prime time (when I feel my best).	☐	☐	☐	☐
7. I take work home with me in the evenings/at weekends.	☐	☐	☐	☐
8. Business trips cause me to spend time waiting for planes, people, etc.	☐	☐	☐	☐
9. Actual travelling time interrupts my normal work routine.	☐	☐	☐	☐
10. I get to work on time.	☐	☐	☐	☐
11. I leave work late.	☐	☐	☐	☐

	Rarely or never	Occasion -ally	Fairly often	Usually, if not always

Organising

12. I can locate things (filed correspondence, stationery, etc.) easily. ☐ ☐ ☐ ☐

13. I discard outdated documents, letters and memos. ☐ ☐ ☐ ☐

14. I report to more than one superior. ☐ ☐ ☐ ☐

15. I know the extent of my responsibility and authority. ☐ ☐ ☐ ☐

16. I am aware of the extent of my subordinates' responsibility and authority. ☐ ☐ ☐ ☐

17. My job involves much paperwork and red tape. ☐ ☐ ☐ ☐

18. I have all the equipment/ facilities I need. ☐ ☐ ☐ ☐

Staffing

19. I operate with a full staff complement. ☐ ☐ ☐ ☐

20. Other staff bother me with personal problems. ☐ ☐ ☐ ☐

21. Other staff are over- dependent on me. ☐ ☐ ☐ ☐

Directing

22. I am involved with routine deals. ☐ ☐ ☐ ☐

23. I perform the 'hands-on' aspects of my job. ☐ ☐ ☐ ☐

24. My colleagues take their work seriously. ☐ ☐ ☐ ☐

25. My subordinates/colleagues work well as a team/with each other. ☐ ☐ ☐ ☐

26. I am a perfectionist. ☐ ☐ ☐ ☐

	Rarely or never	Occasion-ally	Fairly often	Usually, if not always
27. I tolerate mistakes.	☐	☐	☐	☐
28. I make all the decisions in my work unit.	☐	☐	☐	☐

Controlling

	Rarely or never	Occasion-ally	Fairly often	Usually, if not always
29. The telephone interrupts my train of thought.	☐	☐	☐	☐
30. I have drop-in visitors at my desk.	☐	☐	☐	☐
31. I say 'no' to the requests/ invitations of others.	☐	☐	☐	☐
32. Information/documentation from others is often incomplete/delayed.	☐	☐	☐	☐
33. I deal with unpleasant and less interesting tasks firsts.	☐	☐	☐	☐
34. Some tasks that my subordinates tackle are left unfinished.	☐	☐	☐	☐
35. My subordinates' work meets my expectations.	☐	☐	☐	☐
36. My subordinates have their work done on time.	☐	☐	☐	☐
37. My work unit contains elements that are visually distracting.	☐	☐	☐	☐
38. My work unit's noise level is distracting.	☐	☐	☐	☐
39. People are available for discussion when needed.	☐	☐	☐	☐
40. I miss out on important announcements.	☐	☐	☐	☐
41. I try to know about everything that happens in my work unit.	☐	☐	☐	☐

	Rarely or never	Occasion-ally	Fairly often	Usually, if not always

Decision making

42. I apply for extensions on deadlines. ☐ ☐ ☐ ☐

43. I try to have all the facts before making a decision. ☐ ☐ ☐ ☐

44. I avoid snap decisions. ☐ ☐ ☐ ☐

Communicating

45. I attend meetings. ☐ ☐ ☐ ☐

46. I need to repeat myself when instructing others. ☐ ☐ ☐ ☐

47. I summarise the main points of an instruction. ☐ ☐ ☐ ☐

48. I find myself drawn into conversations with others. ☐ ☐ ☐ ☐

29. I write memos. ☐ ☐ ☐ ☐

50. When listening to lengthy presentations, I lose concentration. ☐ ☐ ☐ ☐

Reading

51. I read all the literature I receive (e.g. articles, letters, memos, circulars). ☐ ☐ ☐ ☐

52. I benefit from reading this material. ☐ ☐ ☐ ☐

Scoring the activity analysis questionnaire

For each question, on the table below, circle the score in the column you checked on the questionnaire. Then total the numbers you have circled, and record your subtotals. Finally, add up the subtotals to obtain your grand total.

	Rarely or never	Occasion-ally	Fairly often	Usually, if not always
Planning				
1.	0	1	2	3

		Rarely or never	Occasion -ally	Fairly often	Usually, if not always
2.		0	1	2	3
3.		0	1	2	3
4.		3	2	1	0
5.		0	1	2	3
6.		0	1	2	3
7.		3	2	1	0
8.		3	2	1	0
9.		3	2	1	0
10.		0	1	2	3
11.		3	2	1	0
	Subtotal: /33				

Organising

12.		0	1	2	3
13.		0	1	2	3
14.		3	2	1	0
15.		0	1	2	3
16.		0	1	2	3
17.		3	2	1	0
18.		0	1	2	3
	Subtotal: /21				

Staffing

19.		0	1	2	3
20.		3	2	1	0
21.		3	2	1	0
	Subtotal: /9				

Directing

22.		3	2	1	0
23.		3	2	1	0
24.		0	1	2	3
25.		0	1	2	3
26.		3	2	1	0
27.		0	1	2	3
28.		3	2	1	0
	Subtotal: /21				

Controlling

29.		3	2	1	0
30.		3	2	1	0

	Rarely or never	Occasion -ally	Fairly often	Usually, if not always
31.	0	1	2	3
32.	3	2	1	0
33.	0	1	2	3
34.	3	2	1	0
35.	0	1	2	3
36.	0	1	2	3
37.	3	2	1	0
38.	3	2	1	0
39.	0	1	2	3
40.	3	2	1	0
41.	3	2	1	0
Subtotal: /39				

Decision-making

42.	3	2	1	0
43.	0	1	2	3
44.	0	1	2	3
Subtotal: /9				

Communicating

45.	3	2	1	0
46.	3	2	1	0
47.	0	1	2	3
48.	3	2	1	0
49.	3	2	1	0
50.	3	2	1	0
Subtotal: /18				

Reading

51.	0	1	2	3
52.	0	1	2	3
Subtotal: /18				

GRAND TOTAL: /156

Definitions

Questions 1–52 are grouped into eight categories, each of which has been found to be important in determining how effectively you function in the work context. The categories are:

Category	Description
1. Planning	Forecasting, setting objectives, prioritising, developing strategies, programming, scheduling, budgeting, determining resources, setting policies
2. Organising	Establishing the organisational structure, delineating relationships, classifying and dividing the work into manageable units, creating position descriptions, improving systems' efficiency
3. Staffing	Selecting, orienting, training, developing
4. Directing	Delegating, motivating, coordinating, managing differences, managing change
5. Controlling	Establishing a reporting system, developing performance standards, measuring results, taking corrective action, rewarding performance, managing interruptions, exercising self-discipline, finishing tasks
6. Decision making	Collecting facts, specifying problems, setting goals, generating alternatives, evaluating consequences, selecting a course, implementing
7. Communicating	Transmitting information, listening, questioning, confirming, managing meetings
8. Reading	Speed, comprehension

Interpretation

When analysing your scores, you will need to look at three aspects:

1. Your subtotals
2. Your individual scores
3. Your grand total

Your subtotals

These reflect the total scores that you have obtained for each of the eight categories/functions defined above. They will give an indication, within each category, of the extent to which you are being stressed while in the process of getting things done. By converting each score to a percentage (e.g. if your subtotal for planning was 20/33, your percentage would be 60.6%) and then comparing the subtotals, you should be able to identify the major areas where there is scope for finding ways to work more effectively (the lower your percentage score the more stressed you are likely to be).

Use the following as a guide:

- 67%+   no major need for attention
- 51–66%   probable need
- 0–50%   definite need

Your individual scores
These are the scores (0–3) that you have obtained for the individual items that you circled under the headings: *Rarely or never, Occasionally, Fairly often* and *Usually, if not always.* They will help you focus on particular aspects of each category to establish the exact nature of the need, demand or stress.

Your grand total
This is the sum of your eight subtotals and reflects your *level of efficiency*. In this context, efficiency may be defined as 'the quality of producing maximum effect with minimum efforts or expense'.

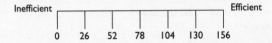

You may choose to plot your own score on the above continuum. This illustrates the range from inefficiency to efficiency, with the midpoint (78) suggesting that you are neither efficient nor inefficient.

The scores you obtain are inversely proportional to the amount of stress that you are likely to be experiencing in your job.

The higher your score, the more likely it is that you are:

- proactive
- managing your job responsibilities efficiently
- coping with the pressure of work
- anticipating fires
- in control of your job.

The lower your score, the greater will be your tendency to:

- be reactive
- be tyrannised by urgent issues
- distort priorities

- put out fires
- manage by crisis.

In short, your job is in control of you!

Stress management programmes at work

Many large companies are moving in the direction of providing stress management training and an employee assistance programmes (EAP) to improve the ability of workers to cope with difficult work situations. Stress management programmes teach workers about the nature and sources of stress, the effects of stress on health, and the personal skills to reduce stress—for example, time management or relaxation exercises. EAPs provide individual counselling for employees with both work and personal problems. Stress management training may rapidly reduce stress symptoms such as anxiety and sleep disturbances; it also has the advantage of being inexpensive and easy to implement. Such programmes can significantly reduce sick leave, and engender a more productive staff.

However, stress management programmes have two major disadvantages:

- The beneficial effects on stress symptoms are often short-lived.
- They often ignore important root causes of stress because they focus on the worker and very little on the work environment.

Organisational change

In contrast to resorting to stress management training and EAP programmes, companies can try to reduce job stress by improving working conditions. This approach is the most direct way to reduce stress at work. It involves the identification of stressful aspects of work (e.g. excessive workload, dangerous practices, conflicting expectations) and the design of strategies to reduce or eliminate the identified stressors. The advantage of this approach is that it deals directly with the root causes of the stress. However, managers are sometimes uncomfortable with this approach because it can involve changes in work routines or production schedules, or changes in the organisational structure.

As a general rule, actions to reduce job stress should give top priority to organisational change to improve working conditions. But even the most conscientious efforts to improve working conditions are unlikely to eliminate stress completely for all workers. For this reason, a combination of organisational change and stress management is often the most useful approach for reducing stress at work.

For managers: preventing stress at work

How to change the organisation to prevent job stress

- Ensure that the workload is in line with workers' capabilities and resources.
- Design jobs to provide meaning, stimulation, and opportunities for workers to use their skills.
- Clearly define workers' roles and responsibilities.
- Give workers opportunities to participate in decisions and actions affecting their jobs.
- Improve communications—reduce uncertainty about career development and future employment prospects.
- Provide opportunities for social interaction amongst workers.
- Establish work schedules that are compatible with demands and responsibilities outside the job.
- Ensure supervisors and managers are able to recognise problems of stress and feel some responsibility for dealing with it.

What might stress at work look like?

Here is a list of possible signs that managers and colleagues may recognise at an early stage so that help can be offered to the distressed employee:

Work performance	*Withdrawal*
Inconsistent performance	Arriving late
Uncharacteristic errors	Leaving early
Indecisiveness	Extended lunches

Work performance
Tiredness
Making complaints
Irritability
Lapses of memory
Resistance to change
Excessive hours

Immature behaviour
Crying
Personality clashes
Sulking
Shouting
Bullying

Withdrawal
Absenteeism
Increased sick days
Lack of commitment

Negative behaviour
Repetitive arguments
Belligerence
Refusal to listen to advice
Using solutions known to be
  inadequate
Vandalism

ACTIVITY 1.2

Does your workplace generate stress?

Place a tick in the appropriate column for each item as it applies to your workplace.

	YES	NO

Management and style of organisation
Lack of clear company objectives and values
Poor communication or lack of information
Lack of consultation or involvement over change

Role in organisation
Unclear role
Conflicting lines of management
Conflicting priorities

Career
Career uncertainty
Frustration over career ambitions
Lack of recognition
Threat to job security
Insufficient training
Threat of redundancy
Restructuring of role

Decision making
Lack of control over work
Low participation in decision making

Relationships at work
Social or physical isolation
Interpersonal conflict
Harassment and bullying

Job and workplace design
Boring repetitive work
Constant dealing with problems and complaints
Significant risks to health or safety
Lack of competency
Fear of technology or training

Pace of work
Lack of control over pace
Sustained over- or under-load
Lack of prioritisation

Work schedule
Unpredictable peak loads
Inflexible work schedule
Unsocial hours of work
Shift work
Excessive required overtime

A high score generated in Activity I. 2 indicates that your workplace has the potential to be quite stressful. So what can you do about it, either as manager or as suggestions from an employee? Here are a few ideas. You may be able to add to these.

To lower stress

- Develop adequate control of hazards
- Produce clear objectives
- Allow greater scope for personal achievement and recognition
- Introduce job rotation to reduce boredom and increase challenge
- Provide good ergonomic designs for work stations

- Make production targets reasonable
- Involve employees in planning and organising own jobs
- Operate in teams
- Train in new skills for restructured jobs
- Give managers training in counselling, conflict management and stress awareness
- Provide contacts for employees in times of crisis.

Environmental stress

In addition to stressful interactions between people and situational stressors (such as work on an assembly line), the environment can contain many stressors. They may be naturally occurring ones, like a heat wave, which generally causes people to be irritable, or they may be man-made. For example, chaotic traffic patterns and unclear signs can be confusing and cause stressful feelings because of a fear of getting lost. It is good to remember, though, that these kinds of environmental factors cause stress to some people, and yet others may gravitate towards them: you may like it best when the weather is very hot, or traffic patterns may challenge your ability to find your way.

Becoming aware of the potential stressors in your environment, and taking actions to minimise their negative effects, could help reduce the stress you are experiencing but may not even be aware of. Often we become so accustomed to the sights and sounds in our environment that we fail to recognise the role they play in making us feel anxious or stressed. We become 'passive adaptors' to conditions that may be hazardous to our well-being and health. And while it is beyond our control to alter some conditions (like the overcrowding in cities or the isolation of rural areas), there are many factors in our immediate surroundings that we can work to change. It is also important to recognise environmental factors that can minimise the negative effects of stress (e.g. fresh air or good lighting), and make sure that these factors are present in our environment.

Environmental stressors seldom come singly. For example, in the inner city we are likely to find both high density traffic and high density buildings. These are associated with simple physical consequences, such as air pollution and noise. They may also be associated with frequent and varied social contacts and/or a highly competitive way of life. All or any of these may be stressful, singly or in combination.

Some specific environmental stressors will now be examined.

Pollution and noise

The physical effects of noxious stimuli are fairly well understood: noise can cause deafness, and air pollution can cause respiratory disease. However, their psychological effects are more complex. As already described, noise can have either an adverse or a beneficial effect on skilled performance. Many people adapt remarkably well to noisy environments. Some workers, for example, learn to lip-read in order to be able to communicate with one another. However, the level of noise around airports causes greater difficulty because of its intermittent nature and because it is not voluntarily endured. People may choose to spend their leisure time at nightclubs and listening to rock groups, even though the noise level may endanger their hearing.

There is a similar interaction between attitudes and the effects of other forms of pollution. Smog and fog are injurious to health. Yet many people spend their leisure time in the smoky atmosphere of a party or a pub, which is worse than most industrial smog. On the other hand, fumes from a new factory may seem so unpleasant that, in addition to any physiological damage that may be inflicted, it may also be a contributory factor in the onset of anxiety or depression in people subjected to this form of pollution.

Crowding and variety in human contacts

Experiments on animals have shown that abnormal behaviour can develop once a certain density of population has been exceeded. In some animals in the wild, the resulting abnormal behaviour can lead to a reduction in the population, as in the case of the lemmings, which are drowned in large numbers during mass migrations. In humans, as in animals, there is a tendency to regard an area of space as one's own and to react aggressively towards intruders. The space that people put between themselves and others is characteristic of how they regard each other. Strangers in a train compartment tend to maximise the distance between them. The greater the intimacy between people, the closer they are likely to stand to each other.

(However, there are very big cultural differences here. For example, Arabs tend to stand closer to strangers than do most Europeans.)

Density of population can be measured in a number of different ways. It has been shown, for example, that the number of children taken into care by the social services, or a high incidence of aggressive acts, correlates most highly with density measured in terms of persons per room. On the other hand, the incidence of psychiatric disorders correlates better with density measured in terms of persons per housing unit. The population density in itself, however, may not be the only reason for stressed behaviour: families with large numbers of children may have many persons per room and have more opportunities to be aggressive, while mentally unstable people may seek a room of their own in large but cheap rooming houses.

It seems reasonable to expect that people living in crowded cities would meet a wide variety of people and develop wider sympathies as a result. Very often the opposite seems to happen. For example, people in cities are less likely to help strangers in trouble. One possible explanation for this is that, in crowded conditions, we protect ourselves from excessive intrusion by erecting conventional but invisible barriers around ourselves. Another explanation is the need to protect ourselves from the possible delinquency of city dwellers. Alternatively, when others are around us, do we hope that they will offer to help and so relieve us of the burden? Darley and Latané (1970), for example, have shown experimentally, in both natural and artificial situations, that people are less likely to talk to or to help strangers when there are other people about. And so, paradoxically, people in cities may so restrict their contacts with other people that loneliness becomes the greatest source of stress.

Competition and the rate of change

Competition and insecurity—the 'rat race'—are often regarded as major sources of stress. They probably are, although claims that life is now more stressful than it used to be are difficult to justify in objective terms. Modern life is objectively *more* co-operative, secure and safe than at any time in the past. Social security payments, health services and the many social services have ensured this. The life expectancy of the individual has increased, and the consequences of professional failure are much less severe than in the past.

Why, therefore, do we perceive our environment as so severe and threatening? One obvious way in which life now differs from life in the past lies in the larger size of our cooperative units and the rate at which these change. Technological and political factors are changing our lifestyles at home and at work faster than at any earlier time. We are much more mobile, in the sense that so many of us now live in a different place from the one in which we were born and reared, and so we are separated from our family and childhood friends. In addition to such special problems as the difficulty of raising children without access to grandparents, aunts and uncles, there is good evidence that change in itself is stressful.

The concept of helplessness proposed by Seligman (1975) is relevant here. He would argue that 'life events' and 'competition' have their greatest effects when we are unable to control them. If by our own actions we cannot influence our situation, we feel helpless. This feeling can become generalised and eventually lead to serious depression or anxiety.

Activity I.3 asks you to examine stressors in your environment.

ACTIVITY I.3

A major stressor in your environment

1. Can you name a major stressor in your work environment or community?
2. Why do you think this is a negative stressor?
3. What is its effect, psychologically and physiologically, on the workplace or community?
4. What would be the first step in alleviating the stress? How would you go about it?

Summary

Stress is any demand that requires some kind of physical or emotional adjustment. It can be a natural and healthy part of living or, if it becomes too great, it can hinder normal living, often resulting in adverse consequences.

There are many sources of stress, and in this chapter we have examined major work-related stressors and environmental stressors, most of which affect us all. By completing the activities in this chapter, you should now have a greater understanding of your work and environmental stressors, and whether you are working at your optimum levels.

Elimination of all stress is not a realistic solution to the problems of our complex society. If stress is a problem in your life and/or career, then the 10 skills and coping techniques in this book should be helpful to you. The aim is to accept that a certain amount of stress is necessary for optimum performance, and that you need to work *with* your stress and not against it. Work through the stress management skills that follow, and choose those that are appropriate to your needs.

Understanding what stress is and how it affects you

Introduction

Understanding the process of stress and how it affects you makes it easier to identify your major sources of stress, to know what feelings and reactions indicate your responses to stress, and enables you to anticipate and plan for stressful events or periods. You will be able to assess what you can realistically cope with in your work and personal life. Hence, before progressing to other stress management skills, it is essential that *you understand what stress is and how it affects you personally*.

Do you know that:

- Even the most conservative medical opinion agrees that up to 80 per cent of all illnesses may have some psychosomatic origin.
- The British Health and Safety Executive reports that British industry loses £370 million stg per year on stress-related sick leave.
- British Institute of Management (1996) reports 270 000 off work each day because of stress—a cost of £7 billion annually in lost production, sick pay and health service charges.
- The UK Department of Trade and Industry reports that one in five visits made by men to their doctor are due to stress.
- An Australian Council of Trade Unions' survey (1997) found that 24 per cent of employees had taken time off, 61 per cent felt depressed and 73 per cent suffered headaches, as a result of stress at work. Stress claims in the public sector in NSW

in 1996 were $35 million (ACTU Stress at Work Campaign briefing, October 1997).

- The American Institute of Stress reports that 75 per cent of visits to doctors, 60 per cent accidents at work and 40 per cent of staff turnover are stress related.
- The EU estimates that 41 million Europeans take work-related stress leave each year.
- Cox et al (2000) suggest that over half of working days lost are due to stress.
- *Karoshi* (death from overwork) is now a social issue in Korea.

There is overwhelming evidence to indicate that when conditions place a person under stress, the body no longer operates smoothly, and if stress continues the person will succumb to physical and psychological ill-health. Stress has been directly or indirectly associated with high blood pressure, ulcers, coronary heart disease, asthma, diabetes, multiple sclerosis, cancer and a range of psychiatric disorders such as severe depression and anxiety (panic) states. Anxiety in our emotional life is equivalent to pain in our physical life and is just as much a warning sign that something is wrong. Recognising the warning signals and managing stress productively reduce the chances of developing stress-related ill-health.

It is impossible to avoid stress. The only totally stress-free state is death! Stressors will always be present because we live in an imperfect and unpredictable world. We experience stress as the body adjusts to the external demands placed upon it. As our body constantly seeks to maintain stability, stress is usually sensed as the body readjusts to too much pressure. Have you ever seen a plastic clown toy that automatically returns to an upright position if pushed over? The clown stays upright because of a heavy base that will always restore it to a vertical position. Scientists use the term 'homeostasis' (*homeo* = the same; *stasis* = standing) for this state of balance at which our bodies function efficiently and comfortably. Stress disturbs homeostasis by creating a state of imbalance. The source of stress may be outside the body or it may originate from within the body in the form of blood pressure, pain, tumours or disturbing thoughts.

Our ability to cope with stressors often determines the amount of stress that we will experience. The graphs in Figure 1.1 show two ways of coping with stress—the healthy and the unhealthy patterns.

Figure 1.1 Stress patterns

The healthy pattern

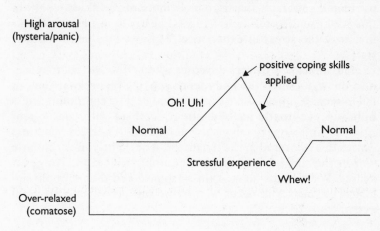

The unhealthy pattern

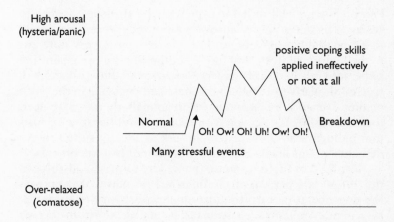

The vertical line on the left of each graph represents two extremes. The bottom of the line represents an extreme state of relaxation called coma and the top of the line a state of hyper-excitation or hysteria. Most people prefer to live at a mid-point between these two extremes.

The healthy pattern recognises that we can assist the body to cope with the stress adjustment process by applying a positive coping strategy, that is, one or more of the skills taught in this book, such as relaxation, physical activity or positive thinking, after the stressful experience. This restores us to a steady state.

The unhealthy pattern develops when either we fail to recognise the signals that the body sends seeking recovery actions, or fail to invoke any effective coping strategy. The continuing stress build-up eventually leads to stress overload with consequent physical and/or psychological breakdown. The reasons stress causes this is located in the innate 'fight or flight' reflex response and in the underlying complex neurophysiological changes it causes. We will now look at this response and the neurophysiological changes that occur when a person perceives a stressful event.

The fight or flight response

Our bodies are well suited to cope with the stressors that had to be faced by our primitive ancestors—but they were conditioned to a nomadic hunter-gatherer lifestyle, obviously very different to the high-tech lifestyle of today. Yet the single aim remains the same: survival. This explains why *Homo erectus* fighting a mammoth reacted similarly to a modern businessman engaging in the stock market. We are still first and foremost animals, therefore we need to assist our bodies to cope with today's stress because our natural biological stress-adjustors are not as ideally suited to the demands of our lifestyle as they were in pre-historic times.

The fight or flight response (named by Cannon and Selye in the 1930s) is a pattern of physiological responses that prepare the organism (that's us) to meet emergency. Our distant ancestors needed chemical responses to enable them to trigger physical responses to survive the perils and pleasures of hunting and inter-clan fighting. The rules of survival are simple and still the same—only the stronger survives. When faced with danger, the two main options are fighting (when you perceive the enemy to be weaker than you) or running away in order to survive. In face of danger, the body changes its inner balance and priorities into high physiological arousal to enable these two functions of fight or flight. These types of responses are inappropriate today. Physically running away from your work-place whenever things got on top of you would not enhance your standing in the organisation. Conversely, if you punch the boss on the nose when he/she gives you a tough time, the resulting dismissal and assault charges will generate considerably greater levels of stress. Consequently we need to develop special skills to deal with most modern stressors—skills of how to cope with and manage stress.

The manifestations of fight or flight are mainly effected through the sympathetic branch of the autonomic nervous system (ANS) and the endocrine system, which are closely inter-connected (Atkinson et al, 1996). The ANS effects many bodily functions instantly and directly, while hormones have slower yet wider effect on the body (Gross, 1998). Both hormones and ner-vous system communicate with cells and create the delicate dynamic balance between the body and its surroundings through feedback mechanisms.

The fight or flight response is crucial to dealing with some short-term dangers, as it triggers our nervous system to release chemicals that convert stored energy into useable energy, but it is incapable of dealing with long-term stress. The grave conse-quences of long-term stress on our body and mind are a direct result of this inadequacy. The 'rev-up' activity is designed to improve immediate performance in the body, but if the stress that launches this activity continues unabated, the body begins to weaken as it is bombarded by stimulation and stress-related chemicals.

The brain–endocrine–immune system

Underlying the fight and flight dichotomy is a very complex physiological interplay between the nervous, endocrine and immune systems. The nervous system, controlled by the brain, regulates the other two systems. In concert, this threesome deter-mines how healthy we are and how quickly and effectively we respond to illness or stress when it strikes. Together these sys-tems constitute a veritable army against toxins, pathogens and psychological stress, which by itself can cause more disease than the others combined.

The stressor initially excites the *hypothalamus* which is the part of the brain under the thalamus controlling body temperature, hunger and thirst. The hypothalamus stimulates the pituitary (a cherry-sized gland at the base of the brain) to release the hormone chemical ACTH (adrenocorticotrophic hormone) into the bloodstream. Once released, ACTH stimulates the adrenal glands to secrete further chemicals, the most important ones being cortisol and adrenaline, to affect various parts of the body. The net effect of this cascade of hormones is that the body becomes charged up, on full alert for a fight or flight response. This is why we often feel tense and highly strung when under a lot of stress. Although the body has a feedback system to settle us down again once the crisis passes, we often stay alert because our thinking continues to trigger off the response. For example, if you have a deadline to meet with a particular project, constant thought of the deadline and all the work you have to process to meet it may cause you to feel stressed.

Adrenaline (epinephrine) is the major stress hormone. Produced and secreted by the adrenal gland as a direct reaction to stressful situations, its powerful effects are similar to those of the sympathetic branch of the ANS (such as increasing heartbeat, blood pressure, sugar levels, muscle activity, etc.). Adrenaline helps to maintain an increased heart rate and will tell the liver to release stored sugar for energy to the body. Other stress hormones do other things—noradrenaline, for example, is associated with anger and will raise blood pressure in most people. Symptoms associated with a stress response might include high blood pressure, panic or anxiety. At the same time the secretion of endorphins (natural painkillers) provides an instant defence against pain.

Besides its hormonal functions, adrenaline is also an excitatory neurotransmitter in the CNS (central nervous system), indirectly controlling its own production. It is therefore by far the most important single hormone operating in regard to stress, taking a major role in the stress response.

The hypothalamus causes blood levels of another important hormone, cortisol, to rise. Cortisol is the major steroid hormone produced by our bodies to help us get through stressful situations. Cortisol is responsible for keeping high levels of fats and sugars in the bloodstream to provide instant energy.

The related compound known as cortisone is widely used as an anti-inflammatory drug, in creams to treat rashes and in nasal sprays to treat sinusitis and asthma. But it wasn't until very recently that scientists realised the brain also uses cortisol to suppress the immune system. These chemical reactions can induce a whole set of behaviours that we call sickness behaviour: you lose the desire or the ability to move, you lose your appetite, you lose interest in sex. These behaviours help us conserve energy when we're sick or stressed so we can better use our energy to fight disease and danger.

Over a long period of time the stress response begins to take a toll on the body because the hormones involved also trigger chemical reactions that stimulate or inhibit the immune system. One of the prime targets affected is the *thymus gland* (sited behind the breastbone, above the heart) which plays a key role in the body's immune system. The thymus gland pumps out millions of lymphocytes each day to patrol throughout the body and kill off bacterial invaders. Killer cells called macrophages literally eat invading bacteria. They operate in all parts of the body and we depend on them for our survival. Macrophages are weakened by the cortisol released by the adrenal gland when we experience stress. A weakened immune system makes us vulnerable to infection and this is why people under stress often experience regular attacks of colds and flu.

Psychological stress has considerable physical ramifications. We can do ourselves a great deal of harm through stressful thinking, which floods the body with stress hormones, and creates a vicious cycle making us more and more stressed, as well as turning off the immune system. If you're severely and constantly stressed, the immune cells are being bathed in chemicals which are essentially telling them to stop fighting. In situations of chronic stress the immune cells are less able to respond to an invader like a bacteria or a virus. This theory holds up in studies looking at high-levels of shorter term stress or chronic stress—for example, in caregivers like those taking care of relatives with Alzheimer's, medical students undergoing exam stress, army commandos undergoing extremely gruelling physical stress, and couples with marital stress. In a series of experiments in the 1990s (Kiecolt-Glaser et al, 1995, 1996; Marucha et al, 1998), researchers observed diminished immune responses as reflected by the time it takes to produce antibodies after a flu shot in chronically stressed populations; and by exam stress negatively impacting various immune-related processes in students, ranging from a delay in the ability to produce antibodies to a hepatitis-B shot to the time it took to heal a minor mouth or arm wound. Wound healing is a primary factor determining hospital stay in post-surgery patients, and other studies suggest that a very moderate level of behavioural intervention aimed at reducing stress ('reading a pamphlet or watching a video about the procedure the night before surgery') have a substantial impact on the outcome of surgery, leading in some cases to a shorter recovery period in the hospital.

Problems between the brain and the immune system can go the other way, too. If your brain can't make enough of these hormones to turn off the immune system when it doesn't have to be active anymore, production could go on unchecked and result in autoimmune diseases like rheumatoid arthritis and lupus, or other autoimmune diseases that people recognise as inflammation. So if you have too much of the stress hormones shutting down the immune response, you can't fight off infection and you're more susceptible to infection. Too little of the stress hormones, and the immune response goes on unchecked and you could get an inflammatory disease. Balance is needed.

Other physiological effects are also evident. Our bodies are hardly static collections of the proteins, fats, and sugars we ingest. Rather, throughout the course of an ordinary day, levels of all of these substances fluctuate widely. A case in point is the level of circulating fat (blood lipids). Changes in the amount of cholesterol and another lipid type called triglycerides go up and down by 20 per cent or so (Stoney et al, 1999). Stoney noted that pervasive, long-term stressors increased blood levels of cholesterol, which can put people at risk for developing atherosclerosis and further heart disease; that the bigger the perceived stress—caused, for example by a major earthquake, flood or bushfire—the greater the fluctuations in blood lipid levels, and that the effects appeared to be completely independent of changes in other health behaviours. Stoney has also conducted studies which examined the effects of much shorter and milder forms of stress—the inevitable stress we all experience in everyday life. Studying the consequences of so-called 'short-term' or acute stress, Stoney detected increases in a host of molecules considered potentially dangerous to maintaining optimal heart health: cholesterol, especially low-density lipoproteins (LDLs, the 'bad' form of cholesterol), triglycerides, and others. Table 1.1 and Figure 1.2 summarise the physiological sequences and their effects.

Table 1.1   Related physiological and stress responses

	Normal physiological state (relaxed)	Physiological state under pressure	Arousal level increased to optimum stimulation level	Over-arousal (stress)
Brain	Blood supply normal	Blood supply up	Thinks more clearly	Headaches or migraines, tremors and nervous tics
Mood	Happy	Serious	Increased concentration	Anxiety, loss of sense of humour
Saliva	Normal	Reduced	Reduced	Dry mouth, lump in throat
Muscles	Blood supply normal	Blood supply up	Improved performance	Muscular tension and pain
Heart	Normal rate and blood pressure	Increased rate and blood pressure	Improved performance	Hypertension and chest pains
Lungs	Normal respiration	Increased respiration rate	Improved performance	Coughs and asthma
Stomach	Normal blood supply and acid secretion	Reduced blood supply and increased acid secretion	Reduced blood supply reduces digestion	Ulcers due to heartburn and indigestion
Bowels	Normal blood supply and bowel activity	Reduced blood supply and increased bowel activity	Reduced blood supply reduces digestion	Abdominal pain and diarrhoea
Bladder	Normal	Frequent urination	Frequent urination due to increased nervous stimulation	Frequent urination, prostatic symptoms
Sexual organs	(Male) Normal; (Female) Normal periods, etc.	(M) Impotence (decreased blood supply); (F) Irregular periods	Decreased blood supply	(M) Impotence; (F) Menstrual disorders
Skin	Healthy	Decreased blood supply; dry skin	Decreased blood supply	Dryness and rashes
Biochemistry	Normal: Oxygen consumed, glucose and fats liberated	Oxygen consumption up, glucose and fats consumption up	More energy immediately available	Rapid tiredness

The consequences of stress

Some of the events in the body resulting from hormonal secretion, preparing it for either a fight or flight response, include:

Figure 1.2   The process and effects of stress

1.   The front of the brain receives stimulus from the eyes, ears, etc. (e.g. awareness of danger); inability to cope with perceived context.
2.   The hypothalamus in the brain activates:
     (a)   the pituitary gland to release hormones;
     (b)   the involuntary nervous system, which then sends signals via nerves to various parts of the body.
3.   These in turn cause the adrenal glands to release the hormones adrenaline, noradrenaline and cortisone, leading to the following changes (points 4–12).

4.   Mentally alert; senses activated for survival vigilance.
5.   Breathing rate speeds up; nostrils and air passages in lungs open wider to get oxygen in more quickly.
6.   Heartbeat speeds up and blood pressure rises.
7.   Liver releases sugar, cholesterol and fatty acids into the blood to supply quick energy to the muscles.
8.   Sweating increases to help cool the body.
9.   Blood clotting ability increases, preparing for possible injury.
10.   Muscles of the bladder and bowel openings contract, and non-life-supporting activity of body systems ceases temporarily.
11.   Blood is diverted to the muscles, and muscle fibres tense ready for action.
12.   Immunity responses decrease (useful in short term to allow massive response by body, but harmful over a long period).

1.   Increased heart rate, blood pressure and respiration pumping more blood to the muscles, and supplying more oxygen and sugars to the muscles and heart-lung system. Increased sugar rates in the blood permit rapid energy use and accelerate metabolism for emergency actions. Symptoms that can be associated with this stress response might include rapid or irregular heartbeats, increased blood pressure.

2. Breathing usually becomes more rapid, to get more oxygen into the body. Symptoms that can be associated with this stress response might include hyperventilation and some forms of asthma.

3. Thickening of the blood to increase oxygen supply (red cells), enable better defence from infections (white cells) and stop bleeding quickly (platelets).

4. Muscles that you would use to fight or flee often become very tight until released by relaxation, massage, stretching or exercise. This is one of the most common responses to stress and has lead to everyday expressions like: 'uptight', 'pain in the neck' (and other places). Symptoms that can be associated with this stress response might include tension headaches, tight jaw, neck/shoulder pain/tension, back pain, insomnia (including trouble getting to sleep, staying asleep, or not feeling rested after sleeping), fatigue, loss of concentration (distracted by muscle pain or tension), learning disabilities, poor communication (listening and speaking)

5. Prioritising of blood-flow/circulation. Blood is directed toward the brain and major muscles for survival. Blood is directed away from surface of skin in hands and feet (for survival—a primitive response so you do not bleed to death if you get cut running away or fighting for your life). Blood is directed away from digestive organs and reproductive organs because it becomes a low priority to digest food if you are threatened. Symptoms that can be associated with this stress response might include high blood pressure, cold hands and feet, upset stomach, migraine headaches, pre-ulcerous/ulcerous conditions, increased colitis, sometimes constipation; additionally, 70 per cent of sexual dysfunction in both men and women can be linked to this stress response.

6. Sharpening of senses. All of your senses are heightened for survival vigilance. You are more sensitive to noise (ringing telephones or door bells), to light, to smells, even to touch. The neocortex (the thinking part of your brain) shuts down and the survival mechanisms in the middle and lower more primitive parts of the brain take over, so you react rather than thinking things through. Basic emotions—fear, anger, sadness and joy (nervous laughter)—take over from complicated, sophisticated higher function thinking and rational judgment. Symptoms that can be associated with this stress response might include emotional irritability, substance abuse to escape

stress through self-medication, anxiety, depression, poor impulse control, poor problem solving and reduced communication abilities.

7. Perspiring, to cool down the body's increased metabolism. Symptoms associated with this stress response might include hyperhydrosis (which can lead to dehydration due to over-sweating).

The general adaptation syndrome (GAS)

The effect of these biological changes is to switch the body's resources from long-term to short-term survival. Everything is optimised to deal with the threat. Under normal circumstances, when the threat has passed the nervous system operates to return the body to its normal state. But if the fight or flight response is constantly being triggered, our bodies never get the chance to return to normal. One of the pioneers of stress research, Selye, believed that stress is essentially reflected by the rate of all the wear and tear caused by life. Taking into account the neuro-endocrine-immune system, Selye proposed a general adaptation syndrome (GAS), a three-stage sequence which if left untreated, always leads to infection, illness, disease and eventually death.

The sequence runs as follows:

Stage 1: alarm reaction

Any physical or mental trauma will trigger an immediate set of reactions that combat the stress, such as increases in blood pressure and a dry mouth. Because the immune system is initially depressed, normal levels of resistance are lowered, making us more susceptible to infection and disease. If the stress is not severe or long-lasting, we bounce back and recover rapidly. We have all experienced the alarm reaction. Can you remember such situations? Perhaps you heard a strange noise when you were home alone, or maybe you arrived at work and discovered there was an urgent meeting to discuss redundancies. Unexpected events like these require some physical and/or emotional readjustment. During the alarm stage, people often revert to more childlike behaviour over which they have little control, such as trembling or needing to urinate. They may faint or even vomit, have sweaty palms and feel their heart racing so much that they fear collapsing. Previous training can be forgotten—for example, someone trained in first aid may forget what to do in an emergency.

Stage 2: Resistance

Eventually, sometimes rather quickly, we adapt to stress, and there's actually a tendency to become more resistant to illness and disease. The immune system works overtime during this period, trying to keep up with the demands placed upon it. We become complacent about our situation and assume that we can resist the effects of stress indefinitely. Therein lies the danger: believing that we are immune from the effects of stress, we typically fail to do anything about it. The body becomes more susceptible and enters the final stage.

Stage 3: Exhaustion

Because the body is not able to maintain homeostasis and the long-term resistance needed to combat stress, we invariably develop a sudden drop in our resistance level. No one experiences exactly the same resistance and tolerance to stress, but everyone's immunity at some point collapses following prolonged stress reactions. Stress-fighting reserves finally succumb to what Selye called 'diseases of adaptation.' The person is now very vulnerable to illness as internal resources are depleted. The severity of any subsequent physical and mental ill-health depends generally on:

- The individual's personal vulnerabilities, e.g. already an asthmatic
- The kinds of stressor that initiated the response and its importance to the individual
- The availability of counselling/support.

Gender differences in stress hormones

Your response to stress may have more to do with your gender than with the stressors you face. Men and women appear to respond differently to stress. What hasn't been clear until now is how or why. Our understanding of the human stress response has been based on the simple fight or flight model, which states that when confronted with a stressful situation, humans either will respond with aggressive behaviour or withdraw.

A study by Taylor et al (2000) provides clues to the biological and behavioural differences in the ways men and women cope with stress. The study found that females of many species, including humans, respond to stressful situations by protecting and nurturing their young and by seeking social contact and support from others, particularly other females. The study refers to this response as tend and befriend. Researchers believe this response is a result of natural selection. Thousands of generations ago, fighting or fleeing in stressful situations was not a good option for a female who was pregnant or taking care of offspring, and women who developed and maintained social alliances were better able to care for multiple offspring in stressful times. Men, on the other hand, were likely to initiate confrontation or sequester themselves.

It is believed the hormone oxytocin, released by the pituitary, promotes maternal and social behaviour, enhances relaxation and plays a role in gender difference. People with high levels of oxytocin are calmer, more relaxed, more social and less anxious. In males, the effects of oxytocin seem to be countered by male hormones but in females, oxytocin may play a key factor in reducing the response to stress. Men are more likely than women to respond to stressful experiences by developing certain stress-related disorders, including hypertension, aggressive behaviour, or abuse of alcohol or hard drugs, Taylor says, while the tend and befriend response may protect women against stress.

These results may help explain such things as why men are reluctant to ask for directions when lost, why men are more vulnerable to the adverse health effects of stress, and why women enjoy a significantly longer life expectancy than men. It would suggest that reaching out is beneficial—protective, even—in times of stress. But for hundreds of thousands of years, men who revealed their weaknesses tended to be undesirable mates. Hiding weaknesses has been biologically advantageous, and men still tend to be less likely to reveal weaknesses, to have very strong tendencies to conceal stressful things and withdraw. Crying is still not acceptable in men.

By changing the way the body normally functions, stress disrupts the natural balance—the homeostasis—crucial for wellbeing. This is why, by learning relaxation and stress management techniques, you'll improve your overall health as well as your odds of living a disease-free life. Stress will cause more health problems and trigger more disease in the twenty-first century than ever before. No single factor has had or will have such an impact on so many individuals. One of the most hopeful aspects of modern medical science is that it tells us that disease is not all in our genes. A growing number of studies show that, to some degree, you can use your mind to help treat your body. Support groups, stress relief and relaxation/meditation may, by altering stress hormone levels, all help the immune system. For example, it has been shown that women in support groups for their breast cancer have longer life spans than women without such psychological support.

The physical effects of stress

We all know from experience how an emotional experience can influence the body. A sudden shock (e.g. witnessing an assault or accident) may cause us to sweat, to start trembling, or we may faint or even vomit. Emotional stress causes certain involuntary physical reactions—for example, a change of facial expression, manner and speech, a pounding heart, rapid pulse, fast breathing, a dry mouth, a rise in blood pressure, sometimes cramps or an uneasy sensation in the stomach, and a generally keyed-up, tense feeling. In primitive humans these were necessary reactions preparing for fight or flight. In modern humans this state of tension does not have such a 'natural' outlet and, unless controlled or relieved, may be damaging.

If only the normal functions of the body are upset, improvement of the condition is often possible with medical help, or without medical help if a change in the situation occurs that eliminates the underlying tension. If, however, these disorders persist long enough, actual physical changes may occur in the organs involved. This now becomes an *organic illness*, which cannot always be cured without leaving some trace of damage. For example, as we have seen, it is normal to have raised blood pressure in moments of excitement. If, however, there are continuous periods of undue stress and repeated increases of blood pressure, changes will be brought about in the blood-vessels and other organs that result in a permanent increase of blood pressure.

Stress and heart disease

Despite all the public interest in cardiovascular disease as a major killer in many countries, we have only recently begun to recognise the relationship between this disease and stress.

Such factors as high levels of cholesterol and fatty substances, hypertension (high blood pressure), obesity, heredity, an inactive lifestyle, a diabetic condition and heavy cigarette smoking have long been associated with cardiovascular illness. However, Selye (1956) maintains that the above-mentioned factors associated with heart disease cause only the *preconditions* for a heart attack, and that they do not by themselves actually bring on an attack. He believes that the decisive factor is excessive stress. But this is more than just a mere belief. Selye has demonstrated in his laboratory that heart accidents can be induced chemically by excessive stress, even without closing of the arteries in the heart. There is also evidence that acute emotional stress may bring on sudden death by unalterably interrupting the rhythm of the heart, even though no actual tissue dies.

Selye mentions the work of Engel, who has taken numerous case reports on sudden death due to psychological stress and has put them in the following eight categories:

1. Due to the impact of death of a close friend or relative.
2. During severe grief.
3. At the threat of losing a close friend or relative.
4. During mourning or on an anniversary.
5. On the loss of self-esteem or of status.
6. When faced with personal danger or the threat of injury.
7. After the danger has passed.
8. During a reunion, triumph or happy ending.

Stress and cancer

Around 25 per cent of deaths each year in Australia are due to cancer. Some researchers believe that this is frequently related to excessive stress. Many patients seem to have their cancers reactivated, after apparently successful treatment, by the onset of some acute form of stress, and in many cases this recurrence proves fatal.

Leshan (1964), of New York's Institute of Applied Biology, studied 450 cancer patients for 12 years. He discovered that these patients had three psychological characteristics in common more frequently than a control group of people not suffering from cancer. Firstly, the majority of them had experienced the loss of a very important personal relationship before their disease was identified. Secondly, almost half of them displayed an inability to vent hostile feelings towards others. Thirdly, more than one-third of them displayed a high level of tension concerning the death of one of their parents, even when the death had occurred some time back.

Stress and other illnesses

The relationship between stress and physical illness is indeed a most interesting phenomenon. Sangomas (witchdoctors) in southern Africa cast 'spells' on victims, who believe that they are helpless to prevent themselves from dying within a short space of time. Among Australian Aboriginals, an equivalent situation arises when bones are pointed at the victim. Ritual execution through the practice of voodoo is a further example of how powerful an effect extreme stress can have upon an individual, especially when social support is withdrawn because a person is then regarded by society as being as good as dead.

Cannon, a noted Harvard physiologist, discovered that the practice of voodoo subjects a person's nervous system to intolerable loads of stress. The heart develops arrhythmia because it is exhausted by overstimulation (i.e. it quivers but does not pulse or beat). Here is a case of self-fulfilling prophecy—believing that death is imminent, the person waits in fear or resignation until they die.

The emotional effects of stress

Undue tension not only has physical effects, but equally damaging emotional effects. Each of us has occasionally suffered some of the more immediate, transitory stress effects like insomnia, undue irritability and losing one's temper too easily. Many of us will have experienced more long-term effects such as general pessimism coupled with a persistent feeling of loneliness and being unloved, mistrusting even our closest friends, lacking in self-esteem and wanting to withdraw socially. Or maybe you have temporarily suffered from a basic insecurity, making you feel that you could not cope with your responsibilities, and even finding it difficult to make simple decisions.

As with physical effects, if the cause of the tension is removed, no permanent damage is likely. But if the tension persists, there could be more severe damage to the personality.

Emotional disorders fall under the broad category of *neuroses* (not to be confused with *psychoses*, which are mental disorders). Neuroses are illnesses caused by circumstances (or one's inability to adapt to circumstances). Someone suffering from a neurosis does not lose contact with reality, but difficulties appear greater for them than for the 'normal' person.

There are several common types of neurosis, including anxiety, depression, hysteria and obsessions.

Anxiety

Anxiety is the most common neurosis. It is not bad in itself—in fact, it is necessary for people's survival because it serves as a danger signal that something is wrong and needs attention. However, too much anxiety, like too much tension of any kind, becomes damaging.

Anxiety is characterised by a persistent feeling of tension and fear that is out of proportion to the cause. Often the person does not know the reason why they are feeling anxious. The effects of anxiety are similar to those of any other form of fear (i.e. fast pulse, dry mouth, distaste for food, abdominal cramps, and a keyed-up feeling that may lead to giddiness or tension headaches and an inability to concentrate). The anxious person may have difficulty in getting to sleep, and have bad dreams when they do. During the day the person may suffer from undue panic and confusion. They may become so tense that they get pains in their chest, or a sensation that their throat is closing and they have to struggle for breath. Some sufferers will realise what is causing their anxiety, while others will become convinced that something is physically wrong with them, thus adding to their basic problems.

Most anxieties are caused by generalised fears, and many people have varying degrees and kinds of fears. Many adults have a mild fear of heights, of being in public places, of speaking in front of a group, of darkness, of certain animals, or of taking examinations or undergoing a performance appraisal at work. When these or similar fears get to be out of proportion to the threat they pose (i.e. irrational), then they are said to be *phobias*.

There are many hundreds of different phobias, and millions of people suffer from severe phobias. The sufferer knows that there are no grounds for the fear, but the fear nevertheless is very real and debilitating. Because they are afraid of being laughed at, many people try to hide their fears, which increases their misery because their terror is real, even producing the physical symptoms a normal person experiences when in danger. People suffering from phobias are genuinely ill, but given medical attention, there is a good chance of recovery.

Anxiety is most common in people who drive themselves too hard, or who are under too much pressure, or who, because of circumstances, have to restrain their naturally aggressive impulses. John may want to tell his unreasonable boss to 'go to hell', but he needs his boss's approval to keep his job. So he restrains his natural impulses, and the pressure builds up.

Depression

Depression is another common form of neurosis and is characterised by feelings of extreme sadness, fatigue, a loss of interest in one's social environment and consequent self-neglect, agitation and insomnia. Unlike the anxious type, the depressed person falls asleep, but tends to wake in the early hours and cannot go back to sleep. Instead they lie brooding about morbid thoughts.

We all have a fit of the 'blues' at times, but when this feeling is out of proportion in intensity and duration to the cause, or when there is no apparent cause for persistent feelings of depression, then a doctor should be consulted. Effective medical treatment suited to the individual person, and free from unpleasantness and risk, is available. In cases of mild depression, many people seem to respond well when they keep busy, and particularly when the activities they undertake boost their self-esteem. A change of scene also often helps.

Depression frequently occurs in compulsive, hard-driving perfectionists who feel that they cannot afford the incapacity of illness. To lessen the misery of their depression, they will engage in hectic work activities, or fall prey to temper outbursts. A lowered self-esteem goes hand-in-hand with depression. To self-treat or boost this, a depressed person may resort to gambling, impulsive sexual behaviour, drug-taking or excessive use of alcohol.

There are two types of depression. The first is a reaction to circumstances, and will usually follow, for example, the death of a loved one, family or money troubles, or retrenchment/redundancy. This is called reactive depression. The other type originates within the person (endogenous depression), and is characterised by severe changes in mood. At one time the person may be very talkative and in an unusually excitable state, then swing drastically to feeling completely down in the dumps, not wanting to talk or to do anything. This type of depression is sometimes experienced by women during menopause, or by men at the corresponding period (mid-fifties to mid-sixties). Older people also suffer from this type of depression, but it is rare in the very old.

Social isolation—living alone, or being in big cities where one does not have close, meaningful human contacts—is the worst kind of situation for the person inclined to depression.

Because it makes people feel so hopelessly desperate and morbid, the greatest danger of depression is that it will end in suicide. Many suicide attempts are a desperate effort to attract attention and to get help. But, tragically, there is often no one to recognise and heed this call for help. The person's own reasoning cannot stop them either because, when suffering from an endogenous depression, they are not in a clear frame of mind.

Hysteria

Hysteria is another type of neurosis. It is a state of panic in which a person has lost their self-control and may display any emotion excessively and uncontrollably—for example, anger (temper tantrums), and fear and happiness/sadness (laughing and crying at the same time). Hysterical behaviour is a subconscious response to extreme emotional stress, which causes a split between what the person wants to do and how they actually respond. In severe grief or shock, this subconscious response may take the form of paralysis or blindness. *Shell-shock* is an example of hysteria. *Amnesia* (loss of memory) is another particular type of hysteria that provides an escape, and which usually follows acute mental conflict.

Hysteria may also manifest itself in constant doubts, chronic hesitancy, an inability to make decisions, feeling compelled to attend to all kinds of unimportant details, and not accomplishing anything, but taking forever to do so. A hysterical person may go through senseless routines of arranging things, or repeatedly washing their hands or checking details before going to bed.

More commonly, hysteria takes the form of a physical illness, which is used as an escape or to manipulate sympathetic family and friends. The hysteric genuinely suffers from an illness or illnesses, which is brought on by their belief that they have that illness. The hysteric makes no distinction between fact and fantasy, truth and falsehood; they may live in a world of make-believe, very much like a child who has little concern for the future. The hysteric is thus unrealistic and egocentric, and often quite a colourful character.

Obsessions

Obsessions, the fourth type of neurosis, are less common. A person suffering from an obsession has a strong and established habit they cannot break. If the routine of doing something at a particular time or in a particular way is upset, the obsessive person becomes very distressed because of the belief that disaster is now inevitable. Obsessions might involve always having a cup of tea at exactly 8 am from the same cup, or always having the desktop arranged in a particular way, or locking the doors in a specific order at night. Such rituals and routines help to keep under control the tensions that typify obsessive people. Many such people will frantically carry out the rituals of religion as a source of comfort and help. Others relieve their feelings by means of frequent ritual hand-washing, for example, as a symbolic act of 'cleansing'.

ACTIVITY 1.1

Make a Stress Diary

The aim of this activity is to create your own personal record of stressful events in your life so that, as you learn the skills and techniques for reducing stress, you can apply them in the circumstances you have noted. (Remember the sources of your stress, your perception of it and your bodily responses will differ from those of other people.)

1. Using a pad of A4 paper, separate sheets stapled together or an actual diary, divide each page into three columns with the following headings:
   - *Stressor (activity, event interaction)*
     Example: Giving a speech at the firm's annual dinner.
   - *Responses (what I felt/how my body acted)*
     Example: My heart pounded, I felt anxious.
   - *Behaviour (what I did)*
     Example: Had trouble getting there on time. Felt sick during the journey. Asked a colleague for moral support. Started the speech very shakily and had to refer to my notes all the time . . .
2. Put the date at the top of the page, and date each subsequent page when you record something in your diary.
3. Remember, stressors can be pleasant or unpleasant, large or small, external situations or internal feelings. Be frank; you will not be sharing the information with anyone else.
4. If possible, complete the stress record each day. Feel free to add categories that seem important to you. For example, you may want to keep track of the place the stress was experienced (e.g. home or work), and who or what was involved.
5. Review your Stress Diary from time to time and become aware of emerging patterns.

Note that you will be asked to refer to and add to your Stress Diary throughout this book.

ACTIVITY 1.2

What are your symptoms of stress?

1. Look at the 'Stress symptoms' list on the next page. Then refer back to your Stress Diary from Activity 1.1 and answer the following questions:
   - Do you recognise any of the stress symptoms in how you behave or respond to stressful situations?
   - Why do you think you might have reacted in the way you described in your Stress Diary?
   For example, it is sometimes easier to be angry and irritable than to take the risk of stating what you want. Learning to communicate directly and assertively can help to reduce stress

that results from unclear or incomplete communications. Sometimes unexpressed anger gets played out in careless behaviour, like reckless and aggressive driving. Adults as well as adolescents can abuse drugs or alcohol by using them to escape from or cover up stressful feelings. There is danger in trying to avoid or mask the symptoms of stress. The use of alcohol and other drugs, for example, interferes with the natural psychological and physical warning signals, thus allowing stress to build up unnoticed.

2. Now look at the 'Signs of successfully coping with stresses and strains', which follows immediately after the 'Stress symptoms' list. Read each sign, and then think of examples of when you have tried or experienced these behaviours, feelings or attitudes. Refer to your Stress Diary if necessary.

Why do you think some of these coping behaviours or attitudes might be hard to adopt? (For example, showing friendliness and love can make you vulnerable to rejection; when you take responsibility, you are responsible for both success and failure; and exercising as a form of fitness and relaxation may be difficult or time-consuming.)

Stress symptoms

Physical or what happens to your body
Increased heart rate (pounding); elevated blood pressure; sweaty palms; tightness in the chest; headache; diarrhoea; tightness in neck/back muscles; trembling; tics or twitching; stuttering; other speech difficulties; pupil dilation; nausea and/or vomiting; sleep disturbance; fatigue; proneness to accidents; slumped posture; shallow breathing; nervous laughter; susceptibility to minor illnesses; dryness of mouth or throat; butterflies in stomach.

Emotional or how you feel
Irritability; lowered self-esteem; angry outbursts; depression; jealousy; feeling 'up-tight'; suspiciousness; diminished initiative; feelings of unreality and over-alertness; loneliness; helplessness; insecurity; frustration; lack of interest; tendency to cry; reduction of personal involvement with others; critical of oneself and others; lacking in confidence; self-deprecation; nightmares; tiredness: exhaustion; desire to escape.

Intellectual or how you think
Forgetfulness; preoccupation; blocking; errors in judging distance; diminished or exaggerated fantasy life; reduced creativity; difficulty in making decisions; mental confusion; lack of concentration; diminished productivity; lack of attention to detail; orientation to past; over-sensitivity to criticism.

Behavioural or how you act
Increased smoking; aggressive driving; having accidents; clumsiness; nervous laughter; panic; increased alcohol or drug use; carelessness; eating too much; fast (even incoherent) speech; chewing fingernails.

Your health
Asthma; coronary heart disease; dizziness; headaches/migraine; skin complaints; dyspepsia; cancer; aches and pains in the chest and limbs; diarrhoea; frequent urination; nightmares; ulcers; loss of sexual interest.

Your work
Increased absenteeism; increased accident rate; less job satisfaction; lower productivity; poor relationships with colleagues; less commitment to job; less creativity.

Signs of successfully coping with stresses and strains
The following are signs of successfully coping with stress:

- ability to carry out jobs efficiently
- ability to take responsibility
- ability to work under authority and rules
- ability to work under difficulties and limitations
- tolerance of frustration
- ability to adapt to changes
- reliability
- sense of belonging
- ability to show friendliness and love
- ability to take recreation, relax and sleep
- sense of humour
- sense of fulfilment
- self-direction
- reasonable sense of independence and self-reliance
- tolerance of others.

Individual reactions to stress

What you have read so far in this book has presented a very general account of the physiological and psychological responses that occur as part of the response to stress. It is important to note that there is no fixed pattern of behaviour or response that follows the impact of a stressor.

People all differ from one another, so it is clear that situations will affect or influence them differently. What is more, the same person may react differently to a similar situation from one day to the next, depending on their 'mood' or what other experiences they have had that day.

Let us look at Harry and Mark working in the same office. Harry hardly hears the noise of the traffic outside, whereas Mark is startled by every screech of brakes. Then suddenly one day Harry is the agitated one. The reason? That morning he had an argument with his wife, lost his car keys and was late for an important appointment. Naturally his reactions to the usual office situation will be different.

Thus, there are many factors affecting an individual's reaction to a stressful event. These factors will now be examined, including an individual's ability to cope, personality, the nature, number and timing of stressful events, prior experience, information available, the degree of social support, and whether the individual has an internal or external 'locus of control'.

Ability to cope

The ability to cope varies from person to person, and may even vary within the same person. This depends on a number of factors, including age, personality, how (and if) someone has learnt from previous experiences, the degree of security experienced from ties with others and state of health. Thus the capacity for 'bouncing back' varies. Some individuals can endure tremendous emotional or mental anxiety and yet seem to emerge unscathed, even strengthened. Others go to pieces when a cross word is said to them.

A person's confidence in their ability to handle a stressful situation is a major factor in determining the severity of the stress. Speaking before a large audience is a traumatic event for most people. But individuals who are experienced in public speaking have confidence in their ability and feel only minimal anxiety.

Emergencies are particularly stressful because our usual methods of coping do not work. Not knowing what to do can be demoralising. People trained to deal with emergencies—such as police officers, firefighters or medical rescue squads—can act calmly and effectively because they know what to do, but the person who lacks such training may feel helpless. Since we tend to fall back on well-learnt responses under stress, it is important that people who may have to deal with particular types of emergencies are taught a repertoire of responses to cope with various contingencies.

Personality

Possibly the simplest explanation of the difference in individuals' reactions to stress is the 'Type A' and 'Type B' personality theory of Friedman and Rosenman (1974). They believe that there is a correlation between the way in which an individual perceives their environment, and the qualities of the individual's behaviour or personality. The qualities of the Type B personality are held to be the opposite of the Type A personality. Type A people are likely to perceive more stressors in the same environment than Type B. They also experience more situations with *potential* stressors than Type B.

Type A personalities exhibit intense drive and ambition, aggressiveness and competitiveness, a need to get things finished, restlessness and impatience. Type B personalities have a more easy-going manner, are patient, and make time to appreciate leisure and beauty. They are not particularly competitive and do not feel the need to set deadlines.

Over a number of years, regular physical examinations were carried out by Friedman and Rosenman on 3500 males between the ages of 39 and 59. It was found that 70 per cent of Type A people developed coronary heart disease and only 30 per cent of Type B.

In a recent review of the literature, Powell (1987) has concluded that one of the most significant psycho-social predictors of coronary heart disease is a competitive, striving and time-pressured lifestyle. This is the Type A personality classification (i.e. the coronary-prone behaviour pattern). Even when the other risk factors (e.g. smoking, cholesterol level) are controlled, the incidence of coronary heart disease and the death rate from that disease are twice as high in Type A than in Type B individuals.

It is argued that, in addition to responding to environmental demands in a less adaptive way, Type A individuals also create stress for themselves by their time-urgent and competitive lifestyle.

ACTIVITY 1.3

Self-evaluation: Stress control lifestyle questionnaire

As you can see, each item below is composed of a pair of phrases separated by a series of seven horizontal lines. Each pair has been chosen to represent two kinds of contrasting behaviour. Since most of us are neither the most competitive nor the least competitive person we know, put a tick where you think you belong between the two extremes (on the scale of 1–7).

Then tally your result.

1 2 3 4 5 6 7

1. Don't mind leaving things temporarily unfinished   __ __ __ __ __ __ __   Must get things finished once started

2. Calm and unhurried about appointments   __ __ __ __ __ __ __   Never late for appointments

3. Non-competitive   __ __ __ __ __ __ __   Highly competitive

4. Listen well, let others finish speaking   __ __ __ __ __ __ __   Anticipate others in conversation (e.g. nod, interrupt, finish other people's sentences)

5. Never in a hurry, even when under pressure   __ __ __ __ __ __ __   Always in a hurry

6. Able to wait calmly   __ __ __ __ __ __ __   Uneasy when waiting

	1 2 3 4 5 6 7	
7. Easy-going	— — — — — — —	Always going full speed ahead
8. Take one thing at a time	— — — — — — —	Try to do more than one thing at a time, while already thinking about what to do next
9. Slow and deliberate in speech	— — — — — — —	Vigorous and forceful in speech (use a lot of gestures)
10. Concerned with satisfying self, not others	— — — — — — —	Want recognition for a job well done
11. Slow at doing things	— — — — — — —	Fast at doing things (eating, walking, etc.)
12. Express feelings openly	— — — — — — —	Hold feelings in
13. Have a large number of interests	— — — — — — —	Have few interests outside work
14. Satisfied with job	— — — — — — —	Ambitious, want quick advancement
15. Never set own deadlines	— — — — — — —	Often set own deadlines
16. Feel limited responsibility	— — — — — — —	Always feel responsible

1 2 3 4 5 6 7

17. Never judge things in terms of numbers (how many, how much)   — — — — — — —   Often judge things in terms of numbers

18. Casual about work   — — — — — — —   Take work very seriously (work weekends, bring work home)

19. Not very precise   — — — — — — —   Very precise (careful about details)

SOURCE: Adapted from R. Bortner, 'A Short Scale as a Potential Measure of Pattern A Behaviour', *Journal* or *Chronic Diseases*, 1969, 22, pp. 87–91.

Total each column here: __ __ __ __ __ __ __

Add all your totals: _____

If your grand total on this stress scale is between 30 and 59, you are a Type B or a low-stress person. If you fall in the 60–79 group, you have an average level of stress in your life. If you fall between 80 and 100 your stress is high, and you may want to start using some stress-reducing techniques. If your score falls between 110 and 133, you are considered a Type A personality, which means that you are stress-prone because of your competitive, impatient and aggressive behaviour. You should introduce a stress-reducing campaign into your life to prevent the possibility of stress-related ailments.

The skills and techniques suggested in this book will help you to cope with stress and to prevent your health from deteriorating. Relaxation plus self-monitoring can contribute to lowering these scores.

Life events or changes

You need to be able to identify when you are under stress. This means that you need to be aware of the nature of stress, your own stress responses, and the types of situation that contain stressors for you personally. The 'Life change stress index' (Activity 1.4 on page 68) emphasises that the way in which an individual responds is greatly influenced by the way they see a stressor. This, in turn, is affected by underlying personality, memory, age, time, previous conditioning and learning experiences.

Any change in an individual's life, whether pleasant or unpleasant, requires some readjustment. The scale shown in Activity 1.4 was developed to measure stress in terms of life changes. The life events are ranked in order, from the most stressful (death of a spouse) to the least (minor violations of the law). To arrive at this scale, the investigators examined thousands of interviews and medical histories to identify the kind of events people found stressful.

Studies using the life change scale have found a consistent relationship between the number of stressful events in a person's life and that person's emotional and physical health. When the life change units added up to between 200 and 300 over a period of a year, more than half of the people had health problems the following year. When the scores came to over 300, 79 per cent of the people became ill the following year.

Of course it is not being suggested that stress alone causes deterioration in health. For one thing, it is difficult to separate the effects of stress from such factors as diet, smoking, drinking and other general health habits. For example, individuals trying to cope with the demands of a new and more difficult job might increase their alcohol intake, eat too much snack food, get less sleep and fail to exercise. An increased susceptibility to illness in such a case is more likely to stem from the changes in health habits than from the direct action of stress on resistance to disease.

Secondly, people differ in their tendency to focus on physical symptoms and in their inclination to seek medical help. A respiratory infection or stomach-ache that one person ignores may send another person to a doctor. Individuals who are unhappy and discontented with their lives are more apt to focus on symptoms than people busily involved in activities they enjoy; they are also more likely to go to a doctor.

Stressful life events therefore clearly play a role in illness. But they do so in interaction with biological factors (pre-existing susceptibilities towards certain disorders), life habits and the psychological characteristics of the individual.

The life events that are consistently rated as most unpleasant and requiring most adjustment appear to be those involving a personal loss, particularly of a close companion, such as a partner or spouse. Some research workers in this area believe that a generalised sense of loss (actual, potential or imagined) or bereavement are significant factors in the onset of disease, and can give rise to an emotional response of hopelessness and helplessness that results in the individual literally 'giving up'. When this happens, the individual can no longer cope, psychologically and biologically, with environmental demands. If the individual has a predisposition to a disease, then being in this psychological state will make the disease more likely to occur because the body will be less capable of dealing effectively with the processes that give rise to the disease.

Many studies have shown, for example, that the recently bereaved are much more likely to develop physical and psychological problems. There is also evidence that the bereaved have a higher mortality rate in the six months following the death of a spouse. In one study in Great Britain, some 4500 widowers were observed for six months after the death of their wives. In addition to high rates of illness and depression, these men had a mortality rate that was 40 per cent higher than expected for their age.

Bereavement is distressing for many reasons, and these will vary from person to person. The grief reaction appears to pass through a number of phases, with recurrent pangs of depression, and again this varies in its duration. It would appear that those who show a strong initial grief reaction, and who are able to express their emotions, are able to make the best psychological and physiological adjustment. By contrast, there appears to be a less satisfactory outcome for the bereaved person who has had an over-reliant relationship with the deceased, who has reacted badly to previous separations, who has limited social support, or who is experiencing other stresses. These individuals appear to be most at risk in terms of their susceptibility to subsequent disease.

ACTIVITY 1.4

Life change stress index

Complete the questionnaire below. Under the 'Scale of impact' column, circle only those events that have affected you personally in the past 12 months, and ignore the others. Transfer the given scores to the 'Stress score' column and add them up to give your total.

Event	Scale of impact	Stress score
Death of spouse	100	_____
Divorce	73	_____
Marital separation	65	_____
Jail term	63	_____
Death of close family member	63	_____
Person injury or illness	53	_____
Marriage	50	_____
Fired at work	47	_____
Marital reconciliation	45	_____
Retirement	45	_____
Deterioration in health of a close family member	44	_____
Pregnancy	40	_____
Sexual difficulties	39	_____
Gain of new family member	39	_____
Business readjustment	39	_____
Deterioration in financial state	38	_____
Death of close friend	37	_____
Change to different line of work	36	_____
Increase in number of arguments with spouse	35	_____
Mortgage more than double your annual income	31	_____
Foreclosure of mortgage or loan	30	_____
Change in responsibilities at work	29	_____
Son or daughter leaving home	29	_____
Trouble with in-laws	29	_____
Outstanding personal achievement	28	_____
Spouse begins or stops work	26	_____
Beginning or completing school	26	_____
Change in living conditions	25	_____
Revision of personal habits	24	_____
Trouble with boss	23	_____

Change in work hours or conditions	20	_____
Change in residence	20	_____
Change in schools	20	_____
Change in recreation	19	_____
Change in church activities	19	_____
Change in social activities	18	_____
Mortgage or loan less than twice your annual income	17	_____
Change in sleeping habits	16	_____
Change in number of family get-togethers	15	_____
Change in eating habits	15	_____
Vacation	13	_____
Minor violations of the law	11	_____

TOTAL

SOURCE: T.H. Holmes & R.H. Rahe, 'The Social Readjustment Rating Scale', *Journal of Psychosomatic Research*, 1967, II, pp. 213–18.

Your score on the 'Life change stress index' scale indicates your probable level of resistance and how likely you are to become ill from the changes you have been through during the past year.

It should be emphasised that these are probabilities. Given a group of people who have filled out the rating scale and received the same score, all of them will have the same probability (or odds) of becoming ill as a result of the changes they have experienced. But interestingly enough, only some of those people will actually become ill. Part of the reason for this is that those who cope successfully are more likely to be healthy, regardless of how much change they have been through.

It is important to remember that your score is just that, a score. Whether you remain well or eventually become sick will depend more upon how you live and cope from here on than upon what your score was. A high score, however, should serve as a warning that you may need to attend to the stress in your life and devote yourself to more effective ways of coping. You can interpret your score as follows:

Total score	Change of illness or injury	Your level of resistance
12–149	Low (10–34%)	High resistance
150–299	Moderate (35–50%)	Borderline resistance
300 or more	High (51–85%)	Low resistance–high vulnerability

Changes in your life are not necessarily to be avoided. The very nature of human growth and development requires changes at various stages of life. But too much change in too short a period of time exacts its toll on the body's adaptive capabilities, thus raising the risk of major health problems.

Evaluating your score
Look at the items you marked and think about the following:

1. Which events had a negative effect on your life and which had a positive effect?
2. How did you respond to each event?
3. In future would you respond differently if a similar event occurred?
4. Do you have a few major problems, or many small ones, or none at all?
5. Did the exercise help you to discover possible ways of managing stress?
6. How did you feel doing the exercise?

Prior experience

Experimental studies have shown that rats subjected to a certain amount of stress early in life can 'cope' much better with later stress than rats who have not received this early stimulation. From such studies, as well as related observations on child development, it has been concluded that infants who are stimulated have various advantages in later adaptation to stressful environments.

More specific experience with stressful situations also appears to result in an improved ability to cope. In a study of parachutists, it was found that experienced and inexperienced parachutists showed quite different reactions prior to a jump. The experienced ones reported becoming progressively less fearful from the time of the decision to jump up to the actual jump, whereas the reverse was found for the inexperienced group. Experienced parachutists were apparently able to anticipate and deal with the stress of the jump in advance so that, by the time of the jump, they were less likely to experience anxiety that would interfere with performance.

Specific experience of this type therefore provides knowledge about a situation, and places the individual in a more predictable position where they can be aware of how their own behaviour will affect and be affected by a potential stressor.

Information

This arises directly from the point made above (i.e. experience can provide the individual with information about a coming event). It is also possible to provide people with information in order to facilitate their adaptive reactions to stress.

In a series of studies of surgical patients (Redman, 1988) it has been shown that providing the patient with information about the operation and post-operative pain can aid the recovery process. However, it seems that the success of such prior information is at least partly dependent on the style of coping adopted by the patient.

Social support

Research on the impact of stressful events has shown that a person's social environment can have an influence on their reactions to stress. One aspect of the social environment that appears to be important is the support of or access to helpful or sympathetic individuals. Certainly emotional support plays an important role in early emotional and social development, which in turn can considerably influence later behaviour.

There is even evidence that severe emotional deprivation in early life can give rise to serious physical problems, such as deficiencies in growth hormone. Thus, in general terms, insufficient early social support can give rise to physical and behavioural abnormalities, including a reduced ability to withstand stress.

There is a great deal of evidence to suggest that people will cope more successfully with a stressful situation if they have access to a social support system. It has been shown that the recovery of people who have suffered strokes can be significantly affected by the understanding and empathy shown by members of the family, and that individuals who have had a close and confiding relationship with another person are less likely to develop psychiatric problems.

Divorce, the death of a loved one or serious illness are usually more devastating if one is alone. Sometimes, however, family and friends can increase the stress. Minimising the seriousness of the problem or giving a blind assurance that 'everything will be all right' may produce more anxiety than no support at all. For example, people who are realistically supportive of those taking crucial examinations ('I'm worried, but I know you'll do the best you can') are more helpful than people who deny any possibility of failure ('I'm not worried; I'm sure you'll pass'). In the latter case, the student has to worry not only about failing the exam, but also about losing the respect of their supporter.

Stress is also easier to tolerate when the cause of the stress is shared with others. Community disasters—floods, earthquakes, tornadoes, wars—often seem to bring out the best in people. Individual anxieties and conflicts tend to be forgotten when people are working together against a common enemy or towards a common goal. For example, during the intensive bombing of London during World War II, there was a marked decline in the number of people seeking help for emotional problems.

ACTIVITY 1.5

Developing support systems

Some people experiencing severe crises or major life changes find individual counselling beneficial. However, for many kinds of crises—such as frequent moves, job retrenchment/redundancy or worker/supervisor conflicts—no counselling help is available.

1. List some crises that have been experienced by people you know. What support systems were available to assist them? What support systems were needed? Have any of these systems been developed since these crises occurred?
2. What different types of support systems do you think could be organised to help people manage crises? Below are a few possibilities, some of which already exist:
   - newcomers' club
   - babysitters' cooperative
   - crisis hot-line
   - infirm elderly people or potential child abusers (or others in need) receive two check-in phone calls per day
   - meals on wheels
   - AIDS hot-line
   - community watch
   - support group for the families of the mentally ill

- support group for parents who both work
- redundancy club
- dial a 'listener'
- the 'say no to suicide' line
- support group for children of divorced parents
- support group for families of terminally or chronically ill individuals
- alcoholics anonymous.

Can you add any further suggestions to this list?

3. You might consider ways you could provide an active support system either individually or collectively in an organisation (work or community) for other people experiencing a crisis. How would you help these people to recognise alternatives for managing change?

Locus of control

Locus of control refers to another personality difference that influences the individual's perception of a stressful event and its impact on behaviour. Locus of control refers to the degree of control that individuals think they have over what happens to them.

Persons who see themselves as having control over their environment are less likely to be affected by stress. Such people have an *internal* locus of control. Others feel they are like flotsam and jetsam, that their lives and what happens to them are determined by others or by outside events. They do not believe they have control (i.e. they have an *external locus* of control philosophy), and stressors will tend to play havoc with their lives.

There are a number of human and animal experiments that indicate that lack of control over unpleasant or stressful stimuli is associated with a greater vulnerability to physical illness.

In the case of human beings, many harmful and distressing situations appear to be aggravated when individuals feel entirely helpless, believing that nothing they can do will significantly alter the outcome.

Seligman (1975) has called this condition *learned helplessness*. He regards some human depressions as a form of learned helplessness, and has successfully treated people by encouraging them to succeed, at first with simple tasks and then with progressively more demanding ones.

ACTIVITY 1.6

Locus of control

Complete the following questionnaire by circling the number in the relevant column:

	Strongly agree	Agree	Disagree	Strongly disagree
1. People who never get sick are just lucky	1	2	3	4
2. Most people can be successful it they try	4	3	2	1
3. We might as well make decisions by tossing a coin	1	2	3	4
4. Much of the time the future seems uncertain to me	1	2	3	4
5. I will often stick at things when they are hard because I believe I can overcome them	4	3	2	1
6. War between countries is inevitable	1	2	3	4
7. If I take care of myself I can avoid illness	4	3	2	1
8. Life is mostly a gamble	1	2	3	4
9. What I do and become depends mainly on me	4	3	2	1
10. I can affect the way others behave towards me	4	3	2	1
11. I have little influence over the things that happen to me	1	2	3.	4
12. Getting a good job is a matter of being in the right place at the right time	1	2	3	4

Score this questionnaire by adding up the numbers that you circled. The lower your score, the more you are an *external* locus of control person. The higher your score, the more you are an *internal* locus of control person. The maximum score is 48 and the minimum is 12. Remember that an external locus of control person (a low scorer) will perceive not only more stress, but will be less able to do anything about it. They will feel helpless in the face of stressors. Such a person must try the stress management skills and techniques discussed in this book, such as relaxation, positive thinking, self-concept enhancement and assertive behaviour, in order to create more personal control of the environment.

The role of perception in stress

What we see, hear or feel is not always a true reflection of reality. Each of us organises our perception of events into something that is meaningful to us as individual—that makes sense to us. Perception is an active process in which 'distortion' of 'reality' can occur. The same happens with stress. Activities 1.7 and 1.8 demonstrate the role that perception plays in how we see 'reality'.

ACTIVITY 1.7

The Lady

Look at 'The Lady' illustration (Figure 1.2) and then answer the questions at the top of the next page.

Figure 1.2 The Lady

SOURCE: Originally drawn by W.E. Hill and published in *Puck*, 6 November 1905. It was first used for psychological purposes by E.G. Boring, 'A New Ambiguous Figure', *American Journal of Psychology*, 1930.

1. Is the lady young or old?
2. Is she pleasant-looking or lined and tired?
3. Does she seem to have a large nose or a normal-sized nose?

The chances are that some of you will look at the illustration and see the face of an old woman, while others will see a pleasant-looking young woman. In fact, once you have settled on one interpretation, it may be hard for you to let go of that perspective long enough to see the alternative possibility. By going through this simple exercise, you will discover first-hand the role of perception in shaping your experiences.

ACTIVITY 1.8

The process of perception

Look at the Muller-Lyer illusion below (Figure 1.3). Which of the two has the longer centre line, A or B?

Figure 1.3   The Muller-Lyer illusion

If you measure the two horizontal lines, you will see that they are exactly the same length. The Muller-Lyer illusion points up an interesting fact: you seldom see an object all by itself. Instead, you almost always see an object in context or in relationship to the other objects around it. In the Muller-Lyer illusion, the two horizontal lines have 'tails' at either end that affect your perception of the lines themselves.

Now look at Figure 1.4. The two centre dots are exactly the same size, but they do not look the same.

Figure 1.4   The illusion of the centre dots

Can you read the word in Figure 1.5? You will have to decide which is figure and which is ground.

Figure 1.5 Can you read the word?

The impact of emotional states on perception

It does not require a parade of scientific findings to demonstrate that emotional states and moods tend to influence perception. Folk wisdom has recognised this relationship since time immemorial. The lover, we say, sees everything through 'rose-coloured glasses'. The child's happy optimism makes the world appear to be their oyster.

Experiments designed to investigate the influence of moods and emotional states are relatively straightforward. The experimenter induces a mood or emotional state in the subject, and then compares their responses in a perceptual test situation either to the subject's normal responses, or to those of a matched control group, who are not under the influence of an emotional state.

Leuba and Lucas (1949) hypnotised three subjects, and by means of suggestion induced three different moods in each subject: happy', 'critical' and 'anxious'. While in each mood, the subjects were presented with six pictures, which they were asked to describe following a brief observation period. In general, the descriptions corresponded to the induced moods. For example, one picture shown to the hypnotised subjects was that of a wounded man being carried by soldiers to an aeroplane. Subject A, in a 'happy attitude', gave the following description: 'Wounded soldier. Good thing men were there to help him and get him to a hospital. The men in this war are well taken care of.' When Subject A was put in a 'critical attitude', this was his description of the same picture: 'Wounded or killed soldier; one more in a million who are just killing each other off. That's war, I guess. We must think it's fun or we wouldn't do something so useless as murder and destruction.' Finally, while in an 'anxious attitude', the same subject described the picture in this fashion: 'He is wounded and they're taking him to a plane, but he's in bad shape and may not live, even though the plane will rush him to a hospital.'

How expectations influence our perception

People's perceptions are much influenced by their expectations. Kelly (1950), doing experimental work in this area, told a class of students that, as their lecturer was away and the class was to include discussion, he would give them a brief description of the personality of the lecturer's replacement. Half of the students were given a sheet describing 'a rather cold person, industrious, critical, practical and determined'. The other half were given the same description, except that the words 'rather cold' were changed to 'very warm.'

The replacement lecturer arrived and took charge of the discussion. Afterwards the students were asked to give their impressions of him. The analysis of these impressions showed that the students who were told he was warm described him as 'more considerate of others, more informal, more sociable, more popular and more humane' than did those who had been led to believe he was 'rather cold'. In addition to analysing what the students said about the lecturer, the experimenter had noted the number of times each student had taken part in the discussion, and he found that the behaviour of the two groups was different—those who had more positive feelings about the lecturer participated more. Clearly, then, the students' expectations were affecting both their experience and their behaviour.

As we have seen, our needs, motives and feelings influence our perception of events and people. Our perceptions, how we view an event, can sometimes make the difference between feeling that something is acceptable or finding it distressing. Not feeling good about ourselves, for example, can make us misjudge situations. We may feel that we have to do something, even if we are not comfortable doing it, because we are afraid of not being liked. Family attitudes or cultural values can also affect how we perceive stressors. A person who is taught that occasional failure in the process of learning is normal, for example, will not be distressed when they try something that does not work out just as planned. Instead, the person can perceive the failure as a way to learn.

The same stressful event can be perceived quite differently by two people depending on what the situation means to them. The objective facts of the situation are less important than how the individual appraises them.

Stress management strategies

The goal of stress management is not to eliminate the stress response, but to determine and control *individual optimum stress levels*—that is, where stress will work *for* you and not *against* you.

Stress management involves several strategies that may be employed to help control your responses to stressful situations. Effective management of stress involves two stages:

1. *Awareness*   Identifying your own stress reactions and your stressors.
2. *Control*   Working towards self-responsibility.

After signs of stress have been identified and the sources of the stressors determined, you are ready to move on to a management plan. An individual's particular stress management plan can utilise one or more of the remaining effective skills and techniques outlined in this book (Skills 2–10).

ACTIVITY 1.9

Stress sources and reactions

Using all the information you now have about the sources of your stress and your stress reactions, write down at the end of your Stress Diary (from Activity 1.1 on page 57):

1. Your major stress sources.
2. Your stress reactions.

Consult your Stress Diary and any information from the previous activities that will help you. You might want to write out the stress sources and stress reactions in a table like this:

My stress sources	My stress reactions
Pressure of work	Panic. Sweating. Can't think straight
Elderly invalid parent always complaining	Irritation and angry outbursts

Try the 'Stress questionnaire' that follows. It will help you to see which stress management skills you will benefit most from.

Stress questionnaire
Read the following statements and tick the ones that seem to describe the way you think, feel and behave.

1. I make strong demands on myself. ☐
2. I may seem easy-going, but I won't let anyone push me around. ☐
3. I feel lonely much of the time. ☐
4. I get angry when things don't go my way. ☐
5. Happiness is more important than money. ☐
6. I try very hard to be a good person. ☐
7. I work hard and play hard. ☐
8. When I'm tired or unwell, I often sleep quite late. ☐
9. I hate to disappoint anyone. ☐
10. People seldom come up to my expectation. ☐
11. I live in the present and take things as they come. ☐
12. One of my faults is that I try too hard to please everyone. ☐
13. I have a great need for praise, recognition and flattery. ☐
14. I enjoy all sorts of people. ☐
15. If I'm belittled or criticised, I tend to brood about it. ☐
16. I'm an aggressive, go-getting sort of person. ☐
17. I don't mind having to work under pressure. ☐
18. I often feel people are talking about me behind my back ☐
19. I tend to have strong likes and dislikes. ☐
20. Sometimes I like to loaf around the house alone. ☐
21. I can't bear being near people who are rude or unfriendly. ☐
22. When I see a man/woman I like, I often pursue him/her. ☐
23. I find it hard to hold a grudge for very long. ☐
24. Sometimes it's very difficult for me to say no. ☐
25. I feel I have to push to get what I want, ☐
26. I like men/women who are amusing, agreeable companions. ☐

27. If I'm upset, I try not to show it. ☐
28. I'm never totally satisfied with my accomplishments. ☐
29. On the whole, my life seems quite full and enjoyable. ☐
30. To me, love is one of the most important things in the world. ☐
31. I find it hard to slow down or take things easy. ☐
32. I like to compete, even if I don't always win. ☐
33. I'm a giving person. ☐
34. I have a low tolerance for disappointment or frustration. ☐
35. I love to take impromptu trips and excursions. ☐
36. I worry about what people think of me. ☐
37. No matter how well things are going, my ambitions are seldom satisfied. ☐
38. I'm fairly calm about my love life. ☐
39. Sometimes I'm overwhelmed with feelings of hopelessness. ☐
40. I detest getting sick and tend to ignore minor ailments. ☐
41. I like to meet new people. ☐
42. It seems to me that life is cruel and that rewards are very rare. ☐
43. I don't like to waste my time on trivialities. ☐
44. I would not work for a dishonest or reprehensible boss. ☐
45. When I lose a friend or lover, my whole world crumbles. ☐
46. I tend to demand perfection from my mate or lover. ☐
47. As long as it's in fun, I don't mind being teased or baited. ☐
48. I consider myself extremely thoughtful and tactful. ☐
49. I always try to be impeccably dressed and groomed. ☐
50. In someone I really like, I can overlook many flaws. ☐
51. I often become ill after an emotional upset. ☐
52. Watch out, I'm a dangerous person to cross. ☐
53. On the whole, I have a live-and-let-live attitude. ☐
54. I try to see the good in people rather than the bad. ☐
55. I tend to feel tense and defensive when I'm around important successful people. ☐
56. It doesn't bother me very much to admit I'm wrong. ☐
57. When asked for help, I find it very hard to refuse. ☐
58. Criticism or nitpicking tends to make me furious. ☐
59. I feel pleased when a friend scores a big success. ☐
60. I work very hard to live up to my ideals. ☐

Stress questionnaire: Feedback sheet

In the following table, circle the numbers of the items that you ticked in the questionnaire:

X	Y	Z
1	2	3
4	5	6
7	8	9
10	11	12
13	14	15
16	17	18
19	20	21
22	23	24
25	26	27
28	29	30
31	32	33
34	35	36
37	38	39
40	41	42
43	44	45
46	47	48
49	50	51
52	53	54
55	56	57
58	59	60

Now count up the number of responses you have circled in each of columns X, Y and Z. The column containing the most circled numbers represents your primary mode of reacting to stress. The one containing the fewest represents your least frequent mode of reaction.

The mode X person

Mode X people are ambitious, aggressive strivers who work without let-up to maintain their self-image. They cannot tolerate failure or criticism because these will reawaken the feelings of worthlessness that they dread. They find it difficult ever to relax or slow down, because that, too, might allow self-doubt to catch up with them.

Mode X people react to stress by denying it, rising above it, fighting against it. They see adversity as another obstacle that must be overcome. They fight any weakness within themselves, either physical or emotional, with great determination.

Since people in this category often ignore the early symptoms of an illness, they are more apt than other people to succumb to serious diseases. Research has shown that the mode X type is much more prone to heart attacks than other groups.

Stress management for the mode X person
The mode X person will benefit most from therapeutic techniques that help them to slow down and take life easy. Time management, meditation, self-concept enhancement, relaxation exercises and similar methods can be very helpful in reducing the effects of stress. Perhaps more important, with the help of such techniques, the mode X person should come to the realisation that they now *are* a strong, dynamic, successful individual, and no longer need to be goaded by the fear of personal inadequacy.

The mode Y person

Whatever their other characteristics, mode Y people are those who in childhood were conditioned to feel secure, perhaps even complacent, about themselves. Carried over into adulthood, this allows them a self-esteem that cannot easily be shaken by illness, failure or adversity.

Unlike the mode X person, they see no shame in coddling themselves when ill or fatigued. They can also acknowledge emotional or physical weaknesses without feeling invalidated by them, and will take minor or even major failures in their stride, regarding them as temporary setbacks rather than proof of worthlessness.

All this gives the mode Y person pliancy in the face of stress that is lacking in the other two modes.

The mode Z person

Mode Z people are sometimes so unselfish and self-sacrificing that they seem almost saint-like. They tend to put other people's wishes above their own, and have difficulty in asserting themselves or expressing hostility. Emotions like anger and rage are turned inward, against the self, resulting in feelings of guilt and worthlessness.

Mode Z people work extra hard in order to expiate the guilt and prove that they are 'good' after all. They have difficulty in coping with the effects of stress, which are particularly severe for this type of person and often lead to disease or depression.

According to Leshan (1964), cancer is the highest-risk disease for mode Z people. During a 25-year study, Leshan found that 76 per cent of cancer patients had a mode Z life history pattern, as opposed to only 10 per cent among non-cancer patients.

Stress management for the mode Z person
The mode Z person will benefit from the techniques that help them to release blocked emotions: self-enhancement, assertiveness training, decision making and similar positive behaviours. Mode Z people need to overcome their fear of rejection and to become more positive in asserting their own needs and desires.

How do you respond to stress?
If you checked more answers in the Y column than any other, you are basically pliant and adaptable, and able to turn a period of stress and pressure into an opportunity for growth.

If Y was your second most frequent answer, you still possess fair adaptive powers and can probably take many of life's upheavals in your stride.

With Y as your least frequent answer, after both X and Z, you show a relative vulnerability to stressful events.

Summary

The key points to remember about *Skill 1: Understanding what stress is and how it affects you* are:

- When stressed, people experience a number of physiological responses.
- Excessive amounts of stress over prolonged periods can lead to serious illness, including heart disease and cancer.
- Excessive stress can have equally damaging emotional effects.
- Reactions to stress differ from person to person, depending, for example, on personality, prior experience, social support, an individual's ability to cope, and our own perceptions or 'distortions' of reality.

By completing the activities in this chapter, you should now have a clearer understanding or your own reactions to stress, and the types of events that you, as an individual, find stressful.

This understanding of what stress is and how it affects you forms the foundation for learning the remaining nine skills in this book. Without this increased self-awareness, it will be difficult to gain the maximum benefit from the stress management skills and strategies taught in this book.

SKILL 2

Improve your decision making

Introduction

It may seem strange that decision making is the second skill to be learned in stress management, after understanding what stress is and how it affects you. But if you cannot make decisions, you may never be able to positively decide to adopt the eight major stress management skills that follow. So let's learn to make that decision.

ACTIVITY 2.1

Can you make decisions?

For each of the following statements, circle TRUE or FALSE (i.e. most nearly true or false for you).

1. I often have difficulty in making up my mind.   TRUE   FALSE
2. I am good at thinking of alternatives in most situations.   TRUE   FALSE
3. If I have an important decision to make, I always weigh up the advantages and disadvantages of each choice.   TRUE   FALSE
4. If I make a decision and it doesn't turn out to be a good one, it is still my responsibility and I can 'own' it.   TRUE   FALSE
5. There are some occasions when it is better to delay making a decision.   TRUE   FALSE

If you are good at making decisions, you should have answered the above like this:

1. False.
2. True.
3. True.
4. True.
5. True.

One problem that those who experience stress often face is that they find it difficult to make decisions. When under stress, having to make a decision causes even more stress. But decision making, like relaxation and assertiveness, is a skill that can be learnt, and stress can thus be reduced. You will no longer need to worry about having to make a decision or what decision should be made. You will no longer have to say to yourself, 'Oh dear, I don't know what to do or say.' Being able to make decisions gives you confidence, and is part of the positive outlook on life and on the self that you will develop from applying some of the techniques that follow.

Decision making and locus of control

When you were learning about *Skill 1: Understanding what stress is and how it affects you*, you completed a questionnaire (Activity 1.6) and read about locus of control. Remember that people who give up at the slightest barrier are often called *externally directed* (or 'externals'). They are said to have an external locus of control. They believe that external events control their lives—for example, luck, powerful others and destiny. Those who are *internally directed* (or 'internals') have an internal locus of control and believe in their own ability and power to change themselves, or to overcome feasible barriers. Externally directed people are fatalistic and passive; they *allow* things to happen to them. Internally directed individuals are active, know where they want to go, have a plan and *make decisions* to ensure that their plan works out. They will decide, for the most part, what they can be and achieve, taking into account their own limitations and assets, aiming to maximise the latter and improve on the former.

Some of you may remember the hilarious and somewhat far-fetched successful activities of the 'A Team' on television. They are an extreme example of self-directed 'internals', who plan their lives to achieve their specific aims, not allowing others to direct their lives.

The externally directed person feels far more stress from a situation because they believe they cannot do much about it. They feel resentful, sometimes guilty, and of course experience stress when making decisions. In their view, their decision may be wrong or have no effect.

Constraints on decision making

Of course there are situations where the environment imposes constraints and restrictions on decision making. There are some social, physical, legal and environmental factors over which we cannot have any influence. For example:

- We cannot change the rainfall of an area because we have decided to grow different crops.
- We cannot choose to drive ourselves in the family car to work rather than going in the bus if we have been banned from driving.
- We cannot choose to become a flight attendant if our height is not within a specified range.
- We cannot choose to watch an alternative TV channel if there is no local transmitter for that channel.

You may think that you have no choice about whether you go to work, whether you get up in the morning, or whether you even wear any clothes! Of course you *do* have a choice. But the problem is that the consequences of making an unrealistic or inappropriate decision can be very serious. Where the constraint on decision making does not stem from you but from an environmental reality, the options between which you choose must be realistic ones. You do not have complete freedom, but you probably have more choices than you imagine.

The problem is that external barriers on some decision options make some people feel so irritated and tense that they simply 'give up'. While laws, social customs and economic conditions might restrict our activities, remember that (a) there are many options still open within those restrictions, and (b) laws often have exemptions of which we may be unaware. So do not always take everything for granted. Check first with people who are in the advice/counselling business.

Remember, too, that if you are an 'internal', you have the personal drive to try to overcome environmental restrictions in socially approved ways. If you never try, you can never succeed. It is vital that you do take some decisions and have some control over your own life and over what happens to you and what you become. It is only by being committed to make the best of yourself and of your situation that life can become meaningful and pleasurable, rather than unhappy and filled with resentment and stress.

Self-imposed constraints

Restrictions that you place on yourself are due to a combination of personality, values and previous learning experience. You may tend to avoid making a decision because such avoidance worked for you in the past, or because you have a tendency to be an 'external'.

Some people cannot face up to making decisions: 'I don't know what to do,' they complain. Or they depend on friends and relatives to make decisions for them. We often restrict our lives and choices by saying, 'I am no good at . . .' or 'I'll never cope with . . .'. But it is amazing what we *can* do if we put our minds to it. Few people ever operate at their full potential. A little more effort, confidence and interest will reveal a greater range of activities, behaviours and options that are open to everybody. Self-imposed constraints such as 'I can't', 'I never had a chance' and 'I am a failure' mean a loss of choices for alternative actions, and remove the chance of developing in a variety of *possible* directions.

ACTIVITY 2.2

Self-imposed constraints

Have you ever made any of the following (or similar) statements, either to yourself or to other people?

- 'I can't . . .'
- 'I am no good at . . .'
- 'I'll never pass . . .'

- 'I don't think I could manage to . . . '
- 'I just can't be like that . . . '

1. Write down the issues relating to the situation where your responses were similar to any of the above.
2. Do you feel that you missed an opportunity?
3. What action do you think you could have taken instead of responding in this way?

The biggest thief of time is indecision. On arriving at the point of decision many people vacillate, procrastinate or in other ways refuse to decide. Not only does indecision waste time, but it also involves worry. It may cause worry, result from it or simply accompany it. And worry is so destructive that it makes a person tired before they can even make a start.

Even if you do feel powerless, frustrated and tense because you believe you have so little control over your own life and future, do not give in. What decisions you do make may be small ones, but you have to try and make them, and make them in a way that faces up to the reality of the situation in which you are. It is too easy to avoid facing up to reality. Refusing to confront things will prevent you from doing anything to change them. Once people give up trying to have some control over their own lives, they become psychologically numb and more liable to manipulation by others. They become powerless and alienated from work, society and life itself.

As you will see, despite your previous experience and behaviour in decision making, the external constraints of society and the environment, and your self-imposed constraints, you do have greater freedom to make choices.

ACTIVITY 2.3

What are the real constraints?

We have seen that there are real constraints on our choices in some situations: legal, physical, environmental and even self-imposed. Make a list under the two headings in the sample table at the top of the next page. Write down items that are important to you, your future and the sort of life you want to lead. Some examples are provided to get you started.

Things I am unable to change	Things I can change
Age	Overweight
Height	Lack of confidence
...	...

1. Look at your list of things that you decided you are unable to change, and put an X next to any item that, if you are really honest with yourself, you think you are able to change. (If you prefer, ask a friend to mark the items.)
2. Now look at your list of 'Things I can change' and write down what you regard as the advantages to yourself and others if you implement some of these changes.
3. In the light of what you have discovered in 1 and 2 above, revise your list. Do you see that you have far more choices than you may have previously believed?

Your moods, habits and behaviour *can* change if you really want them to. So look at your lists again and see if you can give yourself a 'face-lift'. Trying out new ways of behaving—particularly those that help you build more positive relationships with others—as well as trying new ways of thinking about yourself that encourage more self-confidence, cheerfulness, resourcefulness and stress control can be your choice just as much as trying out a newly advertised breakfast cereal or a new hairstyle.

You may also choose to refuse or delay making a decision. Provided this is done for the reason of waiting for more information or for other matters to be resolved first, this is fine. *What you must not do is refuse to make a decision in order to avoid having to make any decision at all.*

No one can avoid making decisions, particularly the far-reaching ones such as, for example, those that occur during adolescence to do with subject choice that will affect any future career. Many decisions we take affect other people, too, and so their views and reactions must be considered. Some young couples, for example, have to decide whether career should come before parenthood. This decision obviously affects both partners and the future earning/spending potential of the couple. Should a young person get a job to keep their widowed parent, or should they continue with their studies, leaving both of them with little money now but a potentially healthier financial situation in the future when they are qualified? These and many other similar stress-provoking decision situations may come your way.

How can you make decisions about really important matters with a minimum of worry and stress? *Risk is implicit in all decisions*. You will never have all the facts. Every decision is *an* attempt to balance gains, costs and risks.

How do you make a decision?

The simplest explanation of decision making is that people choose the alternative that leads to the greatest amount of positive benefit to them in terms of their interests and values. However, it is not possible to jump immediately from this general principle to making excellent decisions. On the pages that follow, the DECIDE model of decision making, and the 'balance sheet' method of decision making (which can form part of the DECIDE model), are examined.

The DECIDE model

There are several steps in making sound, satisfying decisions, and you are likely to go through all of them, either consciously or unconsciously. Very briefly, these steps are:

D Determine or define the problem or difficulty.
E Express your aim(s) or purpose.
C Collect information (find sources that are reliable).
I Interpret the information; assess the possible solutions.
D Decide what to do; choose the most appropriate solution that most satisfies your aims.
E Examine your decision later (i.e. review and see if it is working out).

This is the DECIDE model of decision making. Each of the steps in the DECIDE model will now be examined.

Determine or define the problem or difficulty
The first step in decision making can be very easy, or just the opposite. Usually it is clear that you have a problem that needs to be solved. For example, if you need to lose weight or increase your income, you are quite aware that the problem exists. No one

can begin to make any headway against a problem without first recognising that there is one. A husband may be spending so much time on sporting activities that his relationship with his wife is beginning to suffer. But he may be unaware of this fact and its effect—and thus be unable to do anything about it—until, for example, a supervisor comments on his poor work.

Sometimes it is harder than this. A person may have a vague sense of dissatisfaction with life, or even feel extremely worried, stressed or upset without being able to put a finger on any specific problem. But even then, as soon as the person can say 'I am not happy; maybe I can change myself or my environment to make things better,' the solution to the problem is underway.

The necessary first step in any kind of personal problem solving is to acknowledge that a problem exists and to believe that change is possible. Can you acknowledge that you have stress and that it is affecting your behaviour and your health? For example, a manager may be worrying about their time management, but until the cause of the poor performance is located, it is impossible to make sensible plans to improve the situation. The reason could be too heavy a workload, ill-health, family problems, poor work habits or a host of other possibilities. Merely deciding to 'try harder' is not likely to produce satisfactory results.

The simple process of talking your problems over with someone may help you see it more objectively.

Exploring the difficulty, however, does not always involve a search for underlying causes. Very often all that is necessary is to define the problem a little more narrowly. For example, if a person feels that their problem is a lack of money, they should not stop at this point and accept such a vague definition. They should ask themselves: 'Why is this lack of money making me feel so uneasy? Is it because I am short of money for necessities, or because my debts are overwhelming me, or is it because I desire some luxuries in my life?'

Express your aim(s) or purpose

Analysing the problem, finding its causes and narrowing it down to manageable size all help you to know your aim. In general terms, your aim will be to remove the problem once you have determined what it is. The aim is what you want to achieve, and if possible you should state it in very specific terms. It is no good simply saying 'my aim is to improve my health'. This is too vague. You will have a better chance of making a decision about the best way to go about it if you state your aim with specific goals in mind. So your aim now becomes 'to begin a reputable diet plan and reduce my weight by 20 kg, and to start jogging every day'. Once you have a specific aim like this, it is possible to see whether you can achieve your aim or not. In addition, the decision you have made, selected from a number of different choices, can be evaluated (i.e. was it the best decision?).

Collect information

The next step in decision making is to gather all the information that may have a bearing on your final plan. In making personal decisions, two kinds of information are essential: information about yourself and information about the situation.

Information about yourself

The better you understand yourself—that is, the more you know about your likes and dislikes, your strengths and weaknesses, and your attitudes and values—the more likely you are to make decisions that will be right for you.

It is neither possible nor necessary to be cold-bloodedly objective about yourself. But it is possible to isolate a few characteristics that have a bearing on the particular decision that needs to be made. For example, Barbara is offered two part-time jobs, one in the university library and the other at a fast-food restaurant. Which one should she take? She knows that she likes a quiet atmosphere, enjoys reading and has good verbal skills. She also has good manual dexterity, likes to cook and handle food, and enjoys people. These qualities by no means describe everything there is to know about Barbara. But they are a few of the characteristics that she thinks may have a bearing on which job she should choose. The important thing is that she recognises that her own personal characteristics are an essential ingredient in deciding which job to take.

Information about the situation

Without facts about a situation, reliable decisions cannot be made. What kind of work would Barbara be doing at the library? Would it involve working with office machines, talking with students at the circulation desk, re-shelving books or keying in catalogue information on a computer? What do the two jobs pay? How far away is the restaurant? Would transportation be a problem? What are the hours for each job? What are the supervisors like? Barbara should be extremely careful to get the facts right. She should not assume, for example, that because the restaurant manager is friendly, the hours will be convenient.

In collecting information at this stage, you should try not to eliminate any possibilities. Sometimes one can make the mistake of closing one's options too soon. If your need is for a quiet place to work, do not rule out 'far-fetched' ideas like an empty room, a park bench, a garden shed or the air-conditioning room in your office. These may turn out to be terrible ideas: the places may be noisy, unavailable when you need them or physically uncomfortable. But do not let fears about the impracticality of a solution stop you from considering it as a possible option.

This is the creative stage in decision making. Use your imagination, your experience, your reading, your colleagues and your friends to list every possible solution to your problem. (Of course, it is not entirely possible to keep yourself from weighing alternatives and judging solutions as soon as you think of them. No human mind is that compartmentalised. But you must certainly refrain from making snap decisions at this stage.) Go ahead and get the facts about each possible solution. Criticism (evaluation) of the different possibilities comes later.

Interpret the information

Perhaps the most important part of decision making—and unfortunately the most neglected—is sorting and weighing information about the various alternatives. Most of us do not use our brains to full capacity to process the information we acquire.

Most decisions involve more than immediate consequences, and most have more than two alternatives. Usually several possibilities are available, and the important consequences of each one are often difficult to calculate. For many of us, our experience has poorly prepared us to sort and interpret the large amounts of information that have to be handled to arrive at a good decision.

Also, we sometimes do not foresee the consequences of our actions, even when information is available. When undesirable consequences do occur, we wonder why we chose as we did. We must weigh up each possible solution in the light of the aim(s) that we have set for ourselves, and then choose the alternative with the most advantages. (We will be working with a 'balance sheet' (page 99) to have a look at this stage of the decision-making process when choices involve consequences for other people as well as for ourselves.)

Decide what to do
This stage of the DECIDE model involves re-evaluating the alternatives, taking a risk and being objective.

Re-evaluate the alternatives
After all this problem defining, information collecting and weighing up of alternatives, it might seem that making the actual decision would be relatively easy. Most people, however, have trouble making choices. When one alternative is clearly better than another in all ways, there is, of course, no conflict in deciding between them. But often we find that one alternative is better in some ways, and another is better in other ways. Because of this, we experience *conflict* in choosing among the alternatives. In such a case, the practicality of each alternative must be re-evaluated.

Similarly, one is often faced with a decision in which no alternative seems better than any other. In this type of situation, you will probably depend on your 'state of mind' or on what you assume (without evidence) to be the advantages of one course of action. In some cases, to avoid unpleasant uncertainty, you may convince yourself that one choice is better than another even though there is no clear-cut advantage.

Take a risk
Most decisions contain an element of risk, for no one can know precisely what will result from the choice of any given alternative. The problem is to choose the alternative that offers the best positive pay-off and the highest probability that the pay-off will take place.

In life, decisions often occur in sequence. Information available for later decisions is likely to depend on the nature and consequences of earlier decisions. This suggests that a single decision has some relationship not only to decisions that were made before it, but also to decisions that have to be made after it. This interdependence makes present decisions more important and, in a sense, more risky, because you cannot know all the ways in which a decision may affect your future range of choices.

It may be encouraging to recall, when thinking about risks, that most successful people have not become so by avoiding risks. Marie Curie and the Wright brothers, to name only two examples, took reasonable chances and kept going despite repeated failures. Risk-taking is a part of every decision and every meaningful life.

Be objective
No doubt you have been told many times to be *objective* when making a decision. This simply means that your judgment should be unaffected by your feelings, and the advice is given in the hope that your choice will be made on the basis of what will be best for you in the long run. Unfortunately, few if any guidelines can be suggested to help you become objective. No matter how objective you try to be, there are elements in every decision that are subjective. Your personal characteristics, needs and values definitely influence the choices you make. For example, in some individuals the drive to achieve success is greater than to achieve security; hence they will be more inclined to take risky choices.

Examine your decision later
It is never too late to change the course of your life. Although certain options may be closed because of earlier decisions, there is always something that can be done to *improve* a bad situation.

For this reason, examining the consequences of a decision makes a lot of sense. The sooner the consequences can be evaluated, the more likely it is that you can get back on the right track, if you find you are not on it. Minor adjustments made early can make a big difference to your final destination.

An example of the DECIDE model
Let us now look at a simple example of this DECIDE model in action.

A computer-buying expedition:

1. *Determine or define the problem*
   You want to buy a new computer immediately.

2. *Express your aim(s) or purpose*
   To buy as cheaply as possible a new PC that is available now and has:

   - At least a 2-year warranty
   - A Pentium 3 processor or better
   - At least a 40Gb hard disk
   - A processor speed of 2.0GHz

- RAM of 256 MB
- 128 bits full duplex sound card
- 56X CD-ROM drive
- Multi-media speaker system
- 56bps internal modem.

3. *Collect information*
   The main information required is:

   - The price of the different makes and models.
   - The type of processor in each of the different makes and models.
   - The capacity (speed, memory and hard disk size) of the different makes and models.
   - Compatibility with other computers (e.g. at work).
   - Whether each is in stock and their respective warranty periods.

   (You could add other factors if you wish.)

4. *Interpret the information*

	Model X	Model Y	Model Z
Price	$2000	$2500	$2750
Processor type	Athlon 1900	Pentium 3	Pentium 4
Hard disk size	30Gb	40Gb	40Gb
Processor speed	1.9GHz	2GHz	2.4GHz
RAM	128MB	256MB	256MB
In stock	Yes	Yes	No
Warranty period	2 years	2 years	1 year
Full duplex sound card	128bps	128bps	128bps
56X CD-ROM drive	Yes	Yes	Yes
Multi-media speaker system	Yes	Yes	Yes
56bps internal modem	Yes	Yes	Yes

Brand Z is eliminated because it is not in stock, the warranty period is less than required and many other aspects are the same as the slightly cheaper Brand Y. Brand X also fails to meet the requirements although the cheapest. Thus Brand Y seems to be the best choice.

5. *Decide what to do*
   The decision will be made on the basis of the final evaluation in 4 above, weighing cost against hard disk size, RAM, type of processor and warranty period. You have made the choice yourself and must be responsible for the outcome. (Of course,

one decision can be not to buy now but to save more money for the more expensive one, or hope that the price will be reduced.)

6. *Examine your decision later*
   Your review will help you decide whether the computer was a good buy. If you are well satisfied, you may recommend the computer to other people. Your decision was successful!

The 'balance sheet' method of deciding

In some situations, you need to consider very carefully how a particular decision will not only help you to achieve your aim and solve your problem, *but how that decision might affect others.*

Remember that decision making has to be socially and ethically responsible. Deciding to buy a particular pair of shoes for oneself, or deciding to do your gardening before your dinner, has little impact on other people. But deciding whether to drive a car after drinking alcohol, or whether to start a family, or whether to accept a job in a distant town, all have an impact on other people.

The 'balance sheet' becomes part of the DECIDE model at stage 4 (Interpret the information), when you have to compare possible solutions and their effects not only on you, but also on others. The following questions have to be asked in weighing up alternative solutions. If I choose this particular option or course of action:

- What gains or losses are in it for me?
- What gains or losses are in it for significant persons in my life?
- What gains or losses are in it for the social systems of which I am a part (e.g. work, family and clubs)?

An example will make the use of the balance sheet clear. Helen has a conflict between her role as a mother and her role as a solicitor. She cannot decide whether to stay at home to look after her young children, or whether to return to work to continue her professional career and increase the family income. She uses the balance sheet to help her make a decision (see Figure 2.1).

Outlining her options on the balance sheet helps her to clarify her ideas. As a result of comparing the gains and losses for all concerned, she decides that remaining home for the time being will enable her not only to give her children the opportunity to develop in a secure environment, but also to provide increased support for her husband in his career.

Figure 2.1 Helen's decision balance sheet on returning to work

Gains for self	Acceptable to me because	Not acceptable to me because
Able to continue my career, thereby maximising my opportunities for advancement Increased family income Using my brain and education	No longer have to feel like a parasite living off husband Will not suffer a break in my career Intellectually more stimulating	The creche is expensive Housework will have to be done at weekends
Losses for self	**Acceptable to me because**	**Not acceptable to me because**
Less time to be with my children during their formative years	I need to get away from constantly being in children's company, and to be with other adults	I think young children need a close relationship with a parent, particularly when very young
Gains for significant others	**Acceptable to me because**	**Not acceptable to me because**
Husband and children can be helped with extra money Children will develop social skills at the creche	I want husband to stop working overtime It's important for children to become independent of the home	I'm not satisfied with the quality of care that the children will receive at the creche
Losses for significant others	**Acceptable to me because**	**Not acceptable to me because**
Children will miss me Husband will have to help more about the house I'll be busier and less available to the family	The children need to associate with other adults and not depend only on me	A family needs a comfortable, unstressed home Husband should be able to relax at weekends
Social gains	**Acceptable to me because**	**Not acceptable to me because**
We can have a higher standard of living	We would like things that at present we cannot afford	Money and material possessions cannot replace lost years with the children
Social losses	**Acceptable to me because**	**Not acceptable to me because**
Family bonds may not be as strong	Not applicable	Family is more important to me than anything else

ACTIVITY **2.4**

Using the DECIDE model

As an exercise, use the DECIDE model (with the balance sheet if necessary) to make a decision about whether to learn the stress management skills being taught in this book. Remember:

- Define what your problem is (e.g. I am always tense).
- Express your aims (e.g. I want to relax and enjoy life more).
- Collect information (e.g. list skills, changes in lifestyle that will achieve your aims).
- Interpret the information (e.g. what is the most appropriate way of doing this?).
- Decide what to do (e.g. go ahead).
- Examine your decision later (e.g. evaluate how you feel).

ACTIVITY **2.5**

Using the decision balance sheet

Using the sample balance sheet decision in Figure 2.1 as a model, create a balance sheet for yourself based on a conflict situation that is at present bothering you, and about which a decision needs to be made. When you have completed the activity, ask yourself the following questions:

1. Has this method given me greater clarity about my problem?
2. Has it made it easier for me to come to a balanced decision?
3. Has this made me feel less stressed about my problem?

Summary

It is hoped that by now you have positively decided to learn the remaining stress management skills in this book. The ability to make decisions—in an unstressed way—is essential for healthy living. Decision-making skills can always be improved and now that you are aware of some of the constraints on decision making and of some tools for assisting decision making (the DECIDE model and the balance sheet method), you should be able to put into practice and reap the benefits of improved decision making.

SKILL 3

Master the benefits of relaxation

Introduction

One important technique in managing stress is acquiring the ability to elicit 'the relaxation response', a mechanism that nature has provided to help us manage or resist stress. There are several methods of achieving the relaxation response. Meditation, autogenic relaxation, biofeedback-aided relaxation and neuro-muscular relaxation are all examples. While the discussion of perception in *Skill 1: Understanding what stress is and how it affects you* was aimed at reducing the likelihood of perceiving events as stressful, relaxation helps people cope with stressed feelings before, during and after the event.

The development of an ability to relax has short-term and long-term consequences. In the short term, relaxation increases our ability to manage current stress, generates pleasant feelings of personal well-being and frequently produces increased creativity and innovativeness. Long-term consequences of continued use of relaxation make life more satisfying for ourselves as well as less stressful for others around us.

Many people have a sanctuary, or a 'time-out' relaxation activity, which they turn to when they feel stressed or distressed. Think about your answers to these questions:

- Do you relax? If so, where?
- What exactly do you do to relax?
- Did you learn how to relax?

Some people try to relieve feelings of stress by smoking, drinking alcohol, taking pills or over-eating. While these remedies may make some individuals feel better temporarily, they do not remove the stressors in the long run, they do not change our personal perceptions and they do not make stressful life events disappear.

A much more useful response to stress, with long-term positive effects, is *conscious relaxation*. In the relaxation response there are specific bodily changes, including decreased heart rate, lower metabolism and a decreased rate of breathing—all of which bring the body into healthier balance. Researchers believe that people can break out of a prolonged state of stress or distress by summoning this relaxation response, which is easily learnt.

Background to relaxation

Jacobson (1938), one of the earliest researchers in this field, developed his technique during the 1920s and 1930s. He used a method of *progressive physical relaxation training* involving muscle tension and gradual release to a state of no tension. He also pioneered the application of electromyography to record the physiological changes that resulted. Initially this method required lengthy training, but it has been refined over the years to provide a relaxation technique that is fairly simple and easy to learn.

When the body responds to relaxation, the effects are the opposite to those induced by stress, as shown in Figure 3.1. Figure 3.2 shows some of the bodily changes that take place during relaxation.

In Germany, a more cognitive (i.e. knowing or understanding) type of relaxation, now known as *autogenic training*, was developed. This involved experiencing warmth and heaviness in different parts of the body. Physiological changes were reported in hundreds of people.

Figure 3.1   The relationship between stress and relaxation

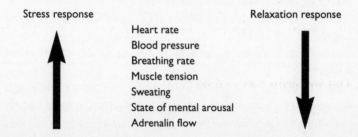

Stress response   Relaxation response

Heart rate
Blood pressure
Breathing rate
Muscle tension
Sweating
State of mental arousal
Adrenalin flow

Figure 3.2   Bodily changes that take place during relaxation

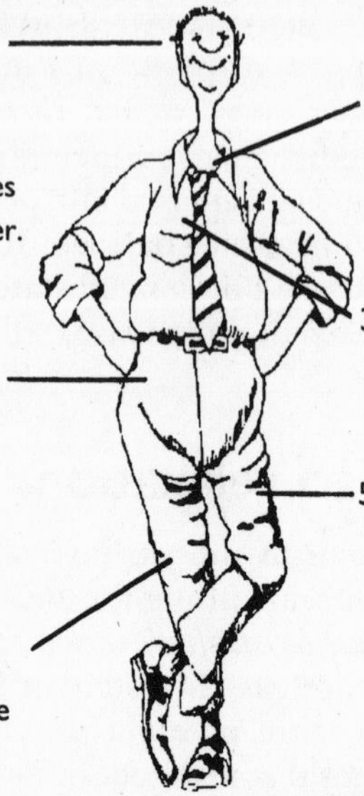

1. The hypothalamus of the brain causes the pituitary gland and the involuntary nervous system to bring about changes; brain waves become slower and deeper.

2. Breathing slows or becomes shallower as less oxygen is needed.

3. Heart rate decreases and blood pressure drops.

4. Adrenal glands no longer produce stress hormones and their presence in the bloodstream decreases rapidly.

5. Sweating decreases markedly.

6. Low electrical activity in the muscles demonstrates marked decrease in muscle tension.

When transcendental meditation (TM) became popularised in the USA in the 1960s, major research projects developed to investigate its effects. *Meditation* generally refers to relaxation attained through the mind attending to a chosen focus. It is an Eastern practice, but may be found in other cultures. For example, contemplative prayer may be regarded as a form of meditative relaxation.

A variety of relaxation techniques are recommended for reducing stress because:

• Relaxation may be approached as a physical skill that can be learnt in similar ways to other skills.
• Relaxation does not have mystical connotations that can put beginners off.
• Relaxation may be successfully learnt in up to 10 short sessions.
• Side effects such as hallucinations do not occur (although these may very occasionally accompany meditative techniques; see page 120).

Benefits of mastering relaxation

Relaxation can be learnt by anyone, and can be applied in every-day life. It involves no drugs or difficult exercises, and it costs nothing. There are six major advantages in practising relaxation:

1. *Relaxation can reduce the stress response.* As we have seen, chronic stress is increasingly being identified as detrimental to health. Many people are aware of this, and want to cope without recourse to medication. Relaxation is becoming a prime strategy in effective stress management.

    The harmful effects of stress may be minimised if the responses are controlled regularly through practising a relaxation technique. This will bring about the following:

    - a reduction of muscle tension
    - calmer and more efficient abdominal breathing (because of less tension in the muscles involved with breathing, and less demand for oxygen)
    - through the first two, other physiological parameters begin to rebalance, and the state of mental arousal is lowered towards the optimum level.

2. *Relaxation can reduce pain.* By decreasing muscle tension through relaxation, aches and pains become less likely. Examples are headache, backache or writer's cramp. Relaxation techniques can also increase the pain threshold, or delay and lessen the perceived pain.

3. *Relaxation can reduce fatigue.* When relaxation techniques are employed in everyday life, economy of effort is the result and fatigue is reduced.

4. *Relaxation can promote sleep.* The body is allowed to rest peacefully and the mind is calmed. There is less tossing and turning in an effort to go to sleep.

5. *Relaxation can improve personal relationships.* It is easier to get along with people when you are relaxed.

6. *Relaxation can increase self-esteem through self-awareness.* Your self-confidence increases when your self-awareness and self-control are improved.

The process of relaxation

Habits of muscle tension are acquired over a lifetime, and so it will take time and practice to learn new techniques and skills.

Relaxation may be achieved for only a few seconds at first. Later it will be possible to reach the enjoyable state of gentle drifting, when the mind idles without conscious effort and cuts off from problems. There are five major components to this process:

1. *Relaxation of the body.* Tension is released and you become aware of the feeling of relaxation in the muscles.
2. *Relaxation of the mind.* Most people who achieve relaxation of the body can go on to achieve relaxation of the mind.
3. *Regression.* When the mind is relaxed, regression can follow (regression is explained below).
4. *New responses.* Once the regression state is reached, new responses may be learnt (calmer, quieter responses).
5. *Transfer to everyday life.* The feeling of relaxation can be maintained during everyday tasks.

Of these five, regression needs some further explanation.

Regression

The mind is capable of slipping back and working at a simpler level of its development. This is called 'regression'. Regression manifests itself:

• as daydreaming
• during the transition between wakefulness and sleep
• as a result of tiredness or mental illness
• as a result of drugs or alcohol.

The essential feature of regression is that we are less alert, and that the critical faculties of the mind become less active.

If we want to learn a new, different response to the old patterns, we must first drop the old ones. This means that first we need to regress to a state where we are free from anxiety. We are then free to learn a new pattern of calm and ease. This is why explanation and persuasion are generally quite ineffective in helping those with tension. The stressed person sees the logic of what is explained, and would like to follow our excellent advice, but they will remain in tension if regression is left out. In all relaxation techniques that are successful, we can assume that regression occurs spontaneously without the participant's knowledge. For when we have attained relaxation of the mind, we are on our way to regression.

ACTIVITY 3.1

Learning the relaxation response

You can remain in your chair for this exercise, or you can create an open space on the floor where you can lie down. Turn off some or all of the overhead lights. Make the room as quiet as possible. The following exercise will become easier with practice; sometimes people do fall asleep, although that is not the goal. (The sleeping state is, in fact, different from the relaxation state we will be trying to achieve; see page 119.)

GROUP CONTEXT

If any of the following relaxation techniques are being done in a group, the leader should read the instructions slowly to the group.

Important aspects of teaching relaxation exercises to a group are the following:

- At first, people may feel 'funny' and giggle or make jokes and act nervously. Explain that feeling nervous about learning something new like this is natural.
- People must be far enough apart from each other to feel that they will not be disturbed, so that they

---

Now do the following to elicit the relaxation response:

1. *Assume a comfortable position.* The best position is flat on your back on the floor. Your eyes should be closed and your arms should be lying loosely at your sides. Uncross your feet and loosen any tight collars, belts or footwear. Initially, lying flat on your back on the floor may seem uncomfortable, but you are urged to try it. Usually once you have started to relax, you do not notice the hard floor, and this position is the best one for your body. (If you choose to sit in a chair, uncross your legs and rest your arms loosely at your sides.)

2. *Maintain a passive attitude.* Do not worry about whether you are successful in achieving a deep level of relaxation. Permit relaxation to occur at its own pace. Do not try to work at relaxing, but do try to disregard distracting thoughts and sounds during the time you have set aside.

3. *Begin to focus on your breathing.* Allow your breathing to become regular and natural as you inhale and exhale through your nose. Remember that breathing is a peaceful, natural process. Each time you exhale, allow some tension to leave your body, and allow the relaxation to enter your body. As you begin to feel more and more relaxed with each breath, try one (or more) of the following to deepen your feeling of relaxation:

    *   Imagine the air that you are breathing as a cloud. The cloud comes to you, fills you and then leaves you.
    *   Imagine your lungs as a balloon (you may want to put your hand on your chest). As you inhale, your lungs expand like a balloon; as you exhale your lungs deflate.
    *   As you inhale, say the word 'in' to yourself. As you exhale, say the word 'out'. (Speak the words aloud for the first few breaths, and then do it silently.)

    Try each of the above at different times to see which works best for you. For some people, the visual images are more powerful, while for others the word formula ('in' and 'out') works better. Try to focus on one of these images or the word formula for several minutes. Tell yourself to relax more and more with each breath. You may discover that your mind will wander from the image or word from time to time. This is normal. Simply return to your word or image and continue to relax.

    You may want to deepen your relaxation even further by using one of the following methods:

    *   Slowly count backwards from 10 to one. With each count allow yourself to feel heavier and more relaxed.
    *   Imagine that you are at the top of a long, winding stairway. Picture yourself descending the stairs. Feel a new wave of calm with each step you take.

4. *It is now important to return.* You will come back to the real world feeling calm and alert. You will feel the benefits of this relaxation throughout the day. Come back to the room slowly by counting from one to five, gradually becoming more alert. At the count of five your eyes should open. Get up slowly. Continue to breathe easily and naturally.

Now reflect on these questions:

1. How did I feel before this exercise?

2. What did I think about during the exercise? Was my mind blank at any point?
3. How does my body feel now?

Refer back to your Stress Diary (Activity 1.1). Look at the column 'Behaviour (what I did)', and think about or take notes on the following questions:

1. If I had used the relaxation response before reacting in my particular situation, would my behaviour have been different?
2. In future will I try using the relaxation response before reacting? If so, under what circumstances do I think it would be most helpful?

ACTIVITY 3.2

Deep muscle relaxation

If you wish, try deep muscle relaxation. This technique involves tensing specific muscle groups and then relaxing them. For each muscle group, a method is described for creating tension and achieving relaxation. Begin by assuming the position for relaxation (eyes closed sitting in a chair or lying on the floor, in a quiet and passive attitude). Now do each of the following twice in a row:

Muscle	Tensing method
Forehead	Wrinkle your forehead. Try to make your eyebrows touch your hairline for five seconds. Relax.
Eyes and nose	Close your eyes as tightly as you can for five seconds. Relax.
Lips, cheeks and jaw	Draw the corners of your mouth back and grimace for five seconds. Relax. Feel the warmth and calmness in your face.
Hands	Extend your arms in front of you. Clench your fists tightly for five seconds. Relax. Feel the warmth and calmness in your hands.
Forearms	Extend your arms out against an invisible wall and push outwards with your hands for five seconds. Relax.

Upper arms	Bend your elbows. Tense your biceps for five seconds. Relax. Feel the tension leave your arms.
Shoulders	Shrug your shoulders up to your ears for five seconds. Relax.
Back	Arch your back off the floor for five seconds. Relax. Feel the anxiety and tension disappearing.
Stomach	Tighten your stomach muscles for five seconds. Relax.
Hips and buttocks	Tighten your hip and buttock muscles for five seconds. Relax.
Thighs	Tighten your thigh muscles by pressing your legs together as tightly as you can for five seconds. Relax.
Feet	Flex your ankles upwards as far as you can for five seconds. Relax.
Toes	Curl your toes under as tightly as you can for five seconds. Relax.

Activities 3.3 and 3.4 describe several more relaxation techniques. Try them, and find out which works best for you.

ACTIVITY 3.3

Autogenic relaxation

This technique involves the use of a word formula that acts as a reminder to each part of the body to relax.

1. Assume the position for relaxation (quiet, eyes closed, lying on the floor or sitting on a chair).
2. Although repeating the word formula may seem like a task, remember to maintain *passive* concentration.
3. Repeat the word formula in the sequence given below. This is done silently. Allow all your body parts to feel heavy, warm and relaxed.

   My right arm is heavy.
   My right arm is heavy.
   My left arm is heavy.

My left arm is heavy.
My arms are heavy and warm.
My arms are heavy and warm.
My arms are heavy and warm; warmth is flowing into my hands.
My arms are heavy and warm; warmth is flowing into my hands.
My legs are heavy.
My legs are heavy.
My legs are heavy and warm.
My legs are heavy and warm.
My breathing is calm and regular.
My breathing is calm and regular.
My body breathes me.
My body breathes me.
My breathing is calm and regular; I am at peace.
My breathing is calm and regular; I am at peace.
I am at peace.
I am at peace.

As you become more experienced at eliciting your relaxation response, some quick methods of relaxation may be useful. Activity 3.4 describes several 'quick release' techniques.

ACTIVITY 3.4

Quick relaxation techniques

These exercises take less time than the preceding methods, but they are most effective only after you have practised the more time-consuming techniques and have become acquainted with your own body and how it tenses and relaxes. As, with practice, you become better at relaxation, it will take less time to achieve the relaxation response. You will still want to continue a regular routine of 15 to 20 minutes of daily relaxation, but the following suggestions can be used to supplement your routine.

Here are some pointers about all the exercises that follow:

- *Position.* Get as comfortable as possible. Some of these exercises can be done at a time when there is nothing to do but wait (e.g. in a doctor's waiting room). It is not necessary to lie down to do them.

- *Attitude.* Remain passive. Just watch your mind work. Whatever thoughts come to mind are okay. Do not work at it, just let it happen.
- *Sounds.* Sounds are a natural part of the environment—just take note of them and let them pass.
- *Breathing.* Focus inward on breathing as a natural, easy process.

Whole body tension
1. Tense everything in your whole body, stay with that tension, and hold it as long as you can without feeling pain.
2. Slowly release the tension and very gradually feel it leave your body.
3. Repeat three times.
4. Think about how this feels.

Imagine air as a cloud
1. Release your imagination and focus on your breathing.
2. As your breathing becomes calm and regular, imagine that the air comes to you as a cloud—it fills you and goes out. You may want to imagine that the cloud has a colour that you find peaceful.)
3. Notice that your breathing becomes more regular as you relax.

Pick a spot
1. With your head level and your body relaxed, pick a spot on which to focus (eyes are open at this point).
2. When ready, count five breaths backwards. With each breath allow your eyes to close gradually.
3. When you get to one, your eyes will be closed. Focus on the feeling of relaxation.

Counting from 10 to one
1. Allow yourself to feel passive and indifferent, counting each breath slowly from 10 back to one.
2. With each count, allow yourself to feel heavier and more relaxed.
3. Every time you exhale, allow the tension to leave your body.

Shoulder shrug
1. Try to raise your shoulders up to your ears.
2. Hold for a count of four, then drop your shoulders back to their normal position.

3. Repeat as often as necessary.
4. Vary this by rotating your shoulders down and around—first one way, then the other and then both at the same time.

Alternate nostril breathing
1. Block the left nostril with one hand and inhale deeply through your right nostril for five seconds.
2. Block both nostrils, holding your breath for five seconds, then exhale slowly through your mouth.
3. Repeat, beginning this time by breathing in through the left nostril.

Breath control and overbreathing

Most systems of relaxation and tension control use breath control. There is a useful link between breathing and relaxation, which can be demonstrated by Activities 3.5 and 3.6. (However, anyone with high blood pressure had better check with their doctor before attempting any of the breath control techniques.)

We are able to affect our breathing pattern consciously because the muscles that contract to bring about inspiration (the diaphragm and intercostal muscles) are muscles that can be consciously controlled. We can decide, for example, to breathe more or less deeply and rapidly, or to hold our breath.

In some cases, breathing patterns that result from such conscious decisions do not meet the metabolic requirements of the body. In time, the resulting carbon dioxide and, to a lesser extent, oxygen levels in the blood, lead to the consciously controlled breathing pattern being overridden by the activity of the respiratory centre in the brain, so that homeostasis is restored.

Occasional negative side-effects of overbreathing

When someone overbreathes (i.e. ventilates the lungs with more air than is required by the body for its level of activity at the time), this has the effect of flushing out the lung alveoli with atmospheric air, which contains more oxygen and less carbon dioxide than residual air. This increases the gradient between alveolar air and venous blood, more carbon dioxide leaves the blood and more oxygen enters. The arterial blood reaching the brain stem thus contains less carbon dioxide than normal, which *may* produce the following effects:

- The activity of the vascular centre in the brain stem is reduced, causing a generalised dilation of the blood vessels in the body and a fall in blood pressure. The fall in blood pressure and the low carbon dioxide levels render the person more likely to feel light-headed and dizzy. In severe cases fainting may occur.
- The respiratory centre reduces its stimulation of inhalation. In *extreme* cases this means that, as forced breathing is stopped, inhalation may not occur again until the level of carbon dioxide in the blood builds up. This stoppage only lasts for up to 20 seconds, and no one should be alarmed, as breathing automatically starts up again quite naturally. The body is simply taking a little time to adjust back into homeostasis (i.e. its normal, balanced state).

While not dangerous in itself, voluntary forced overbreathing can also produce uncomfortable symptoms such as feeling hot and sweaty, and muscular twitching.

When people are asked consciously to *monitor* their breathing—as in an early relaxation class—they often have an initial tendency to overbreathe, and to do this by taking deeper breaths than usual. Generally this is minimal and has no effect, but occasionally someone may overbreathe sufficiently to experience some of the symptoms mentioned above. If this happens, breathe less deeply, or forget about your breathing pattern for the time being. The relaxation, and the fact that you are lying or sitting in a relaxed posture, will tend to minimise the effects of such a fall in blood pressure.

ACTIVITY **3.5**

Breathing exercise for relaxation

Tighten up all your muscles as hard as you can . . . tight, very tight . . . then let go and relax. You probably found that as you tightened up, you held your breath, and as you relaxed you let it go. Now put one hand on your chest and the other on your stomach . . . on the bulge if you have one. Breathe out first, slowly, then breathe in. If you are doing this correctly, your stomach, not your chest, should rise at the start of the breath. Try this several times—

every time you breathe out, do it slowly with a slight sigh, pause a moment and then let the inbreath take over naturally—don't exaggerate, just let it happen.

ACTIVITY **3.6**

Quick release of tension when suddenly facing a difficult situation

Do calm, controlled breathing in the following way:

1. Take two or three deeper, slower outbreaths.
2. Return to normal breathing.
3. Now repeat the two or three deeper, slower outbreaths.
4. Carry on more calmly.

Some useful do's when relaxing

When trying to relax, adopting the following suggestions will help you to relax:

- Relax lying down, as well as in a chair, bus, train, queue, or wherever you are.
- You can put up with some discomfort, but make sure you are warm.
- First relax your muscles, and then your mind. Try following your breathing pattern or listening to a pleasant sound.
- Watching TV, knitting and playing golf are tensing, and so relax somewhere else.
- Relaxation is needed during the day as well as at night.
- Understand your anxiety reactions, practise managing them and think positively.
- Let relaxation happen—trying too hard may be counter-productive.

Occasional negative side-effects

This book is not an attempt to supply therapy or counselling. It approaches the teaching of relaxation and stress management from a 'skills training' and educational perspective. When used in this way, there will be very few, if any, problems resulting from the practice of relaxation. However, there may be worrying side-effects that could occasionally occur, and that you should be aware of. These include:

- Benson (1976) found that eliciting the relaxation response for a long period of time can lead to hallucinations. This may be related to sensory deprivation, and only occurs with meditative relaxation. (For meditation techniques, see page 120 onwards.)
- Anyone already suffering from psychotic illness may have their psychotic symptoms increased.
- Severe depression may be heightened.
- The physiological changes that occur may alter the relationship between a medical condition and the drug that is being used to treat it (e.g. asthma, diabetes, epilepsy). If in doubt, seek medical advice.
- Shaking and crying can occur when someone completely 'lets go'.

Initial obstacles to relaxation

You may experience initial problems in regularly practising relaxation. The following are the most common difficulties, but they are usually overcome with regular practice. (Occasionally these superficial obstacles may indicate deeper resistance to the whole idea of relaxation.)

General problems

There are a number of general problems that may be causing difficulty. These are:

- *Difficulties in getting started.* This may be because of difficulty in:

  - finding time
  - finding an appropriate place
  - finding a comfortable environment or position.

- *Too much noise or silence.* Deep silence is sometimes off-putting, and in this case a low-pitched background noise may be more acceptable.

- *Too many interruptions*, actual or expected. Anticipating, for example, a clock chime can activate logical thought. This anticipation can be more of an obstacle than the actual interruption. Once it has occurred, it should be allowed to pass by, and relaxation should continue.
- *Lack of support*. Friends and relatives need to understand the person's aims if they are to give full support.
- *Initial feelings of guilt* about 'sitting doing nothing'. This is a very commonly stated problem, and it is important to realise that practising relaxation is not a waste of time.
- *Temperature extremes*. In extremes of temperature, it is difficult for the body's metabolism to drop to the required levels.
- *Too soon after physical exertion*. A cooling-down period is needed after vigorous activity to allow the body to stop sweating, the breathing to slow down and the heart rate to return to normal.
- *Too soon after eating*. Doing relaxation exercises straight after a meal can sometimes cause indigestion. More important, relaxation may not have beneficial effects if it is practised within two hours after a meal.

Physical problems

The following are some physical problems that may be causing difficulties:

- *Falling asleep*. If drowsiness is an obstacle to relaxation, a sitting position is more suitable, as you are less likely to fall asleep. It is also helpful to use a 'resolve' (i.e. where you state positively that you will remain awake during practice). To avoid sleepiness, it is better to choose a time of day to relax when you are not too tired, hungry or have just eaten.
- *Pain after maintaining one posture for any length of time*. This is more of a problem for older people. Attention should be paid to the starting position, and people should be allowed to move slightly, if necessary, in order to ease discomfort.
- *Central nervous system arousal* from caffeine and/or nicotine intake. Both are stimulants and may counteract the relaxation response. However, if depriving yourself of these contributes to even more stress, it is important to achieve a balance between the two reactions.

- *Depressant effects of alcohol* on the central nervous system. Alcohol reduces self-control, and difficulty in relaxing may occur.
- *Itching, getting the giggles or having a coughing fit.* These are all symptoms of releasing tension.
- *Eyes that blink or water, and difficulty in keeping them closed.* When fully relaxed, the eyes are not tightly closed but tend to be slightly open. Blinking may be due to difficulty in unwinding, and usually improves with time.
- *Worry about hyperventilation* (see 'Occasional negative side-effects of overbreathing' on page 113).
- *Muscle cramps* as muscles are being tensed or released. The calf muscle is most likely to be affected. Pulling the foot upwards instead of pointing the toes will ease the problem. As the initial tensing is a learning tool, the problem is transitory. Soon you will recognise a relaxed muscle without having to tense it first.
- *Limb jerks* may be indicative of entering a period of drowsiness. They are more noticeable as the release starts to occur after being in marked physical tension.

Subjective emotional problems

Subjective emotional problems can also interfere with relaxation. For example:

- *Fear of letting go and losing control.* It is important to realise that practising relaxation *enhances* self-control. Until this is accepted, you should not feel absolutely bound by the 'rules' of the relaxation technique, but should be free to come in and out of relaxation at will.
- *Claustrophobic feeling.* If you have this problem, try keeping doors or windows open, eyes downcast rather than shut, and keeping the room light.
- *Feeling of panic or choking* during concentration on breathing. This is sometimes present in people with chest conditions. Concentration on an alternative form of rhythm, such as a rhythmic chant (a mantra), may be substituted.

Problems after relaxation

Problems can also occur after relaxation. For example:

- *Feeling cut off from reality.* A firm pattern of moving out of the relaxation should be established to facilitate a return to the normal, alert state.
- *Post-relaxation lethargy and post-relaxation hyperactivity.* These should both disappear once practice becomes regular.

Sleep and relaxation

The relationship between relaxation and sleep is a topic that often comes up for discussion. Briefly, relaxation and sleep have similarities in that they are both states of rest. Relaxation and drowsiness have some points in common. However, the frequently held belief that relaxation is a prelude to sleep, and that sleep is therefore a better state to achieve, is incorrect. The two states are very different, for the following reasons:

- There is a quicker and more marked decrease in breathing, and thus oxygen intake, in relaxation.
- There is a drop in metabolic activity in both relaxation and sleep. In relaxation this happens much more quickly. Oxygen consumption drops by about 12 per cent in three minutes, and returns to normal when the practice stops. In sleep, on the other hand, there is a gradual decrease in metabolic activity over five hours, and oxygen consumption drops by only 8 per cent. Figure 3.3 illustrates this.
- There are some marked differences in body temperature changes, the most marked being that hand and foot temperature often increases during relaxation.
- After sleep, the body seems to need a certain amount of activity to restore it to normal functioning. This is not the case with relaxation.
- During relaxation, all bodily systems drop to a lower level of activity. In most cases, heart rate, breathing rate and blood pressure are lower after relaxation than after a night's sleep.

Some people frequently move from relaxation into a drowsy state and back again when practising relaxation. However, moving into deep sleep is not a good idea, as the benefits of relaxation will no longer occur.

Figure 3.3   Difference between relaxation and sleep (changes in oxygen consumption)

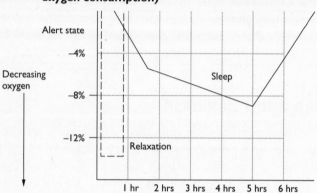

SOURCE: H. Benson, *The Relaxation Response*, Avon Books: New York, 1976.

A word on meditation

When all the hullabaloo is cut away and the semi-religious connotations removed, meditation is one of the important relaxation techniques that can be used for the relief and management of stress. It is a form of deep relaxation that can be learnt without having to accept the religious aspects that sometimes surround it and that make people suspicious of it.

Meditation is an activity in which you seek to gain mastery over the process of attention. There are two forms: *opening-up meditation* and *shutting-down meditation*. There are five ways of achieving opening-up meditation and seven ways of achieving shutting-down meditation. Despite all the claims that one system is better than another, no system of meditation has been able to demonstrate convincingly that it is superior to others. It turns out to be a highly personal matter. It may demand some experimentation, but what works best for an individual is probably the best indicator of the system of meditation that should be used. All five systems of opening-up meditation and all seven systems of shutting-down meditation are dealt with below.

Opening-up meditation

Opening-up meditation consists of using an object in order to emphasise the five senses of the body: seeing, hearing, touching, tasting and smelling. *Any* object may be used to demonstrate the five systems of opening-up meditation. While it may seem silly, remember that the purpose of this is to relax the physical body and the mind. Ten minutes should be used to practise each meditation. Explore each one to see which works best for you. An orange has been used as the object in the examples below.

Seeing

Take an orange and minutely examine the outer skin. Look closely at the colour and texture. Peel the orange and look closely at the edge of the peel. Look at the inside of the peel. Examine the wedges. Break open a wedge and look at the meat of the orange. Examine the small pieces carefully. It is even permissible to use a magnifying glass.

Hearing

Squeeze an orange. Is there a sound? Peel the orange. Bend the peel and listen to the sounds. What sound is it? Close the eyes and break a wedge in half. What sound is there? Rub the fingers along the outside of the peel. Is there a sound? Rub the fingers along the inside of the peel. What difference is there in the sound?

Touching

Close your eyes and rub the fingers along the outside of an unpeeled orange. Feel the texture. Rub the orange all over. Spend five minutes examining the orange with the fingers before peeling it. Peel the orange slowly, feeling each piece. Break the orange into wedges and explore each wedge with your fingers. Feel the inside of the peel. Examine the edges.

Tasting

Close the eyes and place a wedge of orange in the mouth. Bite slowly into the wedge. Bite a piece of the peel. Taste the pulp. Try to establish how many different tastes there are in an orange.

Smelling

Sniff an unpeeled orange. Peel the orange and smell the inside of the peel. Smell a wedge of orange. Bend an orange peel and smell the acid as it explodes from the peel. Smell the pulp. Smell a squeezed wedge. How many different smells are there in an orange?

Obviously the exercise with an orange is 'nonsense'. It has no special hidden or mystical meaning. There is no secret learning to be gained from it. The point of the exercise is that, in extending the senses, one forgets about present problems and is able to relax. By allowing in more than the ordinary amount of information for a single sense, other thoughts are blocked. This is why it is called meditation. Clearly if one can extend the senses to examine an orange, those senses can be used in an even more extensive way during a walk in the bush. Or they could be used on a city block on the way to work or during lunch. It is a handy, quick and efficient way to meditate.

Shutting-out meditation

You will realise that many of the seven systems of shutting-out meditation mentioned below can take many years to perfect. However, this is so only in cases where meditation is not being used merely as a relaxation tool, but in order that an individual may more deeply explore the meaning of life and their own nature.

Here the techniques are being suggested simply as a way to relax and counter stress. For each of the seven systems, an easily learnt method is provided.

In shutting-out meditation, the way to block disturbing thoughts is to shut them out by concentrating on something else. That 'something else' can be *anything else.*

Breathing
Breathing is an exercise that is taught in many disciplines. Each of us knows that anxiety, fear and stress are signalled by shallow breathing. One way to counteract these effects is to practise deliberate deep breathing during an anxious moment or during a period of stress. Here is a simple breathing meditation. Breathe normally, close your eyes and centre your concentration on the nose and mouth. Without much effort, begin to inhale through the nose and exhale through the mouth.

Focusing on a point
This is the meditation system that most people make fun of (i.e. the 'contemplate your navel' meditation!). The point of focus can be a flame, a mandala (a complex figure, sometimes with hidden meanings) or any other object, including religious objects.

All one has to do is set up some object, sit down and stare at it. If intruding thoughts present themselves, redouble the staring. (It is recommended that initially a flame be used as it seems that many beginners find this the easiest.) This type of focusing on a point is one of the exercises taught in the Lamaze childbirth method.

Sounds

Sounds may be internal or external. Transcendental meditation (TM) is famous for its 'secret' special words that serve as a centre of focus. In systems that use an internal sound, the sound is often imbued with special meaning. The systems that use an external sound might ordinarily be called chants, the most famous of these being the Gregorian chants. In the East, a popular meditation chant is the sound 'OM'. Saying the word feels pleasant, and it is very effective in driving away any interfering thoughts. Sit quietly (if a group wants to meditate together, this is an especially good one) and say the sound 'OM'. Stretch out the sound like this: OMMMMMMMMMMMMMMMMMMM. Allow the sound to vibrate through the head. Hold the sound for as long as possible. Take a deep breath and then repeat the sound again, over and over, for about 10 minutes.

Visualisation

This system uses images to block out thoughts. It can be the image of a loved one, a pleasant scene or a religious figure. Here is one visualisation that works for many people. Build a wall of bricks, one brick at a time. Envisage the piece of ground on which it is to be built, level the ground, place the first row of bricks and, brick by brick, build the wall. If thoughts present themselves, build the wall faster.

Movement

Movement meditations are to be found in Sufi dancing (whirling dervishes), worry stones and beads, and saying the Rosary. Here is a movement meditation that needs no equipment. Place both your hands on a tabletop with the fingers spread out. Tap the little finger of each hand on the table top, then the ring finger and so on, down to the thumb. As you do this, count to five, one count for each finger. This technique is usually guaranteed to drive away any intrusive thoughts.

Devotional practices

The meditations that involve devotional practices are familiar to us as prayer (Hail Mary, Our Father), Sufi stories, parables and problems to be solved (koans). For religious people, any number of devotional practices are available at their house of worship. A more secular practice that would be similar would be quietly reciting a favourite poem over and over.

Methodless meditation

It seems that some people are 'natural' meditators. They do not have any particular system, but seem to be able to stop thoughts through a number of ordinary daily practices that are performed only when they seem necessary. Here are several examples of methodless meditation that are common. The playing of a musical instrument provides a combination of sound and movement meditation that gives many hours of relaxation. Simply listening to music is another form of using sound as meditation. Many forms of athletic endeavour can be viewed as movement meditation, as can dancing. Writing can be seen as a form of meditation. In fact, most things that are absorbing can be regarded as a form of meditation for persons who concentrate so much on the task that time and distractions are forgotten.

Any of the seven systems of meditation outlined above hold out the promise of relaxation and the reduction of tension. Try them to see which one or ones work best, and use the technique daily for 10 to 20 minutes. It is also possible to take two- to three-minute mini-breaks to ease the pressures of the moment. While hard evidence is difficult to come by, many have suggested that people who are able to take such mini-breaks are frequently more efficient and more productive.

Summary

The most effective means for eliciting the relaxation response varies from individual to individual. The aim of *Skill 3: Master the benefits of relaxation* has been to highlight the importance of relaxation in combating stress, and to provide guidance as to the various means of eliciting the relaxation response. It is important to choose the method that works best for you.

SKILL 4

Maintain good health

Introduction

In the past 20 years, much research has been carried out that shows clearly that the way in which we minimise stress, maintain good health and even live longer is related to the way we live every day of our lives. There is general acceptance that following seven daily habits can mean an extra seven to 10 years of life for women and 12 to 15 years for men. (This does not mean that nothing else matters, but simply that these seven simple habits have the most evidence in their favour.) The seven factors are:

1. Do not smoke.
2. Moderate your drinking (between zero and two drinks per day).
3. Sleep around seven hours per day.
4. Eat regular meals without in-between snacks.
5. Eat a regular, balanced breakfast.
6. Exercise regularly.
7. Maintain your recommended weight.

More recent research on these daily habits has shown that the three most crucial of these are:

- Do not smoke.
- Exercise regularly.
- Maintain your recommended weight.

Research on the relationship between these basic lifestyle factors and stress is far from complete. However, what we know about the stress response and normal bodily functioning suggests that a healthy diet, adequate exercise and adequate sleep can promote health as well as prepare the mind and body to cope better with stress.

ACTIVITY 4.1

Do you have healthy living habits?

Answer yes or no to the following statements:

1. I do not smoke.
2. I rarely have more than an occasional drink.
3. I sleep seven hours a night.
4. I eat regular meals and no snacks.
5. I eat a regular, balanced breakfast.
6. I take regular exercise.
7. My body weight is right for my size.

If you have answered yes three times or less, you need to reconsider your health practices. If stress should occur in your life, you will not be fit enough to cope with it

A healthy diet

On the most basic level, food is essential for survival. Food contains nutrients that support bodily functions, the six basic nutrients being carbohydrates, protein, fat, vitamins, minerals and water. Each is essential to maintaining health. Carbohydrates supply energy. Proteins build and repair body tissues. Fat stores energy and releases it as we need it. Vitamins and minerals regulate a number of our bodily processes. Water, which makes up 70 per cent of the total body, is necessary for all these processes to take place.

In most Western countries, current eating habits are thought to be among the reasons for the increase in heart disease, strokes and certain forms of cancer. These diseases are called degenerative diseases because they cause the body to degenerate, or weaken, slowly and invisibly over a long period of time. The standard diet in most Western countries has been linked to six of the 10 leading causes of death. We eat too few foods high in fibre and starch, too many foods high in salt, sugar and fat—particularly saturated fat—and too few plant foods that are naturally lower in fat and calories.

Regular mealtimes should be established so that the body becomes accustomed to particular ebbs and flows of blood sugar—rising after meals and falling gradually alter eating. You may recognise that your body has a pretty good memory for time; somehow it always seems to remind you when it is time for lunch or dinner. When we do not respect the rhythms of the body, we put a strain on our system. If your body never knows quite when it is going to get the food it needs, this is an important source of physical stress.

If we do not eat regularly, the only way we can raise the blood sugar level for energy is to release glycogen from the liver. This process is controlled by a chemical called adrenaline, released from the adrenal glands. There are several ways to raise adrenaline levels in the blood, including:

- *Stirring up the body as if for a confrontation*. We get cranky when we are hungry. We are ready to fight because we are stirring up production of the fight or flight chemical.
- *Taking a dose of a drug that stimulates production of the needed chemicals*. One of the most common drugs for this purpose is caffeine. We get tired in the late afternoon, for example, when blood sugar levels are low, and crave a cup of coffee or a cool drink that has caffeine in it. The caffeine raises the production of adrenalin, which controls the release of glycogen from the liver. As the level of blood sugar rises, we have energy again.
- Unfortunately, if you combine the effects of real stress with the artificial boost from caffeine, you compound the effects considerably. A study at Duke University Medical Centre found that even moderate coffee drinking (around four or five cups per day) made the body act as if under constant stress, with a rise of 32 per cent in drinkers' adrenaline levels.

A properly balanced diet is important for all age groups. During their rapid growth periods, children and adolescents need additional protein and energy foods. During pregnancy and lactation, mothers need more protein foods. During retirement, people should have as much variety and unrefined foods as they did before, but fewer energy-giving foods.

Parents should be as diligent about seeing that adolescents have balanced regular meals as they were when the children were small. Some teenagers tend to become overweight (often because they are constantly nibbling at nutritionally poor snacks instead of having regular meals), and this can be a great source of embarrassment to them. If parents set the right example, and also encourage their children to eat only what the body requires of the healthy foods, all members of the family will keep their body mass to what is normal for their size, age, sex and activity level. This is most important.

Not only does excess mass place an additional strain on all organs, which sooner or later disturbs the body's functions and structure, and which may eventually produce illness, but it also places a great deal of strain on emotional well-being. Most over-weight people are unhappy about being overweight. They are ashamed of their appearance. Unfortunately this often leads to self-pity, which in turn causes them to eat more and more as a means of consoling themselves. Take yourself in hand before you get to this stage. Tell yourself that *you* allowed yourself to 'get fat', and now you are going to be sensible enough to get your mass back to what is desirable. Instead of nibbling out of self-pity, keep yourself busy and your mind off food. Many people nibble out of boredom. The solution is to start doing something interesting and worthwhile with your life. There are enough fascinating occupations, interesting hobbies and a host of people needing help, and so you should have no difficulty in finding some meaningful outlet for your energies.

In conclusion, remember these *few truths about eating*:

- Obesity is a threat to health and shortens life, and so culti-vate the lean, lanky look. Stop blaming obesity on glandular trouble. The real cause is overeating and underexercising.
- You reap the most benefit—health-wise, emotionally and economically—by maintaining a constant mass. There is no reason why your mass should be more at the age of 45 or 65 than it was at 25.
- Do not bluff yourself that vigorous exercise will get rid of the excess kilojoules from a sumptuous Sunday dinner (unless you are considering a 20 kilometre hike). Rather, plan ahead

of time and go without Sunday supper, so that the total food intake for the day does not exceed your normal requirement.

It is useful to check your Body Mass Index (BMI) occasionally. BMI is a person's weight in kilograms divided by height in metres squared (i.e. $BMI = kg/m^2$). A BMI of less than 18.5 suggests underweight while normal has a range of 18.5–24.9. Overweight has a value of between 25.0 and 29.9, and obesity ranges from 30 upwards. When we are under stress, the stress reaction in our bodies makes fats harder for the body to process, putting extra strain on us. Yet all too often it is when we are under stress that we are more likely to skip our meals or replace normal meals with high-fat convenience foods like fish and chips, hamburgers, fried chicken and potato crisps.

There is increasing evidence linking excessive salt intake with high blood pressure, one of the most common illnesses in the modern world. Salt, like sugar, can be found in vast numbers of canned and prepared foods. We know that stress increases blood pressure—this is part of the stress reaction. Consequently, the more stressed we are, the less we should be using salt. We could restrict the amount of salt we add directly to our meals, decrease the quantities used in cooking vegetables, and reduce our consumption of products with high salt quantities such as cooked meats, potato crisps, salted peanuts and all bottled sauces.

ACTIVITY 4.2

Assessing your diet and eating habits

On a timetable like the one on the next page, use different colours to indicate (a) when you eat a meal, (b) when you eat a snack, and (c) when you have something to drink. Also provide a brief description of what you eat or drink. Monitor your diet and eating habits for one week.

When you have completed your timetable of diet and eating habits, answer the following questions:

1. How many meals did you eat with others?
2. Did you miss a meal?
3. Did you eat or drink anything while watching television or while doing work?
4. Did you eat between meals? If so, what did you eat?

5. Did you buy any fast foods/takeaway?
6. List the main foods you ate and rate each one as high or low in salt, fibre and sugar. How many different vegetables did you eat? How many times did you drink something sweet (e.g. tea with sugar or a fruit drink)?
7. Did you add salt to your food?
8. How much caffeine did you have (coffee, tea or cola)?

	Mon.	Tue.	Wed.	Thur.	Fri.	Sat.	Sun.
12 am							
6 am							
9 am							
12 pm							
3 pm							
6 pm							
9 pm							
12 am							

Review the information you have now gathered, and judge whether your current diet is healthy or not. What changes do you need to make to turn it into a healthier diet?

Many of us feel tired and peckish in-between meals, and head straight for a snack bar for a chocolate bar or something else sweet. The snack does provide a pick-up, but you may well have been better off walking to the snack bar and back—without getting the chocolate. A 10-minute walk is more reviving in terms of increasing energy, reducing tension and tiredness than a snack. With snacks, the pick-up is short-lived as the sugar is rapidly assimilated.

Undertake exercise

When asked how they cope with stress, a large percentage of people indicate that they use exercise as their primary coping resource. How can an activity that is physiologically almost identical to the physiological response of psychological stress be helpful as a coping technique?

ACTIVITY **4.3**

How fit are you?

Answer 'yes' or 'no' to the following statements about yourself:

1. I always climb stairs rather than travel in lifts.
2. I'm on my feet for between two and three hours each day.
3. I lift something heavy at least once a day.
4. I ride a bike regularly.
5. I run at least 2 kilometres a week
6. I run at least 2 kilometres three times a week
7. I do regular exercises.
8. I do something strenuous each day (e.g. gardening, walking, dancing, ironing, cleaning).

For those readers who gave mostly 'no' answers, it is important to realise that exercise can help ward off stress and make you feel more positive about yourself, as you will see in the following pages.

Physiological benefits of exercise

This involves the detoxification of stress-related compounds. During the stress response, somewhere in the neighbourhood of 1500 biochemical reactions occur in the body. Neurotransmitters are activated, hormones are released and nutrients are metabolised. Some body systems (e.g. the cardiovascular system) accelerate their functions and others (e.g. the gastrointestinal system) slow down their operations in response to stress. Remember the fight or flight response. The body is being prepared for survival. Now most human stress is psycho-social in nature, so the need to respond physically in most cases is unnecessary. Unfortunately the by-products of the stress response continue to circulate in the body and have the potential to create physical illness (e.g. cortisol secretion's impact on the immune system). Regular exercise is useful in removing the by-products of the stress response by providing the opportunity to simulate the fighting or running dictated by the fight or flight phenomenon, thus allowing the body to return to homeostasis faster and reduce the physical impact of psycho-social stress.

Physical activity also acts as an outlet for anger and hostility, which if repressed (not allowed expression and denied) play a role in disease progression. For many, physical activity is a healthy catharsis for this most caustic of emotions. Exercise can provide a socially acceptable means of physically releasing negative energy. Whether one hammers away at a golf ball on the driving range, tackles an opponent in a football game, learns judo or punches their pillow, the physical release of energy appears to dissipate feelings of anger in a healthy way.

Physical benefits of exercise

The major cause of death in this country is heart disease. Diseases of the heart and blood vessels kill more people than all other causes combined, and are responsible for 65 per cent of deaths (excluding deaths caused by accidents). By exercising, you strengthen your heart and prevent the build-up of fatty deposits on the artery walls. In the last 10 years, as more people have become involved in regular exercise programmes, there has been a 22 per cent reduction in deaths caused by heart attacks, and a 30 per cent reduction in deaths caused by strokes. Of course other factors, such as eating food containing less dietary cholesterol and saturated fats, may also be responsible for this promising drop in heart disease.

Perhaps it seems contradictory, but the more regular exercise you get, the more energy you will have for other activities. If your body is fit, it can handle more. So if you are tired and have trouble keeping up with work, study, parties and other activities, the answer may not be more sleep but more exercise. There is evidence to suggest that when you exercise regularly, you need less sleep and you sleep more soundly.

People who are overweight do not necessarily eat more than those with normal weight, but they do move less. The less you move, the fewer calories you burn. The more exercise you get, the more calories you burn, and the more you can eat without putting on weight.

Exercise also helps to regulate your appetite. As you exercise more, you will not be a lot hungrier. In fact, after exercising for an hour, you will generally feel less hungry than when you started. Being overweight (especially in our weight-conscious society) makes many people feel emotionally stressed. But excess weight is also a physical stressor, placing extra demands on the system.

Psychological benefits of exercise

A considerable range of psychological benefits appear to accrue from exercise and activity, beyond the obvious general positive feeling of healthiness.

Certain forms of exercise (jogging, cross-country skiing, swimming, hiking, bicycling) require a fairly consistent repetitive motion that can alter one's state of consciousness. Described by some as moving meditation, the physiological effects of regular participation in these activities is very similar to what happens when one practises meditation. Breathing and movement may in part be responsible for the feelings of calmness and tranquillity claimed by some in response to exercise.

Appropriately high levels of self-esteem and self-efficacy (positive thoughts about self; see Skill 5) have been correlated with increased ability to cope with high stress levels. Exercise cultivates self-esteem and self-efficacy in a number of ways including:

- Whenever an individual knowingly participates in a health-enhancing activity, it is common to experience increased feelings of self-worth as they realise they are doing something which will ultimately benefit them.
- Participation in physical activities that have known social value attached to them promotes social acceptance and status.
- Regular physical activity has the potential to alter one's body image in a socially desirable manner, thus increasing self-image and improving self-esteem.
- Frequent physical activity also promotes consistent physical challenges which, when conquered, foster feelings of self-efficacy.

For some, exercise can be a deliberate, solitary escape from the daily toils and pressures of a stressful society. The escape can be a bicycle ride in the country, the cocoon of a lap pool, an early morning run or any other form of physical exertion that provides a mini-vacation and allows one to recharge energy levels to deal with conflicts when they return. Others use this time to self-reflect on issues of importance, or to stimulate creative problem solving.

The buffering effects of social support are well documented. Recreational activities (netball, golf, a fun run, indoor cricket, tennis) encourage a sense of fun and play with other individuals who have similar interests and can provide a number of opportunities to discuss life situations. The sharing that ensues brings reassurance that one is not alone and that help is available for the asking.

A significant volume of research is accumulating on the positive physical properties of human touch. Some of the research has demonstrated a reduction in stress-related hormones accompanying positive expressions of human touch. Recreational and sporting endeavours raise occasions and provide excuses to touch others in a positive way. As an example, in a culture that breeds homophobia, men are told that it is socially acceptable to hug other men and pat them on the buttocks during sporting events. This behaviour is normally considered taboo, and many men would otherwise have few chances to express emotions in such a physical manner.

During stress, muscles contract (bracing) and lose their normal resting muscle tone. Bouts of physical activity allow muscles to work, thereby releasing stored energy and allowing muscle groups to return to their normal resting potential. This action also reduces the further stress that is precipitated by pain and discomfort associated with muscular tension (e.g. tension headaches, arthritic joint pain, backache, joint dysfunction). Stretching and yoga are also effective in reducing muscular tension.

Catecholamines including beta-endorphins have been shown to increase during physical activity of 20 minutes or more. Chemically similar to opiate compounds, these morphine-like substances have been shown to provide an analgesic (pain-relieving) effect and promote a sense of euphoria, removing anxiety and depression. The physical and emotional symptoms of withdrawal associated with the rapid decrease of physical activity (as occurs with athletic injuries) of physically fit individuals has also been attributed to this hormone. The positive mood states associated with frequent exercise are so significant that some have suggested that this is a more effective treatment for clinical depression than either psychotherapy or the use of anti-depression drugs.

Physical activity can also be challenging—for example, running as fast as one can, swimming as far as one can, or hitting a golf ball as straight and hard as possible. On the far end of the continuum are people who voluntarily involve themselves in high-risk, high-stress physical activities such as extreme skiing, hang-gliding, scuba diving and jumping out of perfectly good airplanes. By constantly testing themselves individuals learn how to take on higher and higher loads of stress. The learning that ensues transfers over to the stress that is experienced in daily life. For example, it would be difficult to imagine someone who had spent all day solo rock-climbing without the use of ropes for safety getting upset over being caught in traffic, when driving back into the city.

Many advocates of competitive sports contend that participants learn a great deal about life and what is necessary for success through their participation. Knowing what it takes to win, how to accept loss, how to set goals, how to deal with high levels of stress and how to get along with others are all mentioned as lessons learned through involvement in sports.

A symptom of stress overload for some is the inability to sleep or get adequate rest. A fatigued individual is less able to perform at a high level. Exercise has been shown to be very effective in helping some individuals fall asleep easily and sleep more soundly. The assumption, however, is that one is not overdoing physical training and becoming exhausted from the activity.

A person who is physically fit has organ systems that are functioning at an optimal level. If this individual should become ill, injured or even pregnant, they will demonstrate more stamina and greater resiliency to fight the discomfort. It is also likely that fit individuals will recover more quickly.

Thus the therapeutic benefits of regular physical activity are many. Someone once said that if exercise was a pill, it would be the most powerful medication known to humankind. The only problem is that it is difficult to get modern men and women to take that pill every day. Inactivity should be considered a disease state. Adults are often told that they should consult a physician before beginning an exercise programme. Based upon scientific evidence, it may be more appropriate to consult a physician before sitting down in a lounge chair in front of a TV with a remote control.

Stressed-out individuals often complain that they do not have time to exercise. Skill 9, concerned with managing time effectively, will provide a strong guide to building a personal schedule that can include all the priorities and yet leave time for activity.

What physical activities are best for stress and emotional health management?

- *It should be enjoyable and invigorating.* Individuals will be more likely to continue activities that they perceive as fun compared to those that are viewed as pure drudgery. If you don't like running, then don't run. Do something you do like, especially with friends. The social support will help you maintain the activity over time.
- *Activities should be non-competitive and ego void.* Although competition was highlighted above as a positive function, for some people winning can become the most important part of competition. This increases stress and leads to depression and loss of self-esteem when they lose, which they inevitably must do at times.
- *Choose activities that promote personal satisfaction.* In general, try to find activities that promote positive feelings regarding your performance. Don't play golf (which has been defined as a good way to screw up a nice walk) if you find trying to hit a small ball hundreds of metres into a tiny hole somewhat stressful. You may want to find something you can do with someone else that is pleasant for both of you.
- *Aerobic vs. anaerobic activities.* From a physical health perspective aerobic activities (e.g. weightlifting) are generally considered superior in reducing the risks associated with most diseases (especially heart disease). Spend time in any busy weight-room and you can almost feel the testosterone being pumped up. The high one gets from lifting weights is not the same as the tranquillity experienced by those who condition aerobically. Weight-lifters feel powerful and confident following workouts. Anaerobic activities (e.g. long-distance running) performed at a long, slow, steady interval seem to have a calming effect on people. From a mental health

perspective, cross-training in both aerobic and anaerobic exercise is recommended to increase variety in workouts while encouraging feelings of both powerfulness and tranquillity.

- *How much exercise.* The frequency and duration of exercise is determined by one's goals. To get in shape more quickly it is recommended that one exercise frequently, as opposed to fewer occasions and longer durations. Weekend athletes don't cut it. In most cases fitness will be lost at less than three sessions a week. Ideally one should attempt to do something physical each day to prepare for the stressors ahead or to decrease the residual effects of stress during the day. Find an activity that you can sustain for at least 20 minutes, that is also vigorous enough to push your heart rate up to 75 per cent of its capacity, and do this at least three times each week.
- *Sexual activity as exercise.* Don't forget to include sexual activity as part of your physical activity. Orgasm is a great release of muscular and emotional tension. Like other forms of physical activity, make sure it is fun and not stressful.

Negative consequences and contraindications of activity

- *Compulsive training.* Overuse of any coping strategy can create additional problems. For some, physical activity can be escape from taking responsibility for their actions. By indulging themselves in their activity, they avoid troubling life situations which are difficult to resolve.
- *Aggressive tendencies.* Although physical activity can be a useful catharsis for aggression, aggressive sport activities can also act to condition a person to become more aggressive. If one learns to be successful by acting overly aggressive, it is not a far stretch to see how some may use aggression to get what they want in other areas of life. Not a very positive consequence of physical activity, and certainly one that can increase stress and negative emotional reactions.
- *Addiction.* Those who exercise on a daily basis often describe themselves as being 'addicted' to their activity. Although considered to be a positive addiction, for some people the withdrawal effects of not being able to exercise can create problems. Whether caused by changes in catecholamine levels (not getting their daily fix of endorphins) or some other mechanism, such individuals should be aware of possible

increases in hostility, anxiety, irritability and depression associated with not working out.

ACTIVITY **4.4**

Health walk/run

This activity helps to release endorphins. It also allows relief of tension and the development of personal health. The health walk/run can be done in the area where you live, starting and ending at your own front door.

No equipment is needed, nor do you need a park or recreation area. The pavements around your home are adequate. (If you feel embarrassed about being seen doing these activities outside, do them in your home, using different parts of rooms for the stations and running on the spot. However, if possible, overcome your embarrassment—exercise outside is definitely more interesting, and you will also benefit from the fresh air.)

The health walk/run is approximately 1.7 kilometres long, with 10 exercise stops or stations built in along the way. It takes approximately 20 to 30 minutes to complete, depending on your speed. Each station features a different exercise. The advantage of the health walk/run is that it provides an excellent starting point if you have not exercised for a long time. Further, it allows you to establish your own pace. It is possible to start out by walking and gradually increase the pace to a rapid run between each station.

The health walk/run is designed in the following way:

1. The starting point may be anywhere. It might be the front steps or the corner of the block. From the starting point, walk or run approximately 200 metres to Station 1.
    Station 1: Touch your toes—bend at the waist and stretch as far as possible; do not bounce. Try to touch your toes with your fingers. Ten times is good, but initially do the number that feels comfortable.
2. Walk or run approximately 150 metres to Station 2.
    Station 2: Waist bend—place your hands on your buttocks and bend at the waist, with your head looking up, until your body is parallel to the ground. Ten times is good.
3. Walk or run approximately 150 metres to Station 3.
    Station 3: Jumping jacks—start with your feet together and hands at the sides. Jump, moving both feet approximately

shoulder-width apart, and clap your hands over your head. Twenty times is good.

4. Walk or run approximately 150 metres to Station 4.
   Station 4: Push-ups—lie on your stomach with hands placed on the ground at the shoulders and toes touching the ground. Keeping your body as straight as possible, push until your arms are fully extended. Try to do this rapidly. Ten times is very good.

5. Walk or run approximately 150 metres to Station 5.
   Station 5: Windmill toe-touch—stand with your feet slightly more than shoulder-width apart and arms extended at shoulder level parallel to the ground. Bend at the waist and touch your left foot with the fingers of your right hand. Continue by alternating hands and feet. Ten times on each side is good.

6. Walk or run approximately 150 metres to Station 6.
   Station 6: Upper-back stretch—stand with feet slightly apart and arms bent at the elbow and at shoulder level. Push your elbows back as far as possible. Hold this position for a count of five and then release. Ten times is good.

7. Walk or run approximately 150 metres to Station 7.
   Station 7: Arm push—find a tree or a wall and push as hard as possible against it with your palms flat against the surface. Hold this position for a count of five. Ten times is good.

8. Walk or run approximately 150 metres to Station 8.
   Station 8: Behind-the-head clasp—stand with your feet slightly apart and place your hands behind your head. Curl the fingers of both hands and lock them together like an S. Pull as hard as possible with both arms, but do not break the lock. Hold this for a count of five. Ten times is good.

9. Walk or run approximately 150 metres to Station 9.
   Station 9: Sit-ups—lie on your back with knees bent and legs at less than a 90-degree angle. Hands are locked behind your head. Lie flat on your back and then come up to a sitting position. Ten times is good.

10. Walk or run approximately 150 metres to Station 10.
    Station 10: Spine stretch—get down on all fours with your back slightly humped. Bend your elbows and move your chest down towards the ground while straightening your back. Ten times is good.

11. Walk or run approximately 150 metres to the end of the health walk/run.

It is possible to design a health walk/run so that it begins and ends in the same place.

Adequate sleep

The mind and body are constantly at work, even when you sleep. During sleep, however, the system has an opportunity to slow down. Energy used during exertion can slowly be restored when the body is at rest.

After exhaustion from excessively stressful activity, sleep and rest can help restore the depleted resources of the mind and body *almost* to previous levels. The word 'almost' is used because excessive or constant stress gradually wears the mind and body down, despite periods of rest. This is why many researchers believe that excessive stress is linked to illness and disease. Different people develop different illnesses and diseases depending, to some degree, on which part of the body is weakest and most vulnerable to stress and strain. Rest and relaxation are two mechanisms for relieving and/or reducing the experience of stress.

Insomnia, or the inability to sleep, is itself a powerful stressor. If a sleepless night follows a hectic day, the chances are that you will not be in any shape to work or concentrate the following day. The stress of trying to get things done when you are tired may mean yet another sleepless night, and the development of a vicious cycle that is very hard to break. Keep in mind that the hormones produced during acute stress are meant to alert you and prepare you for peak accomplishments. They tend to combat sleep and to promote alertness during brief periods of exertion. If too large a quantity of these hormones is circulating in your blood, you will find it difficult to fall asleep.

Scientific studies show that continued sleep loss contributes to nervousness. The *best way* to determine whether you are getting enough sleep is to examine *how you feel*. If you wake up feeling refreshed and full of 'go', you are probably getting enough sleep. But if you feel tired, tense and irritable too often, indications are that you need to get more sleep. Try going to bed earlier and being as regular as possible. It is no good waiting until you are overtired before going to bed.

ACTIVITY **4.5**

A sleep/rest chart

How much sleep and rest do you get? Try charting it by drawing in your Stress Diary a 24-hour clock divided into segments, like the one following:

Using this 24-hour clock (24 is midnight, 12 is noon, 6 is 6 am and 18 is 6 pm), indicate the hours of sleep in any given 24-hour period in one colour, and the periods of rest in a different colour.

After the periods of rest and sleep have been coloured in, look at the chart to see the pattern it reveals. Respond to these questions:

1. Do I sleep at least six hours a day? (At least six hours a day is needed by most of us. Occasionally, there is a *rare* person who really does not need this amount of sleep.)
2. Is my chart lacking in periods of rest and relaxation? If so, plan at least two rest periods during the day that balance out the sleep cycle. For example, sometime during the workday find time to rest, instead of having a coffee break perhaps. Another time to rest is after work and before any social engagements. The people who do not sleep and rest properly are often the ones who are reporting stress and a lack of sufficient energy to do their jobs. Charting can make you more aware of your need for sleep and rest.

This brings us back to the vicious cycle: worry and anxiety cause sleeplessness, making you more tense and irritable, and often unable to get to sleep. Some of the other suggestions in this book should help you to relax, and thus sleep better. Medication or alcohol to induce sleep must not be used, if possible: the brain develops new mechanisms to counteract the effects of alcohol and drugs, and consequently the cycle will be repeated, and stronger drugs will be needed. In other words, people become dependent on drugs or alcohol.

Instead of resorting to medication to induce sleep (drugs are also inclined to leave you less alert the next day), try some of the following suggestions:

- See to it that you have a physical environment that is conducive to sleep. Your bedroom should be quiet and well ventilated, and the bed covers should be neither too warm nor too light. Your mattress should be firm and your pillow soft and not too big.
- Regular, graduated exercise also induces sleep, as long as it is not done immediately before going to bed.
- Before bedtime, avoid heavy meals, coffee, tea or cool drinks containing caffeine.
- Excitement in any form at bedtime should be avoided, whether it be in the form of movies, books, conversations or arguments.

An untroubled mind is probably your greatest assurance of a good night's sleep. The problem, of course, is how to suddenly switch off all the troubles, tensions and worries of the day when you go to bed.

Some of the relaxation exercises provided in this book should help (see *Skill 3: Master the benefits of relaxation*). One thing is certain: worrying about not being able to sleep definitely only worsens the situation. Instead, get up and work on your hobby, or have an interesting, relaxing book handy to read. At least then you do not have to worry about the time wasted while not sleeping.

As you get older, you may find that you do not need as much sleep as you did when you were younger and more active. This is perfectly normal. Apply the same test as we mentioned earlier: how do you feel when you wake up in the morning?

Some older people do suffer from sleeplessness. Either they cannot get to sleep, or they wake up too often during the night and find it difficult to go back to sleep. Check to see if the problem possibly lies in your changed daily routine. If you no longer hold a full-time job, it could be that your days are spent lazing about, and that you are not tired at night.

It could be that you go to bed too early, and are spending too long in bed, or an afternoon or early evening nap may be interfering with your readiness for sleep when night comes. The best remedy for an inability to sleep is to have full, active and interesting days.

If sleeplessness is really a problem and is causing you to become overanxious and exhausted, you should consult your doctor. Worrying about it on your own only makes the situation seem much worse than it really is.

ACTIVITY 4.6

Two case studies

By analysing the two case studies below, you have an opportunity to see the potential use and misuse of diet, exercise and sleep in response to stress. Read the case studies, and then answer the following questions:

1. What is the stressor in each case?
2. What are the signs of stress?
3. How did Julia and Brian use or misuse *diet* to create or reduce stress?
4. How did Julia and Brian use or misuse *exercise* to create or reduce stress?
5. How did Julia and Brian use or misuse *sleep* to create or reduce stress?

Case study: Julia Williams
Up until her final year at university, the world looked pretty good to Julia Williams. She was a star of the university athletics team and consistently came top in her class. Interested early on in computer technology, she had applied and obtained a job at a major computer company.

By any standards, Julia was friendly and attractive. For most of university she had been especially friendly and attractive to David West. To quote her best friend Denise, Julia and David were definitely 'an item'.

Julia and David did everything together. After work, David went through Julia's exercise routines with her to keep her company and to keep them both trim. Both were doing part-time master's degrees and on week-nights they almost always studied together, ending the evening with something to eat at 'Rick's Place'. At weekends they went on trips, partied with friends, watched television or went to a movie. Something was always happening . . . until summer came and David went on a holiday. When he returned, he had a deep tan and a new girlfriend.

After work, Julia can usually be found at the gym or on the athletics track. She works out for long hours. Often it is dark before she heads for home. Instead of looking fit, though, Julia is gaunt and thin. Rumour has it that she lost more than 5 kilograms in only three weeks.

When Julia gets home, she is usually too tired for dinner. More often than not, she grabs a fistful of crackers and a soft drink and heads upstairs to her room. Though Denise has been trying to reach her for days on end, she tells her flatmate she does not want to talk to anyone on the phone.

In her room, Julia tries to study, but finds her mind drifting. Every now and then she even catches herself nodding off. In order to stay awake, she goes downstairs for a cup of coffee and a doughnut for quick energy. Usually it is past midnight before she has all of her study done. As she climbs into bed, she worries that she will have yet another sleepless night. Tossing and turning for the next few hours, she wakes cold and tired to the shrill sound of her alarm. Slowly she pulls herself out of bed to face another day of the same routine.

Case study: Brian Murray

When he returned to his office after yet another rich business lunch, his alertness blunted by a full stomach and several glasses of wine, Brian Murray decided that enough was enough. It had been a very successful luncheon from the business point of view, so why did he feel so depressed? Perhaps it had something to do with the 8 kilograms he had put on in the past two months, ever since he had been promoted to production manager of his company, a position that he had been coveting for many years.

Brian spent a good hour having a serious think about the way his life was going. Every night, and over weekends, he would take work home with him, for he was now striving for a higher position in the job hierarchy, and needed to make a good impression. Supper consisted of precooked pies, or greasy fish and chips from the take away cafe that he passed on his way home. He had completely stopped jogging, and the lunchtime gym he had attended had only lasted for a few weeks—he simply could not find the time. At bedtime he would always take a sleeping pill to ensure that unpleasant thoughts did not plague him during the night. Work and eat: these were his only activities. And now, overweight, unfit and with stomach pains that had recently begun to bother him, he decided to go and see his doctor.

Tests revealed an ulcer. The doctor—an old friend—spent more than an hour telling Brian that his present course was suicidal, and made certain suggestions.

Brian has started to eat small, regular meals, restricts work to business hours, sleeps without the assistance of drugs and has joined a sports club where he has made new and supportive friends and where he is getting fitter by the day. A revitalised man, he has even started to date one of the women at the club.

There is no one right way to manage or reduce stress. Each person must find the techniques or activities that work best for them. It is also important to remember at all times to consider both the short- and long-term health consequences.

In both of the cases above, social support or the absence of social support made a difference to how the stress was experienced. Julia chose to cut herself off from others and was therefore alone with her unhappiness. Brian's acceptance of his doctor's help, and that of his new friends at the sports club, made it easier to cope with the stress of being overweight and needing to diet and exercise.

Research confirms that strong social ties and supports can act as powerful buffers, cushioning the potentially negative effects of stress. One important reason for readers to take their new understanding of stress—and the skills they have learnt to manage stress—beyond themselves to their families and communities is their ability to reduce the effects of stress on others as well as on themselves, by working towards a sense of group and community cohesiveness.

ACTIVITY 4.7

Making charts

Using information that you have supplied in your answers to the questions about Julia and Brian in Activity 4.6, as well as the additional information provided, draw and fill in a chart like the one below, showing the potential links between diet, exercise and sleep on the one hand, and health and stress on the other.

For example, with reference to the role of the six basic nutrients in promoting and maintaining health, you can simply write, next to Health in the Diet column, something like: *Each of the six basic nutrients is essential to health* or *A well-balanced diet is necessary to keep healthy.*

Potential links between diet/exercise/sleep and health/stress

	Diet	Exercise	Sleep
Health			
Stress			

Summary

You have now learnt about the importance of maintaining good health to the effective management of stress. To achieve and maintain good health, there are three essentials:

1. A healthy diet.
2. Adequate exercise.
3. Adequate sleep.

It does not take long to reap the benefits that can be gained by adopting a healthy lifestyle.

SKILL 5

Enhance your self-concept

Introduction

In preventing or coping with undue stress, it is vital that you either possess or develop positive feelings about yourself. An important approach to stress management is the ability to be predominantly hopeful and to see life as a challenge, rather than having a generally negative attitude about yourself, others and life in general.

Your attitude towards yourself, others and life begins to form when you are a baby. *However, this does not mean that as you grow older you cannot cultivate a different philosophy*. You are not a prisoner of your past.

If you are inclined to see yourself in negative terms, are too self-critical or demean yourself, then the rigours of life and its challenges will defeat you before you have even set off. The stresses and strains that come from feeling negative, incompetent and inferior are then supplemented by the stresses and strains of actually not coping in reality, for self-doubt becomes a self-validating prophecy (sometimes called the 'expectancy effect'). You are your own worst enemy.

Figure 5.1 shows how this works with a failure situation. But remember that it also works to the benefit of the person in a success situation, as Figure 5.2 shows.

What is the self-concept?

Psychologists use the term 'self-concept' to mean the beliefs and feelings we have about ourselves. It is important to know who

Figure 5.1   Stress arising from feelings of incompetence and poor performance

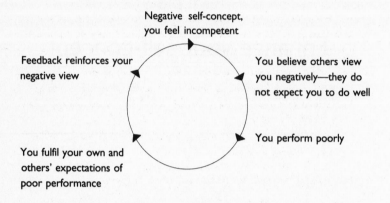

Figure 5.2   Positive feelings about yourself, good performance and positive feedback reduce the likelihood of stress

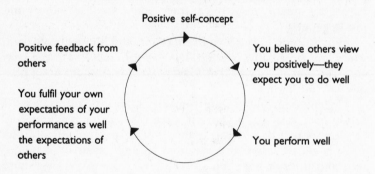

we are, and about our abilities, our needs, our values and our relationships. Certainly we need to know our limitations as well as our potential. But we must be realistic and not self-defeating.

Only by understanding yourself, becoming positive about yourself and building on your strengths, can you get the most out of life both now and in the future, and do what you feel you are able to do. An understanding of yourself provides an internal map that you can study when making decisions about choices that confront you. *Until you know who you are, you will not know what you can become.*

Figures 5.1 and 5.2 are drawn as circular systems because your self-concept, your belief in your competence, your actual performance and the feedback you get, all interact. If at the outset you believe you are going to fail, then that belief creates feelings and actions that tend to make it come true. Have you ever stated some task and said to yourself, 'This is beyond me, I'll never manage it'? The result was almost certainly that you did not. As Alexander Dumas in *The Three Musketeers* wrote:

> A person who doubts himself is like a man who would enlist in the ranks of the enemy and bear arms against himself. He makes his failure certain by himself being the first to be convinced of it.

If you are satisfied with yourself, your self-concept will be positive; you will have a high self-esteem and accept yourself. If you are dissatisfied with what you see, your self-concept will be poor; you will have little self-esteem and have difficulty accepting yourself as you are.

Your self-concept consists of a number of components. The main ones are:

- the *physical self* or *body image* (i.e. how you feel about your physical attributes)
- the *social self* (i.e. how you think others see you)
- the *ideal self* (i.e. how you really would like to be)
- the *self as you are* (i.e. how you see yourself now)
- the *academic self-concept* (i.e. how you see yourself in terms of your intellectual life)
- the *emotional self-concept* (i.e. what emotions you see as being typical of you).

These components are not really as separated as they seem to be in the list above, but are all closely interwoven in your overall view of yourself.

Influence of self-concept on behaviour

There are two extremes of self-concept—low or negative self-concept and high or positive self-concept. While most of us will fall somewhere between these two extremes, it is important to recognise which model of behaviour contains those elements that are often present in your life.

- *Those with a low or negative self-concept* tend to be unhappy, anxious, self-critical people who have difficulty building positive relationships with others. Low self-concept people tend to be shy and therefore avoid others. Some may try to raise their self-esteem by showing off, bragging and boasting. These behaviours are futile attempts to impress other people in order to make themselves more likeable. Unfortunately, such behaviours usually have the opposite effect, making those with a poor self-concept feel even more unworthy and incompetent. They will be afraid to try anything for fear of expected failure in all aspects of life, and will set low goals for themselves.
- *Those with a high or positive self-concept* tend not to be anxiety-ridden, but happy, congenial, friendly and self-reliant persons with a lot of self-confidence. People with a positive self-concept are able to accept themselves in such a way as to include both their weaknesses and their strengths. They feel secure in themselves and therefore tend not to feel stress and jealousy, can tolerate criticism, can express feelings appropriately and have the confidence to cope with most situations.

If we look at the differences in the two extremes of self-concept, it is easy to see that the person with a negative self-concept is likely to respond more stressfully than a person with a positive self-concept.

If you have a positive self-concept, other stress management skills are more easily learnt and used. Examples are building positive relationships with other people (i.e. reducing interpersonal stress) and using assertiveness skills. In general, too, people with positive feelings about themselves will try to centre their lives on their abilities and strengths, and will therefore feel that they are in control of their own life (internal locus of control). Such people have more confidence in their own abilities, are more resilient in coping with life's ups and downs, and are therefore less likely to succumb to stress.

Alternatively, having a negative self-image, low self-esteem and feelings of inadequacy may lead to behaviour that increases the chances of not being accepted and of feeling even more inadequate. The likelihood of having satisfying relationships with others is decreased, and assertiveness and confidence are lowered, leading to feelings of stress that arise from an inability to meet environmental demands.

Evaluating your self-concept

The following activity asks you to examine three components of your self-concept:

1. The *social self* (i.e. how you think others see you).
2. The *ideal self* (i.e. how you really would like to be).
3. The *self as you are* (i.e. how you see yourself now).

ACTIVITY 5.1

What are your characteristics?

Complete the following questionnaire about yourself by working on one column at a time as follows:

1. Fill in the first column as you feel you see yourself *now* (i.e. the self as you are).
2. Fill in the second column as you *think others perceive you* (i.e. your social self).
3. Fill in the third column as you *would really like to be* (i.e. your ideal self).

In each column, give yourself a score of 1, 2, 3, 4 or 5 against each descriptive word, using the following scoring system:

- 1 means that you can never be described that way
- 2 means that you are occasionally like that
- 3 means that you are often like that
- 4 means that you are usually like that
- 5 means that you are always like that.

Description	As I am	As others see me	As I would like to be
Friendly			
Boring			
Successful			
Aimless			
Unimportant			
Stable			
Cautious			
Clever			
Enthusiastic			
Happy			

Description	As I am	As others see me	As I would like to be
Kind			
Tense			
Aloof			
Assertive			
Independent			
Creative			
Aggressive			
Humorous			
Jealous			
Argumentative			
Honest			
Ambitious			
Conscientious			
Complaining			
Generous			
Considerate			
Immature			
Tolerant			
Shy			
Truthful			
Sarcastic			
Reliable			
Patient			
Emotional			
Persevering			
Decisive			
Sensitive			
Stubborn			

In your Stress Diary, answer the following questions:

1. Do you see yourself as others see you?
2. What are the major differences?
3. Are you happy with the way you think others see you?
4. Does your ideal self differ from your real self? In what way?

How did your self-concept develop?

What you come to think of yourself is based largely on what you believe 'important others'—for example, supervisors, friends, parents and teachers—think of you. Other people act as 'mirrors' that reflect back at you how they see you. The way they respond and react to you is a major part of this reflection. Their words, as well as their non-verbal signals, are interpreted by you as indicative of how they feel about you. Of course, you may be correct or incorrect because your interpretation is subjective. But whether correct or not, you will build up a picture of yourself and behave in accordance with that picture.

Self-perceptions may not be correct, but because you hold them and believe them, they affect your behaviour. For example, at some point a teacher may have given you the idea that you were not very bright. You may have believed them, although their impression of you may have been incorrect. And so, based on their perception of you, you decided to leave school, thereby severely limiting your future career prospects. Inappropriate behaviour stems from invalid perceptions. You must try to obtain accurate perceptions and evaluations of yourself on which to base behaviour. An accurate perception of how you 'come over' to others is vital if you are to develop competent social relationships.

ACTIVITY 5.2

Are your self-perceptions valid?

This is an optional activity. If possible, have a friend or work colleague go through your responses to Activity 5.1 with you. Do the two of you agree? Are there any aspects about which you were mistaken? Have you been behaving inappropriately because of any misperception?

Can you see any changes that you could make in your perception of yourself that would help you to see yourself in a more positive light?

The physical self or body image

How you see and evaluate your physical body appears to be a major part of your overall self-concept. Your body is always with you, you can never leave it behind, and as you pass through life, the body changes size and shape, and develops in a variety of ways.

Every person has to adjust to these changes in body image. Some people worry in case they are not tall enough or worry because they believe they are too tall; others think they are too fat; yet others worry because they think that their appearance is not appealing to the opposite sex. Body image as self-perceived is a source of stress to many.

One of our stress management techniques is the use of exercise and diet *(Skill 4: Maintain good health)*. A sensible approach with regard to exercise and diet will certainly go a long way towards improving your body, and thus your body image.

ACTIVITY **5.3**

My body image

Write answers in your Stress Diary to the following questions:

1. Are there any aspects of my physical make-up that I would like to change?
2. Why do I want to change them, and in what way?
3. Is there anything I can do to 'improve' my body image in my own eyes? (An example would be to wear built-up shoes for extra height.)
4. What are my best physical features?
5. If I imagine meeting myself for the first time, what positive features would people notice about me?

Notice that, in assessing one's own body image, it is important to focus on one's positive features and not only on what is 'wrong'.

ACTIVITY **5.4**

The use of aids to improve body image

Make a list of all the aids, cosmetics, dietary or exercise techniques that could be used to improve what you regard as your physical defects.

The emotional self-concept

Your emotional self-concept refers to the emotions that you believe are typical of you.

ACTIVITY **5.5**

What are your most frequently recurring emotions?

1. Here is a list of emotions that we all experience from time to time. Write down in your Stress Diary the four emotions in this list that you experience most often.

nervousness	irritation/annoyance
happiness	enjoyment
jealousy	contentment
anger	love
doubt	depression/sadness
guilt	hate
panic	despair
anxiety	elation

2. For each of the four you have picked, complete this sentence: 'I get this feeling when . . .'

Remember that it is not *wrong* to experience emotions such as sadness, anger, guilt or fear at times. We cannot always be happy. But we must try not to hide these feelings from ourselves by turning to escapes such as alcohol or drugs, or by denying that such feelings do exist. We must all learn to cope with negative feelings in positive ways. Here are some guidelines.

- Express your negative feelings when it is *appropriate* to do so (e.g. be angry when someone has offended or hurt you; allow yourself to feel sad and express your grief when a loved person has died). Do not try to hide your feelings in these sorts of circumstances—be open and honest about how you feel. This is part of being assertive, which is one of the important stress management skills that are taught in this book (see *Skill 8: Learn to communicate assertively*).
- Rather than trying to deny your feelings, avoid situations where negative emotions may occur. For example, if a particular person consistently irritates you, avoid that person if you can.

- Re-appraise the situations in which negative emotions occur and see if there are not some positive things to respond to as well.
- Use relaxation techniques (see *Skill 3: Master the benefits of relaxation*) if stress, tension or anxiety need to be reduced.

How to strengthen your self-concept

It should be apparent to you by now that your self-concept influences your behaviour in quite important ways. With a positive self-concept, you will be happier and less anxious. You will know your strengths, and will be more able to cope with daily life events and challenges. It will be easier to build and maintain productive relationships with others, to perform more competently in the things you do, and you will be more willing to tackle new things. All these attributes will be vitally important in a rapidly changing world where, for example, jobs will be scarce, certain occupations will die out and new ones will emerge as the rate of technological change increases (see *Skill 10: Be prepared for the future*). Values and attitudes will alter as well. The person best able to cope is the one who believes in themselves, who is confident, resilient and resourceful—in short, the person with a positive self-concept who is not 'stuck' but can meet perceived environmental demands and manage their stress levels with confidence.

So how can you strengthen your self-concept? The following pages contain some activities that you should try. But before you attempt them, make sure that you are aware of the fact that the most important way to develop more self-esteem is to develop self-confidence, self-reliance and social skills. To achieve this, you must concentrate on the following points:

- *You need to know your abilities and use them.* This will bring a feeling of success and confidence.
- *You must set realistic standards for yourself*, taking into account those abilities and skills that you have. If you set standards that are too high, you will fail, feel a failure, lose confidence and feel stress when presented with similar tasks in the future.

- *Always think of your positive strengths* and not about those you do not possess. Develop your strengths rather than daydream about the ones you wished you had.
- *Develop your interests* and become a more interesting person as a result. You will gain a lot of positive feedback from others.
- *Do not compare yourself unfavourably with others.* They have their weak points, too, perhaps where you have strengths.
- *Be positive in your relationships.* Give help; do not boast or criticise; others will then be more positive towards you.

Low self-concept people often avoid other people or social events in case they show themselves up as being incompetent to handle a situation. Here are a few basic social skills that will help you to cope and from which you will derive positive feedback:

- Do not always wait for the other person to start a conversation. It is not so difficult to introduce yourself and then let the other person take it from there. There is always *something* to talk about.
- Have something interesting to talk about (i.e. keep yourself well-informed and up-to-date by reading books, magazines and newspapers, or listening to the radio or watching TV).
- A valuable social skill is knowing how to listen. This makes you more likeable because, by listening, you show the other person that you are interested in what they have to say.

The activities that follow will help you to control stress caused by social interactions.

ACTIVITY 5.6

Starting a conversation

You are at a party. Your host or hostess has introduced you to someone new and has abandoned you to your fate. In your Stress Diary, suggest as many ways as you can for opening the conversation. You might even develop a short script.

ACTIVITY 5.7

Topics of interest

You have been 'thrown together' with a stranger at a social event. Write down three or four topics of interest that you could talk about. If you wish, do this in the form of a simple script, or even role-play it with a friend.

ACTIVITY 5.8

What are your positive points?

It is important to realise that *everyone* has some positive points. Before doing this activity, think about your positive points in the light of the following:

- *Intellectual abilities.* Have you shown any ability in problem solving? Do you usually understand things the first time? Do you think clearly and remember well? Can you read well and converse well? Have you achieved something that took a lot of effort?
- *Practical skills.* Have you shown any skills in making things? In repairing things? In designing things?
- *Artistic skills.* Have you developed any artistic skills? For example, can you play a musical instrument well? Can you sing or dance or paint? Is pottery-making, needlework or writing stories something you do well?
- *Relationship skills.* Do you usually get on well with other people? Do you generally show an interest in others and listen to them? Are you trustworthy, reliable and conscientious?
- *Social skills.* Do you enjoy helping others, particularly those not as fortunate as yourself? Do you have the interests of other people at heart?
- *Physical abilities.* Are you healthy and strong? Do you enjoy outdoor activities? Have you any sporting skills?
- *Leisure skills.* Do you have any skills that you practise in your spare time that are interesting or valuable?

Using the suggestions above as a guideline, what do you think are your positive points? What do you feel good about? Write five sentences, starting: 'I feel good about myself because . . .'

Stroking

The positive responses we get from others make us feel valued, worthwhile and accepted, and this makes our self-concept blossom. The American psychologist Eric Berne (1972) has called the positive responses that people give each other 'strokes'. 'Stroking' consists of giving people recognition, acceptance and esteem. Not to be 'stroked' means to be ignored, feeling that you do not count, that you are nobody, and this is obviously very harmful to your self-concept. Isn't it nice to receive praise? Give it to others, too, when they deserve it.

We tend, unfortunately, to focus on errors, faults and failure in others, thereby depriving them of 'strokes' and enhancing their feelings of inferiority and failure.

ACTIVITY **5.9**

Stroking

Keep a record in your Stress Diary for a week of the 'strokes' you have given others. Find opportunities to give subordinates, work colleagues, friends, relatives, in fact anyone, some 'strokes', and avoid giving 'put-downs'. If you are positive towards others, they are most likely to be positive towards you, thus decreasing the chance of tension for either of you.

ACTIVITY **5.10**

Put-downs

Look out for 'put-downs' during the next week. Keep a record in your Stress Diary of those that are imposed on you. How did you feel? Did you notice the effect of 'put-downs' on others? What happened?

The need for success

Success often brings further success, while failure causes discouragement and loss of self-esteem. *Everyone can be a success at something.* Those who have not found what they can gain success in often try obnoxious ways of being 'someone' (e.g. vandalism or bullying). Remember, if you feel 'good' when you receive praise or are successful, other people feel the same way if you recognise their 'success'. This not only helps us all to develop positive self-feelings, confidence and motivation, but it also improves personal relationships, as no one needs to behave 'badly' to be noticed.

Remember that success can mean a variety of things, and is available in many different areas of activity. For example, a nervous person might feel successful if they manage to ask a question in a public meeting for the first time, or someone who has never managed to gain more than 70 per cent in an examination might manage to get 85 per cent.

If a group situation is available, the following three activities are useful. If not, skip these activities.

ACTIVITY 5.11

The importance of praise

GROUP CONTEXT
1. Form groups of four.
2. Each member takes it in turn to sit in the middle for one minute.
3. The other three tell the one in the middle about the positive things they see in that person. This can include physical, intellectual, spiritual or any other attributes.
4. The person in the middle has to remember what was said about them. Everyone has a turn in the middle.
5. Each person writes up in their Stress Diary the positive things that were said about them
6. Finally, come together as a group and discuss the following:
   - How does it feel to be praised?
   - Why is praise important?
   - How can we give praise more often?
   - In what ways can we give praise/recognition/support/acceptance?

ACTIVITY **5.12**

Feeling good about oneself

> **GROUP CONTEXT**
> Each member of a small group talks for one minute about a time when they were 'successful'. They should focus on how they felt, what was gained in self-esteem, how feeling good motivated them to achieve more. The group should then list ways in which one can feel good about oneself.

ACTIVITY **5.13**

Becoming a winner

> **GROUP CONTEXT**
> 1. In small groups, each member in turn chooses a situation or aspect of their life where they would like to experience some success but do not do so at present.
> 2. The group should discuss and suggest in each case how the person might achieve some success in the chosen area, and should also suggest ways in which more of us can be winners more of the time. Obviously any suggestions should be appro-

Summary

As you enhance your self-concept, you will find that fewer demands from the environment are perceived as stressful, and you will feel more confident about coping. Understanding yourself will help you to become more positive about yourself and allow you to build on your strengths and achieve what you are truly capable of.

A positive self-concept also interacts with the next three stress management skills—being positive (*Skill 6: Be positive*), relationship building (*Skill 7: Build relationships*) and assertive behaviour *(Skill 8: Learn to communicate assertively)*—in that each helps to develop the others.

SKILL 6

Be positive

Introduction

In this chapter we will look at some more ways that will help you to manage stress by being positive and constructive in your attitudes towards others, yourself and events. This is a continuation of self-concept development, for if we can be more positive about ourselves, we are more likely to view our environment (people, things, events, contexts) in a more favourable light.

Positive thinking and thought-stopping

The presence of negative statements and other irrational ideas about oneself in one's internal dialogue stimulates self-defeating behaviour. Such behaviour generates stress.

The psychologist Albert Ellis (1977) has catalogued countless variations of the 'musts', 'shoulds' and 'if onlys' of wishful and self-punishing thinking in an analysis that shows how faulty thinking keeps people from facing reality. Here are some of his ideas:

- It is absolutely essential for a person to be loved, appreciated and accepted all the time.
- One must be thoroughly competent and successful in all things if one is to consider oneself worthwhile.
- One should become very upset about others' problems/failings.
- It is very serious when others do not behave as one would like.
- There is invariably a right, precise and perfect solution to human problems, and it is catastrophic if that solution is not found.

- One can achieve maximum human happiness by inertia and inaction, or by passively and uncommittedly enjoying oneself.

Each of these irrational ideas is a source of stress and therefore a stressor that hampers efficient working. If we have these sorts of negative and/or irrational thoughts, one way to rid ourselves of them (and of the stress that accompanies them) is to use *thought-stopping*—we *stop* ourselves thinking such thoughts.

ACTIVITY **6.1**

Thought-stopping

1. Refer to your Stress Diary and identify some non-productive negative thinking that is causing you trouble. For example: 'Other people are so inept and incompetent, I have to do everything myself.'
2. Start thinking about the situation and verbalise your negative stress-inducing thoughts. Suddenly interrupt yourself by saying 'STOP' loudly. Start thinking about something pleasant.
3. Repeat 2 above several times.
4. Now repeat, but say 'Stop' to yourself under your breath.
5. Finally say 'Stop' to yourself in your mind only. Some people find that imagining an open book closing with a bang helps. The closure is the shutting-off of the thought.
6. Continue practising this technique until you can use it automatically to shut down any negative thoughts that cause stress.

Constructive self-talk

We can say many things to ourselves other than 'STOP'. We actually spend much of our time talking silently to ourselves, so much so that we are hardly even aware of it.

ACTIVITY **6.2**

Self-talk

Close your eyes and remain silent for one minute. What was going on in your head during that minute? From your answer it will become apparent that, for most of us, our heads are full of 'noise': thoughts, pictures, stories and sensations.

Some of this 'talking-to-oneself' that goes on can unfortunately work against us, but it can also be made to work in our favour. One thing that we do know is that people tend to believe what they tell themselves. For example, if I have to write a report and I start telling myself 'I'm bound to fail', 'I'm useless at writing reports', 'I'll never get the work done in time', what is likely to happen to me?

Take a personal thought that frequently gives rise to negative self-talk, and write down in your Stress Diary how you could replace it with constructive self-talk. For example, in the case of the report mentioned above:

- 'I've written reports before and managed. I will do OK on this one too.'
- 'This report is difficult, but I've had difficult reports before and have managed to cope.'
- 'I will have to plan my report very carefully.'
- 'I will work as hard as I can. If I fail, I fail. It's not possible to be brilliant at everything. I can only do my best.'

Constructive self-talk is simply what you can say to yourself as you deal with a particular source of stress. It is the old-fashioned device of 'talking to yourself'. The only difference is that you decide *in advance* which thoughts you are going to have in the midst of the stress-producing event. You will want to practise speaking thoughts to yourself that are going to enable you to cope better than you otherwise would.

There are four points in any situation at which you can use constructive self-talk to help manage a stressful experience:

1. You can prepare for a stressful experience before it happens.
2. You can deal with it when it is underway.
3. You can deal with the anxiety of being overwhelmed by it (i.e. if the situation is not going well).
4. You can reward yourself after it is all over.

ACTIVITY 6.3

Constructive self-talk—writing a script

Consider the four situations on the next page. Choose one or more that have relevance for you, and work out a 'constructive self-talk' script, based on the four points listed above.

Situation 1

Alan has just asked his boss for a promotion. She has turned him down. His self-talk is: 'I must be very incompetent. I'll probably never get a promotion here. Well, that's it, never again. I can't face the rejection.'

Situation 2

Sharon has lent some records to Paul, who keeps forgetting to bring them back. Finally, after she has reminded him for the umpteenth time, he loses his temper and is rude to her about her poor taste in music. Sharon's self-talk is: 'Yes, that's what people are like, rude and ungrateful! It's very unfair and I'm really hurt. I'll never ever lend anybody anything again!'

Situation 3

During a ballet performance at a big theatre, Gillian—who is dancing in her first big role—has stumbled and fallen. She distinctly heard some members of the audience laughing. She has wanted to be a ballet dancer since she was a small girl, and has shown a great deal of promise. Her self-talk is: 'Well, that comes of setting my sights too high. I should have taken my parents' advice and become a secretary. I'm finished with ballet, because I'm obviously never going to be any good at it.'

Situation 4

Several of Peter's work friends have gone off to lunch, but he wasn't invited along. His self-talk is: 'What an insensitive bunch! So much for friendship! To hell with them! Who needs friends who are so selfish and think only of their own pleasure? I think I'll find a new job with new friends.'

ACTIVITY 6.4

Constructive self-talk—a personal script

Refer to your Stress Diary. Choose one or more of the situations you have reported (or use a situation that has occurred more recently) and work out some constructive self-talk for each.

Follow this sequence:

1. Find a situation in which your performance was negatively affected because of your thoughts about the situation.

2. Become aware of the nature of these thoughts, and write down a log of the thoughts that occurred before, during and after the situation for approximately a week

3. Analyse your log. Which of your thoughts were self-defeating or not based on fact? Did your negative thoughts seem to occur mostly before, during or after the situation?

4. Construct some positive coping thoughts you might have used, or could in future use during similar situations.

5. Practise using these coping thoughts with imagined or enacted run-throughs of the problem situation. Internalise these thoughts during your practice attempts.

6. As you begin to feel more comfortable with these practices, gradually apply the coping thoughts in any actual situation that may occur. You should use thought-stopping to terminate the self-defeating thoughts, and positive self-talk to replace these with coping thoughts.

GROUP CONTEXT

If in a group context, members in turn can report past or present situations in which they feel (or felt) that their performance is/was being lowered by debilitating anxiety. The group should explore any unrealistic standards and negative self-verbalisations relevant to the situation, and help the member reformulate the standards and verbalisations. The group should suggest one or more coping statements with which the person can instruct themselves before, during and after the situation.

ACTIVITY **6.5**

Using self-reward

Design a self-reward program for acquiring positive self-talk to alter self-defeating thoughts. Write down:

1. Your goal.

2. How you intend to monitor the thoughts that are negative, and which of them are to be replaced in order to establish the new behaviour.

3. The steps in your programme towards achieving your goal, including specific instructions on how and when you intend to reward yourself (i.e. what will you give yourself as a reward?).
4. The steps you intend to take to ensure that your behaviour change lasts once your goal has been achieved.

> **GROUP CONTEXT**
> In a group setting, counsel a member of the group, and together design a self-reward program, based on the outline above, to help them acquire positive self-thoughts.

Positive addiction and enjoyment

Another strategy for stress management involves becoming *positively addicted* to a new activity. The concept of 'positive addiction' is developed in a book with the same title by William Glasser (1976). He suggests that certain physical or mental activities, when done regularly, become addictive in a positive way. Further, he believes that persons who are positively addicted can cope with stress and be successful in what they do. Activities such as running, meditating or riding a bike, when done regularly and chosen freely, can have a positive and soothing effect. Glasser feels that anything a person chooses to do that meets the following six criteria contributes to positive addiction, and will have a favourable impact on the individual.

1. The activity is a non-competitive activity to which one devotes about an hour a day.
2. The activity is easy to do and does not take a great deal of mental effort.
3. The activity can be done alone and does not depend on others.
4. The activity has some physical, mental or spiritual value.
5. The person will improve as a result of performing the activity.
6. The activity can be done unaccompanied by criticism.

Enjoying yourself

The aim of the Activity 6.6 is to engage yourself in some activities that are fun, enjoyable and positive.

People who become depressed tend not to engage in activities that may simply be called fun, whereas non-depressed persons do. One of the most successful treatments for depression consists of encouraging people to engage in activities that they consider to be fun, and this often results in lessening the severity of the depression. By engaging in activities that are fun, the depression that frequently accompanies stress may be avoided, as well as the sense of spiritual 'burn-out' that is a feature of leading a life that seems to lack meaning.

ACTIVITY 6.6

Enjoying yourself

Listed below are seven categories of activities. Read the list, and decide how much fun each is for you. Score each activity as follows:

- 0 = no fun
- 1 = some fun
- 2 = lots of fun

This list by no means exhausts all possibilities. Feel free to add activities to each category. Feel free to add categories that are not listed. Once all the items are rated, select some of the ones rated 1 or 2. Try to do at least one of these activities each day. If possible. do more than one. Once a week, try to plan which activities you will do on which days of the week. Remember, do at least one a day.

Nature
Backpacking
Walking outdoors
Activities associated with the sea
Mountain-climbing
Camping
Studying animals in their natural habitat
Observing natural beauty
Taking a nature walk, observing flowers, plants and animals
Going on a picnic
Canoeing/rafting

Money
Eating in an expensive restaurant
Dressing up

Buying something expensive for yourself
Contributing money to a favourite cause or charity
Betting money on games of chance
Buying something special for someone else
Having your hair styled, or a manicure
Attending sales, auctions, flea markets, garage sales
Buying something special for your home or car
Buying a sculpture or painting

Sports
Watching a sports match on TV
Going to the gym
Going on a fishing trip
Going sailing
Playing a team sport
Taking a bicycle ride or trip
Going horseback riding
Walking or jogging for exercise
Playing your favourite individual sport

Recreation
Going to a movie
Going to a sporting event
Going on a vacation
Going out for a drink with friends
Going to a party
Having a party
Playing table games
Riding recreational vehicles
Fixing something mechanical

Community involvement
Reading your local newspaper
Writing a letter to the editor of the local newspaper
Being politically active (working in a campaign, attending city council
    meetings)
Coaching a youth sports team
Recycling paper and metal products
Visiting sick and infirm people, being a hospital volunteer
Engaging in activities with a service club (e.g. Lions, Rotary)
Volunteering your services to community agencies (e.g. Lifeline,
    tutoring)
Working in a women's shelter

Intellectual
Reading
Writing
Attending speeches, lectures, workshops, classes, conferences
Performing or practising music
Writing music
Working on riddles, puzzles, problems
Meditating
Discussing religion, philosophy, politics, etc. with others
Keeping a journal
Visiting the local library

Cultural
Attending a live musical event
Attending a play
Listening to recorded music
Visiting a museum
Visiting an art gallery
Attending a reading circle
Attending a discussion or lecture

Developing an effective support system

Another positive behaviour that will enable you to manage stress is building up and using an effective support system. Talking with other people, and having people to rely on, has been found to be one of the best guarantees against either too much or too little stress playing havoc with our lives. We all handle stress more effectively if we have other people to help us.

ACTIVITY **6.7**

Using a sociogram

The target sociogram is a way of becoming aware of, analysing and understanding relationships and interactions among groups. Any dimension of interpersonal interaction may be the focus of sociograms.

In this activity, communications, support and power are studied among work colleagues, family and friends, using sociograms as illustrated at the top of the next page.

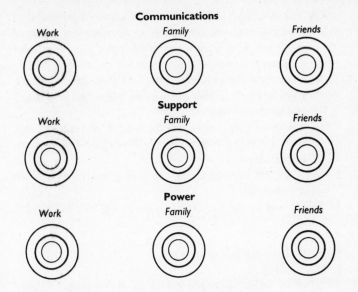

Communications

Work   Family   Friends

Support

Work   Family   Friends

Power

Work   Family   Friends

Instructions for the communications sociogram

1. *Work colleagues.*
   (a) Draw three concentric circles on an A4 sheet of paper (see examples above). Write your initials in the centre of the first circle.
   (b) This innermost circle represents the area of greatest trust. In this inner circle, write the initials of those people at work with whom you would communicate most openly.
   (c) The middle circle represents the area of moderate trust Within this circle, write the initials of those work colleagues with whom you would communicate with moderate ease.
   (d) The outer circle represents the area of least trust. In this case, write the initials of those work colleagues with whom you would communicate least freely.
2. *Family.* Repeat steps (a) to (d) above, substituting family members for work colleagues.
3. *Friends.* Repeat steps (a) to (d) above, substituting friends for work colleagues.

Instructions for the support sociogram

1. *Work colleagues.*
   (a) Draw three concentric circles on an A4 sheet of paper. Write your initials in the centre of the first circle.

    (b) This innermost circle represents the area of greatest support given to you. Within this circle, write the initials of those people at work who you think give you the greatest support.

    (c) The middle circle represents the area of moderate support. Here write the initials of those people at work who give you moderate support.

    (d) The outer circle represents the area of least support. In it write the initials of those people at work who give you the least support.

2. *Family.* Repeat steps (a) to (d), substituting family members for work colleagues.

3. *Friends.* Repeat steps (a) to (d), substituting friends for work colleagues.

Instructions for the power sociogram

1. *Work colleagues.*

    (a) Draw three concentric circles on an A4 sheet of paper. Write your initials in the centre of the first circle.

    (b) This innermost circle represents the area of greatest power. In it, write the initials of the person at work including yourself, who exerts the greatest power.

    (c) The middle circle represents the area of moderate power. Write the initials of the person at work including yourself, who exerts moderate power.

    (d) The outer circle represents the area of least power. Write the initials of the person at work including yourself, who exerts the least power.

2. *Family.* Repeat steps (a) to (d), substituting family members for work colleagues.

3. *Friends.* Repeat steps (a) to (d), substituting friends for work colleagues.

After your have drawn the sociograms, the following questions will facilitate your analysis and understanding:

1. Did the sociograms reveal new information to you? What?

2. What is the relationship between the sociograms? Are support and communication similar or different? Are communication and power similar or different?

3. What suggestions for improving social interaction come out of the sociograms?

4. With respect to power, did you discover that your need for power was not being met?

5. What do the roles of power, communication and support seem to be in the creation or the elimination of stress?

(Be specific and concrete in making applications to yourself, your work colleagues, your family and your friends.)

ACTIVITY 6.8

Where do you need support, and who will give it?

In which areas would you like help from others? Read the list below and for the situations where you feel you need support, write down the names of people whom you can approach.

	People who will give help
1. Someone I can rely on in a crisis	
2. Someone who makes me feel good about myself	
3. Someone I can be totally myself with, who makes me feel wanted	
4. Someone who will tell me how well or how badly I am doing	
5. Someone I can talk to if I'm worried	
6. Someone who really makes me stop and think hard about what I am doing	
7. Someone who is lively to be with	
8. Someone who introduces me to new ideas, interests and people	

Now answer the following questions:

1. Did anything surprise you about your list of names?

2. Did the same few people keep turning up on your list?

3. Were there situations where you could think of no one?

We all need different types of help, and our group of 'helpers' is not complete unless we can think of people to satisfy all our requirements. The following are crucial points:

- Helpers do not all have to be *your friends*. They might, for example, be someone who is marvellous in a crisis, but who is not necessarily a friend. Some people may even annoy you because they always seem to be asking pointed and uncomfortable questions, demanding that you stop and consider a course of action. These are people whom you would not really call 'friends', but who nevertheless provide vital help in stopping you from getting in a rut and becoming bored (i.e. understressed).

- If there are one or two names that come up constantly, you run the risk of having 'all your eggs in one basket'. What happens if one of these crucial people moves away? You do not have to have a huge selection of helpers, but think of the possible consequences of relying totally on only one or two people.

- You need people who will help prevent you from getting both overstressed and understressed.

- If there are gaps in your group of helpers, there are ways of filling them. The first step is to be aware that there is a gap. The next step is to look around for likely candidates. The third step is to create a relationship with these people (see *Skill 7: Build relationships*).

- The main characteristics you should look for in finding helpers are these:
  - They are people who offer help.
  - They are prepared to spend time with you.
  - You know them well.
  - They have gone through a similar experience.
  - You can trust them with what you tell them.
  - You believe that talking about it can make a difference.
  - You believe that they will not laugh at you.

How can we teach ourselves to become better at asking other people for help? There are several major points here. Firstly, we must believe that we have the right to ask for help, and we are more likely to believe this if we are ourselves prepared to give help to others. We must also believe that it is not a sign of weakness to ask for help. Rather, it is a sign of maturity and strength to accept that we are having difficulties and to feel confident enough to share those difficulties with others. It is often those people who have little confidence in themselves who are afraid of letting other people know that they have problems.

We give others permission to approach us with their problems if we approach them first. If we never let on that we have any problems, it will be more difficult for others to approach us with their problems. Asking someone for help is also a way of beginning or strengthening a relationship. Finally, developing relationship-making skills gives us an advantage when trying to extend our support group (see *Skill 7: Build relationships*).

Other tips for being positive

Listed below are a number of general tips that will help you to be more positive and constructive in your lifestyle.

'Work out' your tension constructively

When you are feeling ill-tempered because of frustration, or angry because someone has wronged you, your immediate impulse may be to blow off steam and give the other person a piece of your mind. The truth is that this generally leaves you feeling physically exhausted and foolish about things you wish you had never said, which only adds to your original tension.

How much better it is to work out your anger or frustration on some physical activity that will not only relieve your tension, but also give you a sense of achievement. Dig over the vegetable patch that has been waiting for attention. Help your children build the model plane that they have been begging for. Rather than shout at your employees, take them out for lunch, or show them that you are still a champion on the tennis court after work. This also serves to release *their* pent-up energies.

A hobby is a godsend for the release of tension, especially if it is one that involves physical activity. Not only will you be better prepared to handle the situation after you have given vent, but regular exercise is a great way of keeping yourself in good physical shape, and, as we have seen, an excellent defence against undue tension (see *Skill 4: Maintain good health*).

Learn to accept what you cannot change

You do not benefit yourself or anyone else by getting upset about things you cannot change. If you find the conditions so unbearable that they are causing you persistent tension, it would be better for you to get away from the source of the trouble. This could involve changing jobs or departments, or moving away from a noisy neighbourhood, an interfering relative or a social situation of which you do not approve.

If it is an individual who keeps bothering you, you might try to find out why this person is proving to be so difficult. Could it be that you expect people to behave as you think they should? Would you like to re-make the person to fit your mould? Surely you could spend your time more profitably by appreciating the good points about the person, and also honestly trying to adjust some of your own peculiar ways that might be irritating to others. At least by spending your energy on something that you can improve (yourself), you will feel less frustrated.

You might be able to improve a situation by talking to the person. But you need to decide which will be worse: the tension caused by talking, or the tension in getting yourself to accept the person as they are, and putting up with the inconvenience.

Give in occasionally

Have you noticed yourself feeling very defiant and getting into frequent quarrels with people? It may well be time to take stock of yourself. Could it be that you expect people to behave according to your desires? Or are you just feeling generally cranky? Are there perhaps other frustrations or anxieties that need to be resolved? Could it be that if your manner of interaction with these people changed, you would not get into so many arguments?

Remember, the other person also invariably thinks that they are right, and it is of course possible that they are. Even if they are not, and you have a legitimate reason for standing your ground, consider that it may be easier for you to give in once in a while. 'Winning' is not always the best way to achieve an aim. For example, if you 'back off', this creates the opportunity for the other person to do the same; if you behave in a mature way, the other person will often emulate you.

Do something for others

If you have been too absorbed in your own worries and tensions, get out and do something for someone who needs help more than you do. Besides getting your mind off yourself, it will also make you feel that you have done something worthwhile.

Avoid putting things off

When faced with a task that cannot be avoided, *do not postpone it*. No matter how unpleasant or menial it may be, make a start.

One thing at a time

When you are under undue stress, even your regular job or responsibilities at home may seem insurmountable. Or maybe your regular duties or assignments have mounted to such an extent that they are the cause of your tension. The task may seem so great that you fear tackling even a part of it.

First, try to realise that this is a temporary condition, and that, with patience and plodding, you will be able to work your way out of it or through it. Disregard the enormous total for the time being, and tackle one of the most important or worst parts. Consider carefully how this can be done most efficiently, in the least amount of time, and then get that part done. Once this has been achieved, you will feel better about taking the next step. Before you know it, you will have broken the back of what had seemed so insurmountable (see *Skill 9: Manage your time effectively*).

If you cannot bring yourself to tackle the problem in this practical manner, maybe you should have a quiet, honest look at yourself and the task, and ask yourself whether you are not overestimating your own importance, or the importance of the task. Is it not possible to get someone else to help you get the job done? Maybe simply looking at the situation in a more realistic light will relieve you of some of the tension.

Prepare in advance

Whenever possible, try to *prepare in advance* for common emergencies (e.g. an unexpected meeting). If you are not prepared or competent for a task ahead, *get prepared*. Study, practise, get advice or whatever is needed in order to prepare yourself. Coping with minor crises without fuss conditions you to face bigger ones more calmly and sensibly.

Never expect perfection

If you expect perfection from yourself in everything you do or in all your relationships with people, you are doomed to fail. No one can excel in everything all the time, nor does one have time even to begin to explore all one's interests. Rather, decide which things you have a particular aptitude for, and concentrate on doing these to the best of your ability. The feeling of success you get from doing a few things well is obviously better than the frustration of trying too many things, and failing at most. And should you try something and fail, remember it is not the end of the world. There are many other possibilities for which you may be more suited, or in which you may be much happier. The same applies to relationships.

Avoid being unduly critical

It can be a great source of tension if you expect too much of others, especially work colleagues or close family members on whom you rely, because when they do not measure up, you feel they are letting you down. Remember that each person has good and bad points, and has the right to develop their own personality and character. This includes your employer or employees, or your partner or child. Rather than focusing on other people's weak points and mistakes, use the same energy to concentrate on their strong points, and to help the individual develop these.

Avoid purposeless competition

When people are under emotional stress, they often feel they have to 'get there first', as if this will compensate for their feelings of tension. We see this on the job, on the highway, in the queue and in waiting rooms. Instead of tension being relieved, it is aggravated, because competition is contagious, and the other person can be as obnoxious as you feel. Cooperation is also contagious, and its effects are much more conducive to a peaceful frame of mind. It may even result in your getting there earlier, or in gaining a colleague rather than an enemy.

Whatever the situation that comes your way, consider carefully whether it is really worth fighting for. It might well be that getting there second or last, but cool and collected, is what will score you the needed points.

Get a pet

Pets are a great source of comfort and enjoyment. They give you abundant love and yet almost total freedom. You can hug and love a pet without feeling embarrassed or guilty. Humans need this contact, but are often starved of it because of circumstances of living alone, or of being embarrassed by human affection.

Pets seem to sense your feelings; they make you feel loved by their dependence on you and their obvious joy at your return after an absence. With pets you can be yourself. You do not have to be polite, nor make conversation, nor maintain your dignity. Or if you seek relief through talking, they will listen as long as you have something to say.

Let music soothe you

Whatever mood has ever been experienced through the ages surely has been expressed in music. As a form of *re*-creation it is powerful. It can either make you feel that you are not alone in whatever mood you are, or it can change your mood to one that is more desirable. Play an instrument, or just lose yourself in listening. Try listening to music when you are in a traffic jam— what normally might have seemed like an endless nerve-jangling hassle can become a jive session, or an ethereal escape.

ACTIVITY **6.9**

Stress-building beliefs

How many of these do you agree with?

Perfectionism
Do you feel a constant pressure to achieve?
Do you criticise yourself that you are not perfect?
Do you feel you haven't done enough no matter how hard you've tried?

Control
Do you have to be perfectly in control all the time?
Do you worry about how you appear to others?
Do you feel lack of control indicates weakness?

People pleasing
Does your self-esteem depend on the opinion of others?

Do you keep negative feelings hidden to avoid displeasing others?
Are you a 'yes man/woman'?

Competence
Do you feel your judgment is poor?
Do you feel like an imposter when told your work is good?
Do you feel you can never do as good a job as others?

'Yes' answers indicate potential road blocks to reducing stress. Challenge these negative beliefs and replace them with positive alternatives. Write out some positive alternatives now.

Summary

Being positive puts you in the right frame of mind for effective stress management. It helps you deal constructively with a stressful event—before, during and after the event. Using techniques such as thought-stopping and constructive self-talk can help put you in the right frame of mind. In this chapter, we have examined these and many other skills, techniques and tips for being positive.

One important ingredient to being positive is developing an effective support system. The next skill, *Skill 7: Build relationships*, is vital to being able to develop such a system.

SKILL 7

Build relationships

Introduction

Living a life with minimal stress requires human relationships that are not stressful. Humans are social animals and seek companionship, support, approval and acceptance from others at work, at home and at leisure. Few of us could manage to live like hermits, without any human contact. But sometimes we have to work at developing satisfying relationships. They rarely happen by chance, although luck may play a part in controlling whom we do or do not meet.

Why do we need relationships?

The development of satisfying relationships is important for mental health. If you have difficulty in forming effective relationships with those with whom you work, or the clients, customers or suppliers with whom you do business, you will not be as productive as you could be and you probably find dealing with these people stressful. If you have few friends or social contacts, you can become depressed and anxious, and worry over small things because you have no one with whom to share your concerns. Very minimal contact with others—as experienced by prisoners during long periods of solitary confinement—can lead to hallucinations and fantasy. Mental health and stress management is greatly helped by living in a network of close, warm, sharing relationships in which love, acceptance, support, advice and respect are present.

Medical research has shown that suicide, depression, stress, mental illness and heart trouble are often the consequences of loneliness. Children who have been deprived of warm, close relationships with parents in their early lives tend in later life to be unable to develop deep and lasting relationships, and fail to do as well as other children in their intellectual, social and physical development. Relationships are not just something for love-bitten teenagers, but important for all of us, throughout our lives.

ACTIVITY **7.1**

Why do you want relationships with others?

Look at the following list, and choose the three most important reasons why you feel you need relationships and contact with others.

> **GROUP CONTEXT**
> In a group situation, participants should discuss the reasons that have been chosen, and see whether others have the same or different reasons. Different members can explain to the rest of the group why these reasons are important to them.

1. To feel that I am accepted.
2. To feel that I matter.
3. To stop me being lonely.
4. To feel loved by another person.
5. To stop me being bored.
6. To be able to talk about my problems.
7. To share experiences and happiness.
8. To share problems and help another person.
9. A reason of your own.

ACTIVITY **7.2**

Good and bad relationships

1. Make a list of up to five people with whom you have good, satisfying relationships, and up to five people with whom you have difficult relationships.
2. Explain why you have good relationships with those you mention.
3. Why do you think you have poor relationships with the others you mention? What are the things that cause the difficulties?

ACTIVITY **7.3**

Behaviour that affects relationships

When you have finished Activity 7.2, can you now answer the following?

1. Which of my behaviours help me to have satisfying relationships?
2. Which of my behaviours get in the way of me having satisfying relationships?
3. What behaviours should I alter if I want to develop satisfying relationships and keep my existing relationships on a positive footing?

The personal qualities and skills needed for building relationships

A positive or good human relationship is one in which the individuals engage in a two-way communication at a fairly deep level of feeling. An emotional bond is developed that encourages a mutual concern for each other's well-being. In such a relationship there is honesty, openness and trust. *In addition, you are responsible for the quality of your relationships with others.*

The formation of relationships is a dynamic, value-laden process. As you become aware of the forces that help to create good or bad relationships, you can renegotiate your relationships, building stronger, more open and more caring ones.

Building relationships depends on a number of personal qualities and skills:

- your values, needs and attitudes
- the social context
- your self-concept (i.e. how you feel about yourself)
- your perceptions of others (i.e. how you habitually feel about others)
- your communication skills
- your relationship-building skills.

Each of these personal qualities and skills will now be examined.

Your values, needs and attitudes

The values held by the society in which you live influence the values you hold. Values are those beliefs and concepts that people consider to be most worthwhile, and around which they arrange their lives. Your values affect your behaviour and the way you interact with or relate to others. Because your values are similar to theirs, you find it easier to build up relationships with them. Friendships are often based on a similarity of values. It is far more difficult to relate to people whose values are totally different or even clash with yours. For example, it is difficult for someone who values honesty, cooperation and hard work to associate closely with a person who is devious, sly, deceitful and lazy. Like oil and water, they do not mix. Similarly, a person with strong religious leanings may have difficulty in communicating intimately with a confirmed atheist.

Your values will also be reflected in your style of communication. For example, a highly ambitious person might keep things 'close to their chest', and not want to disclose intimate details about themselves, since they will regard other people as potential rivals.

The social context

The social context influences relationships. If the context is warm and caring, then caring relationships are possible. An example would be a home for the elderly. But if the context has a climate of 'devil take the hindmost' competition, then relationships will be superficial and based on suspicion: 'What is he after, chatting me up like that? He's always ignored me before.' Such a competitive situation may be found in many business environments—for example, an ambitious person seeking promotion may not be able to develop warm, sincere relationships; after all, colleagues are rivals.

Your self-concept

A positive self-concept enables communication and relationships to develop more easily. People who feel positive about themselves do not normally feel threatened by other people. The low self-esteem person is often so concerned with their own performance that their interaction with others—involving withdrawal, critical carping, and defensive and offensive behaviours—

prevents them from developing constructive, caring and warm relationships. The high self-concept person is better able to understand others' feelings and to accept them. The low self-concept person is vulnerable to their fears of being further undermined by others who might become aware of all their presumed weaknesses and deficiencies. (For more about the self-concept, see *Skill 5: Enhance your self-concept*).

Your perceptions of others

There is a very close link between our self-concept and how we perceive others. Low self-concept people tend to be generally prejudiced in an attempt to defend their own inadequate selves: it is nice to feel that there is someone or some group inferior to them. It gives them a little self-esteem, but of course hinders social relationships. So we look at others through the distorting lens of *our own* self-concept.

If we perceive others in stereotyped ways (e.g. 'all male ballet dancers are gay' or 'all accounts departments are difficult to deal with'), then we react to them in a particular way, which affects our relationships. Such misperceptions and inadequate constructions of social reality hamper interpersonal relationships. We must judge each person as an individual. (For more about perception, see *Skill 1: Understanding what stress is and how it affects you.*)

Your communication skills

Communication is the basis of all human relationships. Without communication of some form there could be no relationship at all, for there would be no contact.

Communication can take many forms. The obvious form is *direct verbal communication* (i.e. speech). What we say, and the way it is interpreted by the receiver, affects our relationship with that person. We can communicate by *indirect verbal means* too. This occurs when the person is physically too far away for a face-to-face conversation. Here we would write or use the telephone. Another major form of communication is *non-verbal communication*. It is a very powerful form of communication, because it so accurately reveals how we actually feel about the other person. It is, for example, difficult to tell lies with your non-verbal behaviour, because most of the time you are not even aware of such behaviour.

If you dislike someone, but for some reason feel that you must be polite and friendly to them, the expression in your eyes, tautness around your mouth, in fact your general demeanour (often called 'body language'), will be contradicting your overt behaviour. Such non-verbal behaviour will frequently convey more than words in a relationship.

Non-verbal communication

The saying 'actions speak louder than words' holds particularly true in human relationships. Even though you may express concern for somebody else's problems, if you seem uninterested, the person is likely to feel uncomfortable and confused. Your non-verbal behaviour—eye contact, body posture, hand and arm movements, facial expressions and vocal quality—is the language through which your attentiveness and caring are expressed most directly (i.e. *attending behaviour*). If you are not interested, this is the message that will be sent by non-verbal means. If you look away, never smile and talk loudly (i.e. *non-attending behaviour*), you make it difficult for a warm relationship to develop.

You must learn to use effective non-verbal skills. It is important to realise that merely acting as though you are interested is not enough. The purpose of learning attentive skills is not to enable you to put something over on the other person, but rather to further your ability to develop relationships involving concern and caring for others.

Outlined below are a number of forms of non-verbal behaviour that you use all the time.

Eye contact

Effective eye contact consists of looking directly at the other person when listening *or* talking. The eye contact is spontaneous and relaxed, but serious. Attention is focused on the other person.

Ineffective eye contact consists of not looking at the other person, of breaking eye contact often, of staring either blankly or too intensely, and of looking down or away.

Body posture

Effective body posture includes a slight forward leaning of the body; the body positioned facing the other person; a relaxed but attentive posture; occasional arm and hand movements to emphasise important points; and legs parallel to each other or crossed comfortably when seated.

Ineffective body posture includes leaning too far forward or slouching backwards; the body turned sideways from the other person; a fixed, rigid and tense body position; infrequent hand and arm movements; and arms across the chest.

Head and facial movement

Effective head and facial movements entail occasional affirmative head nods; appropriate smiling; and expressions that match the mood of the other person.

Ineffective head and facial movements entail either constant or very infrequent head nodding; head down; continuous or little smiling; a cold, distant expression; rigid facial expressions; and overly emotional facial reactions.

Vocal quality

Effective vocal quality is shown by a pleasant, interested intonation; appropriate loudness of voice; moderate rate of speech; and natural conversational style.

Ineffective vocal quality is shown by a monotonous tone of voice; and the voice either too loud or too soft.

Personal habits

A final set of ineffective non-verbal behaviours is personal habits that may be distracting to others. Among these are playing with one's hair, incessantly fiddling with something, and tapping fingers or feet while the other person is speaking.

You will need a partner for the next four activities (Activities 7.4 to 7.7), because they all deal with the ways in which people use their bodies to communicate with others and to build relationships. You are urged to try the activities, even though working with a partner may seem a little embarrassing at first, because they will help you to develop your non-verbal communication skills.

ACTIVITY 7.4

Experiencing non-attending

1. Partner A should adopt an attending position. Partner B should violate the rules of attending (they should not face their partner squarely, and so on).

2. Conduct a three- or four-minute discussion on a self-chosen topic.
3. After four minutes or so, change roles so that Partner A now violates the rules of good attending while Partner B assumes an attending position. Continue the conversation for another three or four minutes.
4. Stop the conversation and discuss how you felt in both the attending and the non-attending positions, what impact the other's attending or non-attending had on you, and so on.

ACTIVITY 7.5

Degrees of attending in a one-to-one conversation

1. You are Partner B. While Partner A is talking, do not respond with any facial expression or animations whatsoever. Maintain complete facial passivity.
2. After two or three minutes, respond with a facial reaction that is opposite to the feelings and concerns being expressed by the speaker. For example, if the speaker is talking seriously, smile and look amused.
3. After another three minutes or so, respond with facial animation and expressions that mirror the kind and intensity of feelings being expressed by the speaker. Discuss the different results produced by these approaches.
4. Reverse roles and repeat the exercise.
5. What can you conclude about facial attentiveness? What have you learnt about your facial gestures and what do you want to change? How do you intend to bring this change about? Which non-verbal behaviours had the greatest impact?

ACTIVITY 7.6

Eye contact

1. Stand 1–2 metres away from your partner.
2. Each in turn looks at their partner's forehead, nose, chin, neck and shoulders, in that sequence. See when your partner can tell that you are not looking into their eyes.
3. Maintain eye contact with your partner while paying them a compliment and receiving their response.

ACTIVITY 7.7

Voice quality

1. Make the statement, 'Hello, . . .' (your partner's name). 'I'm pleased you could come', in two ways:
   (a) in a flat, uninterested way
   (b) in a warm, welcoming way.
   Listen carefully to the difference and ask your partner to react.
2. Carry on a conversation from the above opening statement, in the two ways suggested. Get your partner to comment on the quality of your voice.

Your relationship-building skills

In addition to the skills already discussed in this chapter, specific relationship-building skills are needed. These are based on the previously mentioned skills of communication and positive feelings towards oneself and others. In fact, relationship-building skills consist of very specific uses of these skills. Three relationship-building skills in particular are vital. These are:

1. *Convey respect* for others in the way you treat them.
2. Learn to put yourself in the place of the other person and see things from their perspective (i.e. *have empathy*).
3. *Be genuine* in your dealings with others.

Figure 7.1 further explains these skills.

Figure 7.1 Relationship-building skills

	Respect	*Empathy*	*Genuineness*
This behaviour:	conveys to the other person that they are valuable, worthwhile and important to you	informs the other person that you understand how he/she sees the world	shows the other person you are trustworthy and open; and not phoney
It is shown by:	active listening and attending to the other person; giving up your time; asking questions	sharing similar experiences of your own; showing you are in tune with others' feelings; understanding	being natural; not trying to act a role; not being on the defensive; appropriate non-verbal behaviour

These three types of behaviour must be shown to the other person in a recognisable way (i.e. by what you say and by how you convey what you say with body language or non-verbal behaviour). However, in order to have these relationship-building skills, you must possess values, attitudes and a self-concept that will:

- enable you to approach others positively
- enable you to respond positively when others approach you positively
- enable you to accept that each person has weaknesses as well as strengths, an occasional negative quality as well as positive qualities, and that no one is perfect, including you
- enable you to talk openly about yourself when necessary
- motivate you to be with others
- enable you to listen to others and to their points of view
- help you believe that every person is worthy of respect, and is of some worth
- enable you to listen and accept what others say about you
- motivate you to give help to others.

In summary, if you want to be able to develop the relationship skills of respect, empathy and genuineness, you must be able to share yourself with others, and accept others for what they are without necessarily indiscriminately accepting their bad points. You should learn to accept the person, not every aspect of their behaviour. If we tried to accept everything a person does, we would end up being pleased by, and pleasing no one. All satisfactory and effective relationships involve a balance between our expectations of how we would like other people to act, and how they actually behave.

ACTIVITY 7.8

Exercises in relationship-building

1. How can you make another person feel important? List the techniques you can use—for example, eye contact, listening, remembering their name. You should be able to add at least half a dozen more ways.
2. Explain why listening to someone is so important in relationship forming.
3. List the ways you could make someone feel unimportant.

Some behaviours that keep a relationship going

The following behaviours can help maintain a relationship:

- having common interests
- talking to each other a lot
- being able to forgive and forget
- helping when someone is in trouble
- backing each other up
- sharing secrets
- approval from a supervisor
- parental approval in the case of young people
- having friends in common
- understanding each other
- living near each other
- trying to give as well as take
- being dependable.

Some behaviours that harm a relationship

The following behaviours are likely to harm a relationship:

- talking about other people behind their backs
- criticising others
- complaining about others' behaviour
- telling lies
- opposite or antagonistic interests
- unreliability, undependability
- being secretive
- always trying to get one's own way.

So in summary, if you want to build satisfying relationships, you must:

- respect other people, make them feel valued and important
- try to see things from their point of view
- be yourself, be genuine
- be positive about yourself
- try to compromise and negotiate if differences arise
- learn to give as well as receive help
- remember that both of you will change as you grow, but that it is quite possible to change and yet remain friends if you wish to.

ACTIVITY **7.9**

Relationship squares

This is an exercise to help you define those persons in your family, at work and among friends who actually contribute to social health, and those who seem to contribute to social inadequacy. It is a simple, straightforward activity that demands only that you answer the questions 'honestly'. Honesty in this sense means quick first-impression answers. There is no trick. It is a simple technique to help determine those persons with whom we really want to spend time and those with whom we really do not.

List in the appropriate box those people at work who make you feel good about yourself when you are around them. List in the appropriate box those people at work who make you feel bad about yourself when you are around them.

People at work

	Good	Bad
Males	1. 2. 3. 4. 5.	1. 2. 3. 4. 5.
Females	1. 2. 3. 4. 5.	1. 2. 3. 4. 5.

You will now have a list of people in the 'good' column who are the persons in your working life that are natural 'antidotes' to burn-out. The persons in the 'bad' column are those who are contributing to your stress. Contacts with people in the 'good' column should be increased, and contacts with people in the 'bad' column should be decreased, or changed in some way.

Now list in the box below those people in your extended family who make you feel good about yourself when you are around them. Also list those people in your extended family who make you feel bad about yourself when you are around them.

Family

	Good	Bad
Males	1. 2. 3. 4. 5.	1. 2. 3. 4. 5.
Females	1. 2. 3. 4. 5.	1. 2. 3. 4. 5.

The persons in the 'good' column are the ones who help you avoid stress, and more time should be spent with them. The persons in the 'bad' column are persons who are contributing to your stress. Change something about your relationships with these people, or limit contact with them.

Now list in the box below those friends who make you feel good about yourself when you are around them. Also list those friends who make you feel bad about yourself when you are around them.

Friends

	Good	Bad
Males	1. 2. 3. 4. 5.	1. 2. 3. 4. 5.
Females	1. 2. 3. 4. 5.	1. 2. 3. 4. 5.

Contact with friends in the 'bad' column should be reduced or eliminated in favour of those in the 'good' column.

Ending a relationship

No relationship can be guaranteed to be permanent. They end because we move on to other stages in our lives—we change jobs, countries and lifestyles. And ultimately the death of loved ones, relatives and friends ends the longest-lasting relationships.

Ending a relationship can bring pain and guilt. But we must remember that because a relationship ends, it does not necessarily mean that it has failed, or was worthless, or that neither party ever obtained comfort from it. All relationships leave some valuable memories and experiences. And try to remember that a relationship is not measured by how long it lasts, but by its quality. So, (a) think of relationships as coming to an end rather than as failing, and (b) look forward to developing new relationships.

ACTIVITY **7.10**

The end of a relationship

From your own experience, recall a relationship that ended. How was it ended? How did you feel about it ending? Was there anything you could have done to make the ending less difficult?

Summary

Building solid relationships and a positive support system of family, work colleagues and friends will help you to cope with stressful events much more effectively. Your personal qualities, your communication skills and your ability to develop good relationships by conveying respect, empathy and genuineness will all influence the depth and scope of the support system you have in place to help you deal effectively with stressful events.

Learn to communicate assertively

Introduction

As we saw with *Skill 7: Build relationships*, communication skills are a vital component of effective stress management. *Skill 8: Learn to communicate assertively* focuses on the need to be assertive when communicating to ensure you are expressing your feelings and wishes in a constructive way, thereby reducing the likelihood of negative stress.

Assertiveness, non-assertiveness and aggressiveness

Assertiveness is concerned with telling someone face-to-face what you would like, without putting the person down. When you are assertive, you do not threaten, argue, demand or trample on the rights of others. You are stating openly and honestly and in a polite way what you want, to ensure that *you* are not trampled on. It is a social skill in which negative emotions such as anger can he expressed in a constructive way, rather than be bottled up to cause internal misery, or ulterior and destructive behaviour when it can no longer be contained. It is appropriate at times to tell someone you are angry.

Imagine that you are a bottle of lemonade. If you are badly used, thrown around, tossed hither and thither by the unthinking behaviour of other people, then you are likely to fizz up. In the end it becomes too much, and you will be unable to bottle up your anger or frustration. The lid will pop off as your anger and tension surge out. If only you had been able to express your feelings and wishes by allowing a gentle and slow release of such feelings, then no explosive and stressful situation would have arisen.

Non-assertiveness or passive behaviour, on the other hand, leads you to avoid situations or decisions, pretending that no problem exists. You are controlled by the wishes of others rather than trying to take control of your own life. If we are non-assertive, we often feel angry with ourselves for losing out, and this may lead to an outburst of anger and frustration at someone who is perhaps unconnected with the situation. So we still have stress.

Assertiveness is different from aggressiveness. *Aggressiveness* combines an expression of one's own beliefs, wishes and feelings with demands, pressure and threats aimed at winning. No consideration is given to the rights and feelings of others. Aggressiveness may also involve sarcasm, criticism or gossip. If we win, then others lose, and so aggressive behaviour sours relationships with others, may cause guilt feelings and can lead to a lonely life as other people steer clear of us. It is the non-assertive person who may, on occasion, become the aggressive individual, due to the venting of frustration.

ACTIVITY 8.1

Are you assertive?

Find out how assertive you are by taking the following self-report test of assertive behaviour. Then look at page 172 to find out how to determine your score. Indicate how descriptive each item is of you by using the following code:

```
    3  =  very much like me
    2  =  rather like me
    1  =  slightly like me
   -1  =  slightly unlike me
   -2  =  rather unlike me
   -3  =  very unlike me
```

____ 1.   Most people seem to be more aggressive and assertive than I am.*

____ 2.   I have hesitated to make or accept dates because of 'shyness'.*

___ 3. When the food served at a restaurant is not to my satisfaction, I complain about it to the waiter or waitress.

___ 4. I am careful to avoid hurting other people's feelings, even when I feel that I have been injured.*

___ 5. If a sales representative has gone to considerable trouble to show me merchandise that is not quite suitable, I have a difficult time saying 'no'.*

___ 6. When I am asked to do something, I insist upon knowing why.

___ 7. There are times when I am on the lookout for a good, vigorous argument.

___ 8. I strive to get ahead as much as most people in my position.

___ 9. To be honest, people often take advantage of me.*

___ 10. I enjoy starting conversations with new acquaintances and strangers.

___ 11. I often don't know what to say to attractive people of the opposite sex.*

___ 12. I will hesitate to make phone calls to business establishments and institutions.*

___ 13. I would rather apply for a job or for admission to university/college by writing letters than by going through personal interviews.*

___ 14. I find it embarrassing to return merchandise.*

___ 15. If a close and respected relative were annoying me, I would smother my feelings rather than express my annoyance.*

___ 16. I have avoided asking questions for fear of sounding stupid.*

___ 17. During an argument, I am sometimes afraid that I will get so upset that I will begin to shake, or burst into tears.*

___ 18. If a famed and respected speaker/lecturer makes a comment that I think is incorrect, I will see to it that the audience hears my point of view as well.

___ 19. I avoid arguing about prices with sales representatives.*

___ 20. When I have done something important and worthwhile, I manage to let others know about it.

___ 21. I am open and frank about my feelings.

___ 22. If someone has been spreading false and unpleasant rumours about me, I see them as soon as possible and have a talk about it.

___ 23. I often have a hard time saying 'no'.*

____ 24. I tend to bottle up my emotions rather than make a scene.*

____ 25. I complain about poor service in a restaurant and elsewhere.

____ 26. When I am given a compliment, I sometimes just don't know what to say.*

____ 27. If a couple near me in a theatre or at a lecture were talking rather loudly, I would ask them to be quiet or take their conversation elsewhere.

____ 28. Anyone attempting to push ahead of me in a line is in for a good battle.

____ 29. I am quick to express an opinion.

____ 30. There are times when I just can't say anything.*

Scoring the assertiveness schedule

Calculate your score as follows: Reverse the symbols for all items followed by an asterisk (*). Then add up the 30 item scores. For example, if the response to an asterisked item was 2, place a minus sign (−) before the 2. If the response to an asterisked item was −3, change the minus sign to a plus sign.

Scores on this test can vary from +90 to −90. The table below shows you how to interpret your score. For example, if you are a woman and your score was 26, it exceeds that of 80 per cent of women (based on a sample in the United States). A score of 15 for a male exceeds that of 55 to 60 per cent of men.

The results of this test should only be used as a rough approximation of your level of assertiveness.

Women's scores	Percentage	Men's scores
55	99	65
58	97	54
45	95	48
37	90	40
31	85	33
26	80	30
23	75	26
19	70	24
17	65	19
14	60	17
11	55	14
8	50	11

Women's scores	Percentage	Men's scores
6	45	8
2	40	6
−1	35	3
30		
8	25	−3
−13	20	−7
−17	15	−11
−24	10	−15
−34	5	−24
−39	3	−30

If you are not assertive, then you are likely to feel stress from being pressurised and dominated by others, and from over-controlling the anger that you feel. Some of the activities in this chapter will help you to learn assertive behaviour.

ACTIVITY 8.2

Three 'assertiveness diaries'

Read the following diaries out aloud. Diary A should be read quickly and nervously, Diary B lethargically and Diary C in a matter-of-fact way.

> **GROUP CONTEXT**
> In a group setting, volunteers should read aloud to the rest of the group.

Diary A

Monday: Whew! My alarm didn't go off, so I didn't have time for breakfast. Phoned Greg to get a lift to work. What an idiot—he slept late, too! This will ruin the whole day. Then the bus was late, so I ran down to the other bus-stop, but the bus was just taking off as I got there and the stupid driver refused to stop, even though he saw me. I got to work late. When Mr Thomas wanted to know why, I snapped: 'Well, why don't you try taking a bus some time?' At lunchtime I didn't have time to eat because I had to work on the report. The boss insists that it must be on his desk first thing tomorrow. For heaven's sake, who does he think he is? So, to end a terrible day, when I got home I found I'd forgotten to bring the half-done report from the office, so I couldn't work on it I've decided I'll have to get to the office really early tomorrow to get it done. But now I'm so worried, I can't get to sleep.

Tuesday: Oh no! What a mess! The alarm must be broken, it didn't go off again. Now I'm running late . . . the report isn't finished. I've got to get it done, otherwise I lust won't be able to face myself!

Diary B
Monday: The alarm clock didn't go off. Oh well, I overslept. I phoned Greg to see about a lift, but he couldn't manage it. Too bad. I decided not to go to work. My report's late, but I can't talk to Mr Thomas about it anyway, so I went back to sleep. I'd like to talk to him about it some time—but he never seems to have time for me. I just can't finish it. Guess I'll get sacked again. So what's the use of trying? I'm a loser, and I know it I'm a fool to keep trying . . .

Tuesday: I had these nightmares again. I am trying to catch a train, but it passes me by. Just like the other dreams—when I'm at the wrong station . . .

Diary C
Monday: Overslept I called Greg for a lift, but he overslept too. Guess we're two of a kind today. The bus was late, so I was late, but I explained why to Mr Thomas and he wasn't too upset. I've been wanting to ask him something, so I've been practising. It therefore wasn't difficult when I said to him, 'I'm not happy about this, but I just can't get this report done on time. What do you advise me to do?' We talked, and he told me about some resources I can use to help me. Felt a little tense—so after eating lunch I took a walk. It helped me to relax. Then, after work, I went to the library to try to get the books he recommended. Closed early—cutbacks again. I was annoyed, but what can they do when there's not enough money to keep the libraries open at night? So I found a place in the park, and started to do some thinking on the report again. Then I slept pretty well.

Tuesday: Today I'm going to try to finish the report. If it doesn't work out, it doesn't work out, but I'm certainly going to give it my best.

Now answer the following questions:

1. What seem to be the stressors in these environments?
2. How are the stressors handled in each of the three scenarios?

Some possible responses to these questions are:

1. The stressors seem to be being late, uncooperative 'others', the frustration of not being able to finish a report and the closed library.
2. Diary A seems to be coping ineffectively with stress, with angry outbursts and great tension. Diary B is giving up, withdrawing and resigned to failure. Diary C, on the other hand, is relaxed but not excessively so, and has discovered coping skills for minimising stress. In Diary C's life, important ways of minimising stress are:
   - talking and sharing with another person
   - anticipating, by preparing for a conversation with the superior
   - taking time out for lunch and for relaxation and exercise
   - having a personal philosophy of life
   - trying to communicate effectively
   - finding a personal stress level (C knows that a walk—exercise—can release tension).

Now look at your self-report test in Activity 8.1, and answer the following questions:

1. Which style do you seem closest to: Diary A, Diary B or Diary C?
2. What changes might you think about making?

Two of the styles of coping that you have just considered are somewhat like the elements of the fight or flight response: aggressive A—the 'fighter'; passive B—the 'fleer'. People often do not have the benefit of choosing the preferable way—assertiveness. Some 'survive' through childhood by being aggressive in an aggressive family. Withdrawal can be a way of coping, too. But assertiveness—stating what we want or feel, without pushing ourselves on others and without withdrawing and denying our own need—is a much better way of coping with stress, and substantially reduces the likelihood of negative stress.

For example, an insult constitutes a stressor in most circumstances. Insulting someone back does not usually get you what you want, which is an apology. Not responding at all tends to make you internalise your feelings. But stating how you feel and what you want (being assertive) tends to increase the chances that you will not feel negatively stressed by the incident. If a supervisor persists in loading you down with too much work and it is causing you stress, you have several choices: you can get angry, alienating them; you can simply not do it, thus avoiding the situation; or you can speak up, which is being assertive.

ACTIVITY 8.3

Aggressive, non-assertive and assertive behaviour

1. What are some elements of aggressive behaviour and speech?
2. What are some elements of non-assertive behaviour and speech?
3. What are some elements of assertive behaviour and speech?

Some possible responses to these questions are:

1. Elements of aggressive behaviour and speech include using loaded words, accusations, blaming, demanding, being rigid or rude, attacking others and finger-pointing.
2. Elements of non-assertive behaviour and speech include allowing others to take advantage of you, giving up easily, putting yourself down, being apologetic all the time, hedging, hesitating and hoping someone will guess what you want, and looking down and shuffling.
3. Elements of assertive behaviour and speech include expressing yourself openly, acknowledging the needs of others, stating your own feelings, using direct statements, making eye contact and being relaxed.

ACTIVITY 8.4

Four scenarios

Imagine that you are in the following four situations. What would you say? Try to classify your responses as assertive, non-assertive or aggressive.

> **GROUP CONTEXT**
> If in a group, role-play some or all of the following. You could act each one several times, with different actors playing the parts to produce different scripts.

1. You have scheduled a meeting with three members of your staff for 3 pm. Two arrive on time, while the third arrives 10 minutes late. What do you say?
2. You are responsible for producing an important report for your organisation, which must be printed and bound by next Monday. The printer phones you on the preceding Thursday and says, 'We have a very heavy workload and are running a bit late with your job, but—hopefully—we can get it to you sometime Tuesday.' 'What do you say?
3. You have bought a colourful shirt, and the shopkeeper assured you that the colours would not 'run' if you washed it. After the first wash, all the colours 'ran' and it looks a hideous mess. You go back to the shop. What conversation occurs?
4. At the local takeaway you buy some chips. They are cold and greasy. What happens next?

ACTIVITY 8.5

Exercises in aggressive, non-assertive and assertive behaviour

For each of the following, write an assertive, non-assertive and aggressive response. If possible, discuss your answers with a colleague or friend to find out which responses are seen as most likely to retain cordial relationships while allowing open expression of feelings and getting you what you want.

> **GROUP CONTEXT**
> If in a group context, you could discuss the appropriateness of the various members' responses.

1. You have taken a faulty tape back to the music shop. The manager says that you must have damaged it when you first put it on. You say _____
2. A friend asks you to stop in town on your way home from work to pick up their dry-cleaning. You say _____

3. You are invited to a party by a person you do not wish to associate with. You say _____
4. You casually met someone last week and would like to go out with them again. You meet the person again by chance, and you say _____
5. You are in a hurry and have no time to collect an important book that is waiting for you at the library. You want your partner/flatmate to get if for you. You say _____
6. You are at your boss's home for an important business dinner. You have eaten enough when the boss insists you have another helping of dessert. You say _____
7. You haven't understood how to operate the new office machine, which has just been demonstrated to the staff. The boss asks those who aren't clear about it to see her. At the meeting you say _____
8. At your work's Christmas party one of your colleagues comes up to you and insists that you have an alcoholic drink. You really do not want to have a drink. You say _____

The value of assertive behaviour

Being assertive is valuable for the following reasons:

- It allows both you and the other person to enter a win–win situation; tension is reduced.
- Through being assertive, you avoid bottling up frustration and resentment because of your own non-assertiveness; tension is reduced.
- It allows you to avoid losing friends and making enemies in aggressive confrontations. You have no need to be aggressive or feel frustration; tension is reduced.
- You can learn to express your feelings in a constructive way rather than in a way harmful to relationships and health.
- You will be able to improve your social relationships.
- Your opportunities for getting the type of life you want, the friends you want and the career you want will be improved.
- You will be less anxious, more confident, possess higher self-esteem and be generally more positive about yourself.
- You will be more in control of your own life (i.e. proactive), rather than letting things just happen to you.

Using 'I' statements

Often we may want to tell another person how we are feeling, but we are afraid that the other person will react negatively. We cannot control the person's reaction but, by selecting our words carefully, we can reduce the chance that they will become defensive. The other person will usually get defensive if they think we are blaming, criticising, judging or threatening them.

The key to telling someone how we feel without putting that person on the defensive is to use 'I' statements rather than 'you' or 'it' statements. An 'I' statement says, in effect, 'I know and take responsibility for myself and my feelings; I am not blaming you; and I am letting you know what part you play in my life'. Such a statement opens the door to effective communication.

Stressful confrontations between people usually involve criticism, ridicule, preaching, diagnosing, ordering, etc. These are your messages. An 'I' message conveys to the other person your own personal feelings about the matter, and in so doing takes ownership for the problem. For example, 'I feel frustrated and angry when you do that' instead of 'you had better stop that right now'. Feel the difference between the following three statements:

1. 'What you just did was a terrible thing to do!'
2. You make me so angry when you do that!'
3. 'It really upsets me when you do that—it's as if you think that I'm not important enough to have my needs considered too.'

An 'I' statement names your feelings, identifies the specific circumstances when that feeling occurs, says how the circumstances affect you and sometimes lets the other person know how you would like to see the situation change. For example:

1. *Name your feeling*
   I feel happy . . .
   I feel frustrated . . .
   I feel disappointed . . .
2. *Identify the specific circumstances*
   When you share what you are feeling with me . . .
   If you don't look at me when we talk . . .
   When you let me down . . .
3. *Say how the circumstances affect you*
   Because I value your confidence in me . . .

Because then I feel I'm not interesting enough for you . . .
Because it seems you don't regard me as . . .

4. *Say how you'd like to see the situation change (optional)*
And I hope the same applies for you . . .
And I'd like you to tell me what your not looking at me means . . .
And I'd like to know if you are aware of my feelings . . .

ACTIVITY **8.6**

Practise making 'I' statements

Use the situations below, or your own situations, to practise making 'I' statements. Note the four parts to such statements.

Situation 1

After buying a shirt and bringing it home (but not wearing it) you notice that the sleeve has a tear in it. You decide to return the shirt for a refund. What do you say to the sales assistant?

1. My feeling: _____

2. The circumstances (be specific): _____

3. How the circumstances affect me: _____

4. What I want to happen: _____

Situation 2

A close work colleague has informed you at the last minute that he won't be coming to your farewell dinner because he is very keen to attend a play for which he has just received a complimentary ticket. What do you say to him?

1. My feeling: _____

2. The circumstances (be specific): _____

3. How the circumstances affect me: _____

4. What I want to happen: _____

ACTIVITY **8.7**

'I' statements—some questions

1. Why are we sometimes afraid of someone else's anger?
2. How do 'I' statements open the door to effective communication?
3. What are the differences among the following?
   - 'You're a terrible . . .'
   - 'You make me so angry . . .'
   - 'I feel hurt . . .'

Saying 'no'

There can be times when you want to say 'no' for a variety of good reasons, but the situation makes it difficult. You may find yourself going along with something you really do not want to do because you cannot immediately think of a way to say 'no'. There is no point in getting yourself caught up in behaviours that are not 'you', and this means you must be able to say 'no' successfully. Saying 'no' assertively is truly a fine art. Here are some general rules:

- Get your point across firmly, and stick to it. Be consistent. Be honest about your reasons for saying no.
- Do not 'put down' the other person in the process, or act in a way that might lead to a real confrontation.
- Maintain control of your mind, body and actions.

ACTIVITY **8.8**

Practise saying 'no'

Saying 'no' when you want to reduces the likelihood of stressed feelings. Like most skills, this one improves with practice. There is no one way to say 'no'. Practise by responding to the following two requests:

1. 'Please do this for me. It will only take an hour or two. I know you have to leave early, but you're so clever and quick. Please! just this once.'

2. 'Come on! Let me take you home. I haven't had that much to drink—only three or four beers. You know I'm a safe driver.'

Cultural blocks to assertive behaviour

There are cultural blocks to being assertive. We have all been taught to hide our feelings, not to impose ourselves on others, and to be polite and reticent. We often fear that expressing our real wishes and feelings may embarrass others, who will feel obliged to do what we suggest, even though they may not agree with us.

Parents, and sometimes teachers, can prevent children from developing self-assertion, often resulting in the development of non-assertive and aggressive interactive behaviour, because they do not encourage the expression of opinions by children. 'Children shall be seen and not heard' is an old expression that adults still frequently use. Being obedient, and doing what you are told, are 'rules' that we all learnt when young. We even received praise from our parents and teachers. This encouraged us to fall into a pattern of being obedient and not ever contradicting an older person, and, later, any other person.

People are more likely to accept our assertive behaviour if we express positive feelings about them first. Only then should we follow up with requests and complaints.

ACTIVITY 8.9

Positive statements in assertive behaviour

Practise putting a positive statement in front of your assertive statements in each of the situations in Activity 8.5. For example:

Situation 1: 'I have bought a lot of tapes from your shop and they have all been in perfect condition, and so I was very surprised when I played this one and it was faulty. Would you like to put it on your cassette player and listen to it? I am certain it is the tape, because my cassette player has no problem with playing the other tapes I've bought here.'

Practise being assertive

Do not try to take on the 'big guns' before you have *learnt* to be assertive where it is appropriate. Practise assertive behaviour first in situations that are not too challenging (e.g. with a friend who is trying to push you into doing something you do not want to do, or a shopkeeper who is trying to sell you defective goods). Get used to hearing yourself insist on, for example, replacements for shoddy goods you have bought, or expressing your true feelings. The point is that *you* must eventually decide how assertive and how passive you are going to be at work, with your peer group and with your family.

And remember, assertiveness is not an insistence on getting your own way or riding roughshod over everyone else, but the ability to openly express your views and feelings in a sincere manner, which ensures that all parties understand each other, and that decisions take account as far as possible of each person's wishes. This makes for more caring, warm relationships in which no one considers that they have been overpowered, put down or ignored.

ACTIVITY **8.10**

Modelling sessions

For this activity you need a partner. If this is difficult for you, skip the activity. But do it, if possible, as you will find it useful.

Plan modelling sessions based on the situations below. Break up each of the situations into two or three segments, each containing specific behaviours. Consider every detail: appearance, timing, gestures, posture, sequences, words, tone and facial expression. Then carry out each modelling segment with your partner giving feedback on your performance.

1. Enter an office to ask for a job.
2. Convince someone that you are late because your car broke down.
3. Make a complaint about a purchase.
4. Rebuke someone who has jumped a queue.

Activities 8.11–8.13 should be done by those who feel that they are too passive (i.e. not assertive enough).

ACTIVITY **8.11**

Create an assertiveness 'script'

1. Write down as many situations in your life as you can in which you feel that you are not being assertive enough.
2. Identify any recurring themes regarding:
   - the kinds of situation in which you find assertion difficult
   - the kinds of people with whom you find assertion difficult
   - your feelings, physical reactions, thoughts and behaviours in situations and/or with people where assertion is difficult for you.
3. For one or more of the situations identified in 1 above:
   - set yourself an appropriate assertiveness goal
   - generate and write out at least two 'scripts' for handling each situation in an assertive way
   - formulate some relevant coping statements for instructing yourself before, during and after the situation
   - practise role-playing in your imagination, acting assertively in the situation
   - if appropriate, try out one of your assertive behaviour 'scripts' in real life.

The following hints will assist you to improve your assertiveness skills:

- Practise your script if possible. Until you are skilled in assertive behaviour—knowing how to say what you want to say, and adapting your words to suit the situation or other person—it is a good idea to rehearse or plan your 'script'. Work out in advance what you are going to say. This will enable you to appear confident and calm when stating your case or point of view. You will not hesitate or be vague. You will be able to say concisely and precisely what you want to convey to the other person without any excuses or long-winded diversions. Always start with 'I', and show the other person that you are effective in your presentation of your feelings and wants, and can take personal responsibility for them.

    However, there is a danger in planning and rehearsing a script *too well*, for your behaviour might be too mechanical or inflexible, making it inappropriate to the situation. In planning your script, therefore, keep in mind that modifications will have to be made in the light of the other person's responses.

• Use appropriate non-verbal behaviour. If possible, try to maintain eye contact, as this helps social interaction. If your eyes are lowered or you look away, the other person is likely to gain the impression that you feel guilty, embarrassed or shy, and will not be impressed by your unconvincing performance.

Look relaxed, do not pigeon-hop from foot to foot. Smile where appropriate, but do not laugh or giggle nervously.

ACTIVITY 8.12

Identifying people and situations where you have difficulty being assertive

Answer these questions in your Stress Diary.

> **GROUP CONTEXT**
> If in a group, discuss the questions.

1. Which person or persons do you find it most difficult to be assertive towards? Why?
2. Which person or persons do you tend to be aggressive towards? Why?
3. Which person or persons do you tend to be non-assertive towards? Why?
4. What are the situations in which you find it most difficult to be assertive? Why?

It was noted in the introductory chapter that bullying has become a major source of stress in the workplace. An assertive 'I' response, well-scripted, succinct and rehearsed so it is spoken naturally, is a fairly stress-free and effective way to counter the bullying and eliminate it. The assertive statement puts you in charge, controlling the rest of the interaction.

For example:

'I am sorry you feel the need to humiliate me in public but I will not tolerate it and it has no place in this organisation.'

Notice how this comment achieves a number of *hits* on the bully. First, it indicates that there is no obvious reason and therefore there must be a personal *need;* second, it makes clear that the victim is not prepared to accept the behaviour; and third, it intimates that the organisation as a whole has no use or place for such behaviour. But remember, this type of strategy can only be effective where the body language of the victim does not contradict the message which they are verbally delivering to the bully, as a bully is often able to sense fear just as efficiently as any dog. The victim should therefore closely monitor their posture, tone of voice, shifting eye contact or any other form of body language which may lead the bully to believe the victim does not have the necessary self-confidence to see out the confrontation. It should be remembered that if a bully wins the confrontation at this stage, it will be difficult for the victim ever to recapture control of the situation in the future.

ACTIVITY 8.13

Practice makes perfect

Many of us have difficulty in:

- making complaints
- refusing requests
- starting conversations
- giving compliments.

Take one or two of these assertive behaviours and try them out when the opportunity arises. Practice is the only way to learn how and when to use assertiveness.

Summary

Being assertive has many benefits. Key points to remember are:

- Know what you want to achieve.
- Know what alternatives are available when negotiating.

- Express compliments and appreciation if others make a move to meet your wishes.
- Ask for assistance and make requests of others.
- Express justified annoyance and hurt feelings in a calm way.
- Turn down requests politely.
- State personal opinions in a sensible way without showing anxiety about how they will be received.
- Recognise when it is appropriate to be assertive. Appropriate use of assertiveness is not 'accepting the status quo' or 'turning the other cheek'. It is an awareness of the consequences of behaviour, and the ability to weigh up the advantages and disadvantages of alternative strategies.

Remember that:

- Assertive people can state their views without demanding.
- Aggressive people step on others to get what they want.
- Non-assertive people do nothing and feel resentment at their treatment.

An assertive person is not 'better' or 'worse' than an aggressive or passive person. But anyone has an increased chance of relieving feelings of stress by responding assertively.

Manage your time effectively

Introduction

The Moving Finger writes; and, having writ, Moves on . . .
Edward Fitzgerald, 'The Rubaiyat of Omar Khayyam', 1859

Perhaps there's no such thing as time management, because it boils down to self-management, and that's the key to making time your ally rather than your enemy. There are only 24 hours in your day, just the same as everybody else's. So how do you end up stressed, frustrated, angry, behind in your work, and dead on your feet? Maybe because you don't know how to use those 24 hours to your advantage.

Time management refers to the process of actively structuring one's time in ways that facilitate the reduction of stress, and increase the probability that personal and professional goals will be attained. You can manage time by structuring your own activities in such a way as to reduce the number of stressors that have to be confronted, and by organising your day so that there is enough time to accomplish the essentials in day-to-day activities. You should observe several rules in scheduling the time in your day:

1. Do not overload the schedule; overloading dooms one to failure.
2. Schedule time for tasks that produce personal enjoyment.
3. Follow the schedule conscientiously.

Everyone needs to set priorities, both for the short term and the long term. It is easy enough to slide along doing what is easiest, what other people would have one do and what is habitual. You can let others spend your time for you, or you can spend it yourself on what will bring you the best returns—the choice is yours. The rule is to plan ahead by working backwards.

Do you have the time?

Many people under stress claim that they do not have the time to do everything they need to do. They panic and do nothing well. They fail to establish priorities because they are poor decision makers. Not getting things done creates even more stress. They are overwhelmed.

ACTIVITY 9.1

Do you manage your time well?

Answer TRUE or FALSE next to the statements that are most nearly true or false for you.

1. I never seem to have enough time for things.	TRUE	FALSE
2. I rarely get things done on time.	TRUE	FALSE
3. I can always find time for myself.	TRUE	FALSE
4. I always know why I'm doing what I'm doing.	TRUE	FALSE
5. I keep lists of things I need to do.	TRUE	FALSE
6. I plan my day by setting objectives/priorities.	TRUE	FALSE

If you are a person who has learnt how to manage time, you will have answered like this:

1. False
2. False
3. True
4. True
5. True
6. True

If you did not match this pattern, then you may be encountering stress because you have not developed the skill of managing your time.

When people say they 'do not have the time', they really mean they have not sorted out their priorities. We all have 24 hours in each day; some manage, while others do not because they have not worked out their priorities. Are you clear on what is really important to you, what is less important and what is of no importance? If you are not clear about this, you are likely to hop from one task to another, not completing any one properly. If you can plan your time, you are not going to be busy all day long. You will be able to plan relaxation and leisure in your life, for these must have some part in your priorities.

If you can place things in a system of priorities by setting aims for yourself, you will have more control over your life. With more control, there will be less stress in finding time and doing what seems to need doing, and there will be more time for deliberately planned relaxation. It is not *what* you plan, but *how* you plan.

Figure 9.1 illustrates the cycle of stress reduction that can be achieved through effective time management.

Figure 9.1   Reduced stress through effective time management

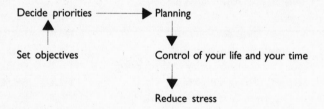

First steps

The first step toward improved time management is a comprehensive task review to identify exactly what you need to accomplish, and when. Many people have a general idea of what they'd like to achieve but never take the time to analyse the steps that need to be taken to complete the tasks at hand; others have settled into comfortable routines without taking the time to periodically review and reorganise. If it's been a while since you last reviewed your duties and priorities, make time to do so. Simply analysing your work and setting broad goals can, in itself, boost your efficiency.

Next, make a list of all the tasks you perform and how often they need to be done. This doesn't have to be done all in one sitting; taking notes as you work and compiling the list over a period of a few weeks will help ensure that your list is comprehensive. Another approach is to keep a diary of tasks performed and associated time values. Just as some dieters keep diaries to monitor and limit their food intake, you can use a diary to put your schedule on a 'diet' and monitor progress toward your goals.

Now you're ready to categorise tasks according to priority and urgency (this morning, today, this month, this year). This is the time to identify and weed out tasks that are no longer necessary or can be delegated to a technician, clerk or junior pharmacist.

Time-management tools

Planning grids are one of the best tools for organising your workload and making sure routine tasks are performed, and performed on time. Use a 12-month planning grid to monitor what you have to do. Similar grids that break down the overall workload into weekly or monthly increments can help target specific problem areas and fine-tune workload scheduling.

After developing an annual schedule, prepare a monthly calendar to help you allocate your time on a weekly schedule. At the beginning of each quarter, spend an hour with your calendar to enter all important dates. Then estimate the time needed to undertake tasks. If your presentation to management is due in eight weeks and it usually takes you four weeks to prepare a paper, start work on the paper six weeks before it is due, allowing yourself an extra week for typing and an extra week for disaster. If you stick to this schedule, you'll amaze yourself by having the paper finished in the seventh week.

At the start of each week, transfer important items from your monthly calendar to your weekly schedule. This helps you to avoid things that might otherwise sneak up on you. Be sure to schedule time for your fitness routine and other personal recreation.

Keep in mind, however, that even the best tools can become time drains if not used correctly. For example, making a list and maintaining it daily can be helpful, but those who compile several lists each day may soon find their lists, and their efforts, scattered. A better approach is to keep one perpetual list and make daily adjustments.

How do you spend your time?

You cannot set objectives and decide priorities until you know *how* you now spend your time.

The next few activities are designed to make you aware of what you spend your time on now, and what you would prefer to spend your time on.

ACTIVITY **9.2**

Your timetable

Draw yourself a timetable for the week, like the one below.

The time can be split up into whatever periods you feel are most appropriate. They should not be too large. Two-hour blocks seem to be a happy medium.

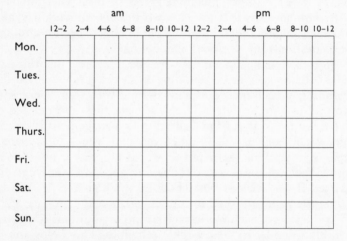

Timetable for one week

	am						pm					
	12–2	2–4	4–6	6–8	8–10	10–12	12–2	2–4	4–6	6–8	8–10	10–12
Mon.												
Tues.												
Wed.												
Thurs.												
Fri.												
Sat.												
Sun.												

For the next week write down every night before you go to sleep what you did during the day.

It is important to fill in the timetable each day, as people very quickly forget what they have done.

The following week, make a list of the activities you have described.

Then calculate the percentage of time you spent doing each activity.

Now answer the following questions:

1. Does anything surprise you about the way you have spent the past week?
2. Was there anything unusual about your week?
3. What return are you getting for your time investment (i.e. how satisfied are you)?
4. Are there any changes you would like to make?
5. Can you see ways of saving time, if you wished to, so that you could invest it in something else?
6. Are there any gaps where you cannot recall what you were doing?
7. You will never have that week again. Was it a good way of spending your time?

ACTIVITY 9.3

My objectives

Draw a circle like the one below and divide it according to the amount of time you spend doing things (get this information from your timetable in Activity 9.2). The circle has been divided arbitrarily as an example.

Now draw another circle and divide it according to the way you would *prefer* to spend your time, keeping in mind that you must still sleep, eat and work. This is your circle of satisfaction.

Now answer the following questions:

1. Does anything surprise you about either of your circles?
2. Are there any differences between your circles of time and satisfaction? If so, what are they?

3. What does this say about the way you are living your life?
4. Is there anything you can do to get your circle of time spent into closer agreement with your circle of satisfaction?

Now complete the following table:

How I used my time last week

	Fill in this column
1. What is my overall impression of how I have spent the week?	
2. How much time have I given to what I like to do?	
3. How much time have I spent on what I don't like to do?	
4. How organised was I each day knowing what I wanted to achieve?	
5. Did anything not 'get done' that I wished had been done, because I 'put it off until another time'?	
6. Have I wasted other people's time? If so, how?	
7. Have I found time to relax?	
8. Have I 'wasted time'? How much? How?	
9. How much time was given to what I think is important?	
10. Did I use any time particularly successfully last week? Can I build on this next week?	
11. Have I spent time on routines or habits I would like to break?	
12. Did I use time spent waiting or travelling constructively?	
13. How much time did I allocate to my priorities?	
14. Have I given myself a reward for time well spent?	
15. Have I set myself some deadlines and met them?	

	Fill in this column
16. Did I ask myself frequently, 'What's the best use of my time right now?'	

Establishing your priorities

You may have come to the conclusion by now that you waste some of your time, and that you could use your time more fruitfully.

You now need to work out your priorities—that is, what *must* you do, what *can be delayed* and what can be done *if you have time left*.

ACTIVITY **9.4**

My priorities

Write out two lists:

1. What I *have* to do next week (or tomorrow).
2. What I *want* to do next week (or tomorrow).

Take each list in turn and put five ticks beside the most important item in each list, four ticks beside the next most important item and so on.

Now, taking the five most important items from each list, make a combined list of the 10 items and order them in priority from one to 10, with one being the most important. This list consists of *your priorities for the week (or tomorrow)*. Put it up somewhere where you will see it regularly, refer to it and strike off the items as you complete them. If anything is left, it must go into the priorities for the following week. Try to continue this activity every week (or day), so that you continue to use your time effectively.

How do you remember all the things you have to do? Some people trust their memories, others may use the proverbial 'knot in the handkerchief', but the best way is a list. You made lists in Activity 9.4. A list can be written on a piece of paper, in your diary, on your calendar, or it may take the form of an electronic organiser. There are now also several computer software programs available that are designed to help you establish and keep track of your priorities. Whatever form you use, the basis of all these options is a list. The benefits of a list are that it:

- takes away the worry
- ensures you do not forget
- helps you work out what is important.

Look at your list of priorities for tomorrow. You can colour-code it. For example, use red to underline or mark the things that must be done, green for things that would be useful to get done and blue for things that will not matter if you do not manage to get them done. As you finish a task marked in red, cross it off. It is very rewarding to see a set of red items crossed off at the end of each day. Carrying a diary with you is useful, too. You can carry a duplicate list in it and mark in advance events that must be dealt with—for example, planning a meal for your wedding anniversary or a meeting you must attend.

As these events arise, they can be built into the priority list for the day.

Doing the things you want to do

Time can be classified in three ways:

1. *Time to sell* is that time which, as adults, we sell to an employer, or as students we sell to a school, college or university. The pay-off is skills, occupational qualifications or education. Sold time goes beyond actual hours spent on the job. For example, it includes work done at home and travelling time.
2. *Time to keep things ticking over* is time spent in maintaining oneself (sleeping, eating, cleaning, dressing, etc.) and in maintaining others (supervising others, cooking for a family, baby-sitting, running errands, etc.).
3. *Time to choose* is what remains. We are free to spend this as we like.

If you work out your priorities as in Activity 9.4 and use a list in some form, you should increase your time to choose when you can do the things *you want to do*.

ACTIVITY 9.5

Activities you enjoy

Complete the table below and then, based on the information you have gained, answer the following questions:

1. How much time do I spend doing the things I enjoy?
2. How consciously and deliberately do I build into my life activities that I enjoy?
3. If I wanted more time to do more of the things that I enjoy, what would I have to change?
4. Do I want to do that?

The table can also be headed *Eight things I don't like to do*, and completed accordingly, focusing on how much of your time can be spent on activities that give little satisfaction. This can be compared quite usefully with the first list as a basis for reevaluating how you spend your time.

Eight things I enjoy doing

List eight things you like to do	Alone or with others (A or O)	Planned or spontaneous (P or S)	New or old (N or O)	How long since you last did it	Done freqently (F), sometimes (S), rarely (R), never (N)	Rank order 1–8 —Most like (1) to least like (8)
1						
2						
3						
4						
5						
6						
7						
8						

Saving time

Planning how best to use your time should allow you to feel a great deal more relaxed. You can save time if you are organised.

ACTIVITY **9.6**

Ideas for saving time

Can you think of ways to save time? Here are some ideas:

1. Do not waste waiting time. For example, if you ever find yourself waiting for a bus, an appointment, etc., instead of regarding this as a waste of time, see it as a gift of time. What are you now going to do with it? It could be time to relax and enjoy yourself thinking pleasant thoughts, time to think about a decision, time to review your daily checklist, time to catch up on some work-related reading, or time to read a book (always carry spare paper and a pen with you, and a book you must or want to read).

2. Make a daily checklist and prioritise the items. If you have priorities, you are less likely to waste time on your blue-marked (i.e. least important) items.

3. Set realistic deadlines and then write them in your diary.

4. Combine activities. For example, if you have something to discuss with a work colleague or friend, do it over lunch.

5. Have a place for everything.

6. Have a filing system. Buy some folders where you can file away papers, letters and documents. If you have access to a filing cabinet, use it

7. Think on paper.

8. Have a notebook by your bed, on your desk or in the kitchen. Never lose an idea because you have nowhere to record it. It might not come back again.

9. Give yourself time off and reward yourself for completing tasks. Without this, you might not want to save time.

10. Constantly ask yourself: 'How can I best use my time right now?'

Cultivating good habits

Without steps to cultivate and maintain good work habits, your time management efforts will be defeated. The following tips can help you stay on track:

- *Conquer the clutter.* Schedule 10 to 15 minutes each week to clear your work area of junk mail, old papers and other accumulated clutter. Change habits that lead to messes.
- *Defuse distractions.* Little distractions can add up to a major drain on productivity. If you're spending too much time on the phone or the Internet, keep an eggtimer at your desk. Learn how to terminate calls politely. If co-workers often drop in to chat, close your door. If you're constantly walking around obstacles, consider a change of floor plan. Take steps to reduce distracting noise.
- *Learn to say NO* once your priorities are set. Turning down an invitation doesn't mean you'll never be asked to do something again. Weigh the consequences. Making a decision based on what you know is best for you at the time leads to greater respect from your friends, not to a reputation as a party-pooper.
- *Stay away from the telephone* or turn off the mobile when you're trying to get work done. If it's really important, they'll call back.
- *Eliminate redundancy.* Analyse every process you use to determine if any steps can be eliminated. Common problems include multiple signatures for approval, extra steps designed to circumvent systems or correct problems that could be addressed more directly, and generating multiple copies that are no longer required.
- *Share the burden.* As any quilter knows, many hands make light work, especially when tackling tedious or large tasks. Performance of dreaded chores like the annual inventory can take on a party atmosphere when many are involved and frequent breaks are scheduled.
- *Seize the moment.* We all have a tendency to put off minor, less important tasks, and we also spend significant chunks of time holding on the phone or waiting in line. Can you see an opportunity here? Make a list of tasks that take five, 10 or 20 minutes, and keep the materials you need to do these tasks handy. That way, when you're put on hold or stuck in line, you can pull out that small job and finish it up.

- *Procrastination is the thief of time.* Procrastination masquerades in a million disguises. Avoid at all costs these common excuses:

'One more day won't make any difference; I'll just put that off until tomorrow.'

'It won't matter if I'm a few minutes late; no one else will be on time.'

'I can't start on this paper until I know just how I want the first paragraph to read.'

'I work best under pressure.'

'I'll watch just 15 more minutes of TV.'

By incorporating these simple time management strategies into your work day, you'll be more efficient, more organised—and much less likely to let tasks build up to a crisis level or slip through the cracks.

Taking time out

Persons under stress often report a sense of being overwhelmed with requests, problems and the concerns of others. Their sense of time is that they have no time for themselves. Periodic built-in blocks of time for catching one's breath and using one of the briefer relaxation or meditation techniques as a regular part of your daily schedule will reduce stress.

ACTIVITY **9.7**

Time out

This activity involves you in planning time for relaxation. 'Time out' is a way of relaxing for short periods during each day, especially while travelling to and from work. It is a way to relieve the stress of the day and to help avoid the stresses that immediately confront many of us as we walk through the doors of our homes. It is meant to be done daily. It should become a regular part of our lives so that other members of the family expect it to be followed. It is a routine that will occur automatically after a time.

- *Step 1:* At the end of the workday, take three to five minutes before leaving the workplace. Sit quietly, breathe deeply. Inhale through the nose to a count of four and exhale through the mouth to a count of four. Sit quietly breathing for these three to five minutes before going home.

- *Step 2:* If at all possible, try to find several different routes home. If you are privileged enough to live in a scenic area, try to explore a different route on different evenings. Make the drive home as pleasant as possible, and try to avoid the mad rush that is observed in so many commuters.
- *Step 3:* Try to find a scenic place on the way home. Stop there and take a little time to walk, relax or meditate. One way of 'meditating' is to accentuate one of the senses. For example, while walking and keeping your eyes open (but not paying much attention to what there is to see), listen carefully to the sounds of birds, trees moving in the wind, gravel crunching under your shoes, or even the sounds of traffic. Try it. It is a relaxing experience.
- *Step 4:* If driving, after you get home and the car is parked, do not go into the house right away. Sit and let the song on the radio finish. Or take a little time to think over the coming evening and plan it quietly in your mind. Take some time and walk around the block before going in. If you are a train or bus commuter, do the same. If at all possible, do not let anyone meet you at the station. Walk home.
- *Step 5:* Insist on a rule that for the first 15 minutes after any person who works arrives home, they will not be asked questions or informed of any crises of the day. The first 15 minutes is quiet time. It is a time to change clothes, fiddle around or do whatever you want. But until those 15 minutes are up, no problems, no crises and no gossip should be shared. Too many of us are confronted at the door every evening with the 'terrors' of the day. Insist that time be given to collect thoughts and get a sense of 'being home' before any new stresses have to be confronted.

Summary

The main points to remember about *Skill 9: Manage your time effectively* are:

- Establish and schedule your priorities.
- Ensure that you are spending your time in the way that *you* want to spend it, and in the way you have to spend it to achieve your goals and objectives.

- Adopt the method of time management that works best for you. While some type of a list forms the foundation of any time management strategy, this may take different forms (e.g. on paper with colour-coding, an electronic organiser or computer software).
- Take time out. Time for yourself—however you want to spend it—is vital for a balanced and stress-reduced life.

Taking control of your life and time will significantly reduce your stress levels.

SKILL 10

Be prepared for the future

Introduction

Two issues facing us that are likely to cause stress in the future, since we are actually experiencing them now, are:

1. A rapidly changing world
2. Increasing occurrence and awareness of disasters.

We must prepare as best we can for both of these stress-inducing conditions.

A rapidly changing world

To give some perspective on the rate of change, we can divide the past 50 000 years into about 800 lifetimes of 60 years each. The first 650 lifetimes were spent living in caves; writing has only been available for the last 70 lifetimes; print for the last six; and the electric motor for the last two. The introduction of most material goods and technological advances have been crammed into less than one lifetime! This is illustrated by Figure 10.1.

Things have always changed. The printing press took over from the quill pen; the petrol engine replaced the steam engine. The rate of change in modern civilisation has accelerated to such a degree that enormous numbers of people are experiencing disorientation and stress—something Alvin Toffler had predicted and named as 'future shock' in the book of the same name in 1980. Hardly do we become used to one change when another more extensive one is underway, particularly in the communications and mass media sphere. Human biological evolution is lagging behind developments in technology and lifestyle. Physiological and psychological stress emerge as the result of a growing deficit between daily demands and coping resources. Change generates stress by forcing us to make adjustments in our lives in a climate of uncertainty and unpredictability. There always seems to be background stress, like static on a poor transmission.

Figure 10.1 Technology time scale (not drawn to scale)

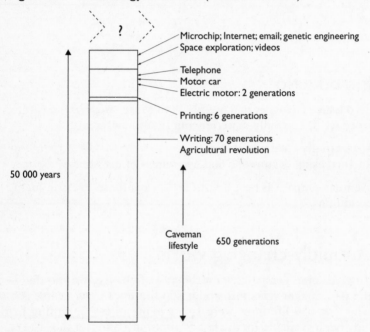

ACTIVITY 10.1

The rate of change

List the number of things you use each day at home, at work and in leisure activities that have been introduced in the last five to 10 years. Ask an older person about the changes that have occurred in their lifetime and note the contrast between the rate of change in the past and the current rate.

It is clear that many futurists such as Toffler (1980) and Ellyard (2000) see us moving into the twenty-first century as a post-industrial society. What we are experiencing is a worldwide transformation in production and processing methods, a move from heavy industry to professional services, and a move from local economies to massive regional and world economies controlled by multinational corporations and non-elected bodies like the WTO (Greider 1997). Of the top 100 economies 51 are corporations and some, like Exxon, have economies bigger than some African and South-East Asian states. Whether this should be the case, or how we as a society might cope with such issues and transformations, is for debate elsewhere. However, what is apparent already is that the impact of the technological future allied with a global economy underlain by an ill-balanced, so-called free trade system has already changed the social, economic, employment and future lifestyle for the generation at present in schools and colleges, and for future generations, particularly in less developed countries beset by the depredation of their natural non-renewable resources, unfair free trade, environmental issues and deskilling. Many big brand corporations employ no factory workers at all—outsourcing manufacture to create a corporate weightlessness, making nothing, but selling a brand which they morph into a lifestyle of aerated rubber footwear, multi-coloured logoed shirts and reversed caps. The global economy is not so much global in operation, but global in its ability to move freely to wherever next appears a more profitable production base or market (Barnet and Cavanah 1994). The whole context provides for multi sources of stress.

Technological change

Many terms have been used to designate the current technological revolution, many linked with the word 'age' such as 'computer age', 'robot age', 'microelectronic age', 'the knowledge age' and so on. Other terms describe new versions of society, such as 'information society' and 'postindustrial society'. We have other labels like the 'third wave', the 'global village', 'planetism' and so on. But whatever the name we prefer, it is indicative of a major discontinuity with the past. No matter what label future generations give this period, it will be remembered as an era of social, economic and industrial transformation that impacted on every aspect of life.

Change is an inevitable part of life and has been a feature of every era, impacting on social, economic and political life. Previous major changes in the way life was organised, the agricultural and industrial revolutions, both had massive effects in transforming the way people lived, where they lived and how they earned their livelihood. The latest change, the technological revolution with its microelectronics, communication super highways, nano-technology and bio-technology is no different in its impact on the way work and life itself will need to be reorganised. The shift will bring, among other things, new values, new pressures, new products, new services, new relationships, new ways of living out one's life, new sources of identity and esteem, new career structures, new demands for coping with change and new opportunities.

By its very nature, 'high tech' means constant transitions and change, and this means consistently high levels of stress from adapting to these changes. Our primitive mechanisms for adjusting to change are often overwhelmed by the high-tech world of change that we need to live and work within. Virtually everyone agrees that negative transitions such as job insecurity due to downsizing ('right-sizing', etc.), to financial insecurities (credit card debt, mortgages, college fees, stock market swings, etc.), to health challenges (sickness, chronic illness, injury, emotional symptoms of stress, etc.), to relationship insecurities (divorce, dating, family role changes, two-income families) and to international or regional political upheavals (as presented 'up close and personal' in our homes on television) are viewed as stressful, with potential downsides to our health and well-being. (A more detailed account of the effect of technology on work and lifestyle can be found in my 2002 book, *The Adult Learner at Work* 2nd edition (revised), Business and Professional Publishing Pty Ltd, Sydney.)

'Good' change: same results

Transitions and change are not always bad. However, even positive change can create responses within our primitive response mechanisms that can lead to negative symptoms of physical and emotional stress. Just in the past 10 years, the high-tech advances have increased expectations of productivity, and often time commitments to responding to the pressures from work. Do you remember life before fax machines, voice mail, email, cellular phones, cellular faxes, and yes, even the Internet? Sure, you can turn them off, ignore them, control them(?), but the pressures of response and keeping up with the changes of hardware/software technologies are still there, even if you do bury your head in the sands of denial.

Changing organisational structures and work patterns

Workforces themselves are becoming split between core and peripheral workers, many of whom are casual, part-time, agency-leased or on contract. A chasm is opening up between the permanently employed core employees who owe allegiance to the company and those on a variety of contract, part-time, contingency, agency-leased conditions who owe no allegiance. This can easily lead to a perception that there is second-class employment from which the employee benefits little, with risks being borne by the employee and employers bearing little risk or cost. The definitions of employee, employer, workplace and workday are reformulating in these conditions. One in five Australian workers are now casual (ABS, 2002).

Even the workplace is morphing into a blend of traditional brick and mortar elements and cyberspaces. Many workplaces are no longer a physical place but a bundle of services and settings that support workers no matter where or when they work. The pace of work is now, and is going to be, much more rapid and the virtual office door will never close. As physical location is no longer critical, 'going to work' becomes meaningless as work becomes what a person does rather than where a person goes. The same time, same place workplace is being replaced by the anytime, anywhere work space. Performance goals will become more explicit and measurement more objective—results will count.

As a result of these technological and economic changes to the structure and processes of work, some workers' jobs are disappearing, while for others who are luckier new job opportunities arise, although possibly accompanied by the traumas of retraining and/or relocation. Many managers and employees at all levels are finding that their tightly planned career paths are evaporating and job satisfaction is not necessarily guaranteed, while new roles in team leadership, and participation in decision making rather than overt managerial control, are the preferred skills for the future. This sort of scenario can seem bleak and threatening to many employees, whether at managerial or lower levels.

Workers entering the labour market today may have up to seven or eight major career changes in their working life. Obtained educational qualifications are no longer a guarantee of a job. Career development is starting to occur laterally rather than through the traditional 'climb the ladder' approach. Recurrent education and training, shorter working weeks, job sharing, term contracts, periods of casual employment, employment and unemployment, cooperative self-help ventures, flexitime, sabbaticals and early retirement are already becoming the building blocks of individually designed and constructed careers. All these changes can lead to traumatic alterations to the textures of peoples' lives, leaving some without an anchor for their psychological and personal identities.

Dual-career couples also face stress as they try to balance the work/home interface. Employers need to face the realities of the conflicting loyalties of such couples and address the organisational implications of these trends. Tensions at one are transferred into the other, there is role conflict and work overload, particularly as work time can spill over into family time. Around 60 per cent of Australian couples are dual-income earners, and women constitute approximately 50 per cent of the workforce (ABS, 2000).

The changes listed above are only a sample. But in order to cope with these challenges you need to prepare yourself with the stress skills already presented as well as carefully evaluate what particular changes are currently occurring in your life and those that have the potential to occur. In this way you will be better prepared to face the future and flow with the tide. Sudden changes may well be avoided and others adapted to with a smoother transition. Activities 10.2, 10.3 and 10.4 are an attempt to start you thinking along these lines and thereby ward off some of the stress of transition.

ACTIVITY 10.2

Your changing future world

Toffler suggested that one way to prepare for the future is by assessing how much time and emotional energy is invested in different aspects of one's life. The next step is to try to predict how our time and energy investments might alter, taking into account the sort of changes that seem likely. Such anticipation and preparation will reduce the effect of future shock stress and tension, and will aid improved coping and adjustment.

Complete the questionnaire below by assessing the percentage of time and the percentage of emotional energy that you now devote to these different activities and relationships. Also estimate the time and emotional energy investment for five years hence. This will be harder but give it a try, and remember your total percentage should not exceed 100.

Part of your life	Now		5 years from now	
	Percentage of time	Percentage emotional eenergy	Percentage of time	Percentage emotional energy
Work				
Study				
Recreation				
Religious activities				
Family				
Friendships				
Spouse/partner				
Parents				
Financial				
Hobbies				
Home				
Other				
TOTAL	100	100	100	100

1. Did you discover any areas that will change in your life?
2. How can you prepare for these changes?
3. Does your distribution of time reflect what you feel is important in your life now?
4. Will the changes enable you to distribute your time and energy better in terms of how you want to live?

> **GROUP CONTEXT**
> In a group context the leader should focus on how the percentage of time differed for different members, whether similar changes were identified, and how different members would prepare for and cope with change.

ACTIVITY 10.3

Changes during the next five years

Under the following headings, list the changes in your life that you think might occur over the next five years: *personal, work, study, family, community* and *nation*. Now answer these questions:

1. Choose the three changes that you think will have the greatest effect on your life.
   - What sort of effect will each of them have?
   - How will you deal with them?
   - What preparation can you start now that may help you to cope with the changes?
2. Which of the changes can you control and which can't you control? Who controls the changes in the latter case?
3. Which changes create the strongest negative feelings and reactions in you? Could anything good come out of them?
4. Examine your list. What can *you* as an individual change for the better?

ACTIVITY 10.4

Identifying personal reactions to future crises

Complete the crisis events list below. The events are divided into three groups of five. The events include crises that might affect your career, family, friends, possessions and self. In each grouping of events rank the items one to five, placing a '1' after the event that if it occurred now would cause the most severe crisis.

Consider whether each event would be as much of a crisis in five years' time by re-ranking them.

Possible crisis event	Rank now	Rank in 5 years
1. A friend/relative contracts AIDS.		
2. You become unemployed.		
3. Your parents get divorced.		
4. Your house is robbed.		
5. You become deaf.		
1. Your father retires.		
2. You (or your partner or spouse) becomes pregnant.		
3. A robot takes over your job.		
4. Your best friend gives you a bad investment tip and makes you bankrupt.		
5. Water has to be severely rationed permanently.		
1. To keep a job, you have to relocate to the other side of the continent.		
2. You become a paraplegic.		
3. A storm destroys your home.		
4. Your mother dies.		
5. A friend joins an urban terrorist campaign in your town.		

After completing the form, attempt the following questions:

1. Do crises that ranked as one and five in each group have anything in common (e.g. all related to family)?
2. Are there any differences between the events that are crises now and those that are crises in five years' time?
3. What skills do you need to handle the crises now and those of five years' hence?
4. How can you start preparing now for those occurring five years' hence?

Post traumatic stress disorder

The second major issue for the future lies in the increasing frequency of disasters with which we have to cope, not usually as participants but as unwilling witnesses to events shown perhaps too graphically on mass media.

What is it?

Post traumatic stress disorder (PTSD) is a stress disorder that can occur following severe stress (traumatic) experiences that produce intense emotional shock and may cause many emotional problems, such as being physically attacked, being in a serious accident, being in combat, being in a bushfire, flood or earthquake disaster, or being in a terrorist event. Even witnessing such events on television can be a traumatic event for some.

Events like these are becoming more common, and more and more people all over the world are becoming involved as victims, as witnesses (either present or through media reports), or as workers/volunteers in emergency response teams after the event. The thousands of people who directly experienced the terrorist attacks on New York and Washington, the millions who saw the resulting death and destruction on television, and the many hundreds who provided the rescue and emergency services, are encountering behavioural and emotional readjustment problems. Schlenger et al (2002) report 11 per cent PTSD in New York, compared to 4 per cent for the rest of the USA, with prevalence related to number of hours watched of televison coverage of the attacks. The New York Academy of Medicine (BBC, 2002a) found that 10 per cent of lower Manhattan residents reported major depression and dreams linked to the atrocity. There was also a significant increase in alcohol abuse, cigarette and marijuana smoking in New York (Vlahov et al, 2002).

Similar effects had been seen earlier after the Oklahoma City bombing. This resulted in 16 per cent of children who lived up to 100 miles away and not directly exposed, reporting significant PTSD symptoms two years later (Pfefferbaum et al, 2000); a year after the bombing, Oklahomans reported increased rates of stress, alcohol abuse and smoking compared to citizens of others cities (Smith et al, 1999). It is likely that events such as the 2002 floods in Europe and China, 2003 bushfires in Australia and California, as well as the Soham murders in the UK, will have their effects far beyond those who were directly involved as emergency crew, police or homeowners. It is apparent that the increasing likelihood of such events entering the lives of normal people will cause significant increases in stress disorders in the future.

After stressful traumatic experiences, people can find themselves having problems that they didn't have before the event. These responses are normal. Many people begin to feel much better within three months, but others recover more slowly, and some do not recover without professional help. PTSD is marked by clear biological changes as well as psychological symptoms. PTSD is complicated by the fact that it frequently causes other related disorders such as depression, substance abuse and memory problems. The disorder is also associated with impairment of the person's ability to function in social or family life, leading to occupational instability, marital problems and divorce, family discord and difficulties in parenting.

Threatened and actual current terrorist acts and natural disasters may result in whole societies questioning their fundamental view of the world as a predictable, just and meaningful place to live. Studies have shown that deliberate violence creates longer-lasting mental health effects than natural disasters or accidents. Re-establishing meaningful patterns of interactions in the community after a trauma may facilitate reconstruction of a sense of meaning and purpose. Many PTSD symptoms are normal responses to overwhelming stressors, but experts agree that the amount of time it takes people to recover depends both on what happened to them and on what meaning they give to those events.

Understanding PTSD

PTSD is not a new disorder. There are written accounts of similar symptoms that go back to ancient times, and there is clear documentation in the historical medical literature starting with the US Civil War, where a PTSD-like disorder was known as Da Costa's Syndrome. There are particularly good descriptions of post-traumatic stress symptoms in the medical literature on combat veterans of World War II and on Holocaust survivors.

Careful research and documentation of PTSD began in earnest after the Vietnam War. It was estimated in 1988 that the prevalence of PTSD in Vietnam veterans was 15 per cent, and that 30 per cent had experienced the disorder at some point since returning from Vietnam. PTSD has subsequently been observed in all military populations that have been studied, including from the Gulf War, in United Nations peacekeeping forces currently deployed around the world, as well as in rescue workers involved in the aftermath of disasters like New York and Oklahoma City, and emergency workers involved in bushfires, earthquakes, hurricanes and floods. PTSD also appears in military veterans in other countries with remarkably similar findings—that is, Australian Vietnam veterans experience much the same symptoms as American Vietnam veterans. PTSD is not just a problem for army veterans and emergency crews, however. A national study of American civilians conducted in 1995 estimated that the lifetime prevalence of PTSD was 5 per cent in men and 10 per cent in women.

PTSD can develop at any age, including in childhood. Symptoms typically begin within three months of a traumatic event, although occasionally not until years later. Available data suggest that about 8 per cent of men and 20 per cent of women who are exposed to a traumatic, stressful event experience some of the symptoms of PTSD in the days and weeks following exposure, and roughly 30 per cent of these individuals develop a chronic form that persists throughout their lifetime. The course of chronic PTSD usually involves periods of symptom increase followed by remission or decrease, although for some individuals symptoms may be unremitting and severe.

How do traumatic experiences affect people?

How serious the symptoms and problems are depends on many things, including a person's life experiences before the trauma, their own natural ability to cope with stress, how serious the trauma was, and what kinds of help and support a person gets from family, friends and professionals immediately following the trauma.

Because most highly stressed trauma survivors and emergency workers don't know how trauma usually affects people, they often have trouble understanding what is happening to them. They may think it is their fault that the trauma happened, or that they got involved in the disaster. They may think that they are going crazy, or that there is something wrong with them because other people who were there don't seem to have the same problems. They may turn to drugs or alcohol to make them feel better. They may turn away from friends and family who don't seem to understand. They may not know what they can do to get better. Specifically, the major symptoms are these.

Re-experiencing symptoms

Trauma survivors commonly continue re-experiencing their traumas—having the same mental, emotional and physical experiences that occurred during or just after the trauma, such as thinking about the trauma, seeing images of the event, feeling agitated, and having physical sensations like those that occurred during the trauma (flashbacks). Trauma survivors find themselves feeling and acting as if the trauma is happening again, feeling as if they are in danger, experiencing panic sensations (heart pounding, shaky), wanting to escape, getting angry, thinking about attacking or harming someone else. They are anxious and physically agitated, easily startled by loud noises or something/someone coming up from behind unexpectedly. They may have trouble sleeping as the flashbacks can occur in dreams. These experiences are not voluntary; the survivor usually can't control them or stop them from happening. These re-occurrence symptoms occur because a traumatic experience is so shocking and so different from everyday experiences that you can't fit it into what you know about the world; and bringing the memory back is actually part of the mind attempting to make sense of what has happened, as if to better digest it and fit it in.

Increased arousal

This is a common response and includes feeling jumpy, jittery, shaky, being easily startled, and having trouble concentrating or sleeping. Continuous arousal can lead to impatience and irritability, especially if you're not getting enough sleep. The arousal reactions are due to the fight or flight response in your body. People who have been traumatised often see the world as filled with danger, so their bodies are on constant alert, always ready to respond immediately to any attack. The problem is that while increased arousal is useful in truly dangerous situations, alertness becomes very uncomfortable when it continues for a long time, even in safe situations. Another reaction to danger is to freeze, like an animal in the headlights, and this reaction can also occur during a trauma.

Avoidance

This is a common way of managing trauma-related pain. The most common expression of avoidance is avoiding situations that remind you of the trauma, such as the place where it happened. Often situations and places that are less directly related to the trauma are also avoided, such as going out in the evening if the trauma occurred at night. Another way to reduce discomfort is trying to push away painful thoughts and feelings. This can lead to feelings of numbness, where you find it difficult to have any feeling, even pleasant or loving feelings. Sometimes the painful thoughts or feelings may be so intense that your mind just blocks them out altogether, and you may not remember parts of the trauma.

Anger

Many people who have been traumatised feel angry and irritable. If you are not used to feeling angry this may seem scary as well. It may be especially confusing to feel angry at those who are closest to you. Anger can also arise from a feeling that the world is not fair, or from frustration over the inability to control PTSD. It can also happen when other things that happened at the time of trauma made the person angry (the viciousness of the terrorist; inability to control the situation). Anger interferes with a person having positive connections and getting help, resulting in job problems, marital and relationship problems, and loss of friendships.

Problems in relationships with others

People who have been through traumas often have a hard time feeling close to people or trusting people. They can get wrapped up in their problems or get numb, and stop putting energy into their relationships with friends and family. This may be especially likely to happen when the trauma was caused or worsened by other people (as opposed to an accident or natural disaster). They can feel detached or disconnected from others, with less interest or participation in things they used to like to do. This can eventually lead to social isolation, through withdrawal and a lack of trust in others, a loss of support, friendship and intimacy. Sexual relationships may also suffer after a traumatic experience. Many people find it difficult to feel sexual. This is especially true for those who have been sexually assaulted, since in addition to the lack of trust, sex itself is a reminder of the assault.

Fear and anxiety

Anxiety is a common and natural response to a dangerous situation. For many it lasts long after the trauma ended. You may become anxious when you remember the trauma—but sometimes anxiety can come from out of the blue. Triggers or cues that can cause anxiety may include places, times of day, certain smells or noises, or any situation that reminds you of the trauma.

Self-blame, guilt and shame

These feelings can take over when PTSD symptoms make it hard to fulfill current responsibilities, or when people fall into the common trap of 'second-guessing' what they did or didn't do at the time of the trauma. Many people blame themselves for things they did or didn't do to survive. For example, some survivors believe that they should have done more to help others. You may feel ashamed because during the trauma you acted in ways that you would not otherwise have done. Feeling guilty about the trauma means that you are taking responsibility for what occurred. While this may make you feel somewhat more in control, it can also lead to feelings of helplessness and depression.

Grief and depression

This involves feeling down, sad, hopeless or despairing. You may cry more often. You may lose interest in people and activities you used to enjoy. You may also feel that plans you had for the future don't seem to matter anymore, or that life isn't worth living. These feelings can lead to thoughts of wishing you were dead, or doing something to hurt or kill yourself. Because the trauma has changed so much of how you see the world and yourself, it makes sense to feel sad and grieve.

Negative self-image

Self-image, self-esteem and sense of identity often become more negative after a trauma ('I am a weak, incompetent, or worthless person'). For instance, a person who thinks of himself as unselfish might think he acted selfishly by saving himself during a disaster. This might make him question whether he is really who he thought he was. It is also very common to see others more negatively, and to feel that you can't trust anyone. If you used to think about the world as a safe place, the trauma may suddenly make you think that the world is very dangerous. These negative thoughts often make people feel they have been changed completely by the trauma. Relationships with others can become tense, and it becomes more difficult to become intimate with people as your trust decreases.

Substance abuse and associated problems

PTSD is complicated by the fact that it frequently causes other related disorders, such as depression, substance abuse, and memory problems. There is nothing wrong with responsible drinking, but if your use of alcohol or drugs changes as a result of your traumatic experience, it can slow down your recovery and cause problems of its own. The disorder is also associated with impairment of the person's ability to function in social or family life, leading to occupational instability, marital problems and divorces, family discord, and difficulties in parenting. Headaches, gastrointestinal complaints, immune system problems, dizziness, chest pain, or discomfort in other parts of the body, are common.

What do trauma survivors need to know?

1. Traumas happen to many competent, healthy, strong, good people. No one can completely protect themselves from traumatic experiences.
2. Having symptoms after a traumatic event is *not* a sign of personal weakness. Many psychologically well-adjusted and physically healthy people, such as well-trained emergency response crews, develop PTSD.

Treatment of PTSD

There is no definitive treatment, and no cure. Some treatments appear to be quite promising, especially cognitive-behavioural therapy, group therapy and exposure therapy. Studies have also shown that medications help ease associated symptoms of depression and anxiety and help ease sleep. At present, cognitive-behavioural therapy appears to be somewhat more effective than drug therapy, but recent findings on the biological changes associated with PTSD have spurred new research into drugs that target these biological changes, which may lead to much-increased efficacy. Scientists are attempting to determine which treatments work best for which type of trauma. Some studies show that debriefing people very soon after a catastrophic event may reduce some of the symptoms of PTSD. A study of 12 000 schoolchildren who lived through a hurricane in Hawaii found that those who got counselling early on were doing much better two years later than those who did not. One-off debriefing after traumatic stress events appears ineffective and longer periods with trained counsellors seems necessary (BBC, 2002b).

Cognitive-behavioural therapy (CBT) involves working with cognitions to change emotions, thoughts and behaviours. *Exposure therapy* is a form of CBT unique to trauma treatment which uses careful, repeated, detailed imagining of the trauma (exposure) in a safe, controlled context to help the survivor face and gain control of the fear and distress that was overwhelming in the trauma. In some cases, trauma memories or reminders can be confronted all at once ('flooding'). For other individuals or traumas it is preferable to work gradually up to the most severe trauma by using relaxation techniques and either starting with less upsetting life stresses or by taking the trauma one piece at a time ('desensitisation').

Along with exposure, CBT for trauma includes learning skills for coping with anxiety (such as breathing retraining) and negative thoughts (positive thinking), managing anger, handling future trauma symptoms, as well as addressing urges to use alcohol or drugs when they occur ('relapse prevention'), and communicating and relating effectively with people ('social skills' or marital therapy).

Pharmacotherapy (medication) can reduce the anxiety, depression and insomnia often experienced with PTSD, and in some cases may help relieve the distress and emotional numbness caused by trauma memories. Several kinds of antidepressant drugs have achieved improvement in most (but not all) clinical trials, and some other classes of drugs have shown promise. At this time no particular drug has emerged as a definitive treatment for PTSD, although medication is clearly useful for the symptom relief that makes it possible for survivors to participate in psychotherapy.

Eye movement desensitisation and reprocessing (EMDR) is a relatively new treatment of traumatic memories which involves elements of exposure therapy and cognitive behavioural therapy, combined with techniques (eye movements, hand taps, sounds) which create an alteration of attention back and forth across the person's midline. While the theory and research are still evolving with this form of treatment, there is some evidence that the therapeutic element unique to EMDR, attentional alteration, may facilitate accessing and processing traumatic material.

Group treatment is often an ideal therapeutic setting because trauma survivors are able to risk sharing traumatic material with the safety, cohesion and empathy provided by other survivors. As group members achieve greater understanding and resolution of their trauma, they often feel more confident and able to trust. As they discuss and share coping of trauma-related shame, guilt, rage, fear, doubt and self-condemnation, they prepare themselves to focus on the present rather than the past. Telling one's story (the 'trauma narrative') and directly facing the grief, anxiety and guilt related to trauma enables many survivors to cope with their symptoms, memories, and other aspects of their lives.

Common components of PTSD treatment

Whatever single treatment or combination of treatments is applied, most of the following four processes are involved.

1. Trauma survivors and their families are educated about how persons get PTSD, how PTSD affects survivors and their loved ones, and other problems that commonly come along with PTSD symptoms. Understanding that PTSD is a medically recognised anxiety disorder that occurs in normal individuals under extremely stressful conditions is essential for effective treatment.
2. Exposure to the event via imagery allows survivors to re-experience the event in a safe, controlled environment, while also carefully examining their reactions and beliefs in relation to that event.
3. Examining and resolving strong feelings such as anger, shame, or guilt, which are common among survivors of trauma.
4. Teaching the survivor to cope with post-traumatic memories, reminders, reactions and feelings without becoming overwhelmed or emotionally numb. Trauma memories usually do not go away entirely as a result of therapy, but become manageable with new coping skills.

ACTIVITY 10.5 _____

PTSD screen test

If you have been exposed to a situation which may give rise to PTSD, please answer the following questions. Your responses will guide you into deciding whether to contact medical and/or psychological experts to receive help.

In your life, have you ever had any experience that was so frightening, horrible or upsetting that in the past month you:

1. Have had nightmares about it or
   thought about it when you did not want to?   YES   NO
2. Tried hard not to think about it or went
   out of your way to avoid situations that
   reminded you of it?   YES   NO
3. Were constantly on guard, watchful,
   or easily startled?   YES   NO
4. Felt numb, detached from others,
   from activities or your surroundings?   YES   NO

Research suggests that the results of this screening test should be regarded as positive if the person answers 'yes' to any two items.

Some guidance for emergency workers

How can you manage stress during a disaster operation?

- Develop a 'buddy' system with a co-worker.
- Encourage and support your co-workers.
- Take care of yourself physically by exercising regularly and eating small quantities of food frequently.
- Take a break when you feel your stamina, coordination or tolerance for irritation diminishing.
- Stay in touch with family and friends.
- Defuse briefly whenever you experience troubling incidents and after each work shift.

How can you manage stress after the disaster?

After the disaster:

- Attend a debriefing if one is offered, or try to get one organised within two to five days after leaving the scene.
- Talk about feelings as they arise, and be a good listener to your co-workers. Talk about what happened.
- Don't take others' anger too personally—it's often an expression of frustration, guilt or worry.
- Give your co-workers recognition and appreciation for a job well done.
- Eat well and try to get adequate sleep in the days following the event.
- Maintain as normal a routine as possible, but take several days to 'decompress' gradually.
- Enjoy some recreation.
- Avoid alcohol and drugs.

How can you manage stress after returning home?

After returning home:

- Catch up on your rest (this may take several days).
- Slow down—get back to a normal pace in your daily life.
- Understand that it's perfectly normal to want to talk about the disaster and equally normal not to want to talk about it; but remember that those who haven't been through it might not be interested in hearing all about it—they might find it frightening or simply be satisfied that you returned safely.
- Expect disappointment, frustration and conflict—sometimes coming home doesn't live up to what you imagined it would be—but keep recalling what's really important in your life and relationships so that small stressors don't lead to major conflicts.
- Don't be surprised if you experience mood swings; they will diminish with time.
- Don't overwhelm children with your experiences; be sure to talk about what happened in their lives while you were gone.
- If talking doesn't feel natural, other forms of expression or stress relief such as journal writing, hobbies and exercise are recommended.

What can other people do by themselves to cope?

- Spend time with other people. Coping with stressful events is easier when people support each other.
- If it helps, talk about how you are feeling. Be willing to listen to others who need to talk about how they feel.
- Get back to your everyday routines. Familiar habits can be very comforting.
- Take time to grieve and cry if you need to. To feel better in the long run, you need to let these feelings out instead of pushing them away or hiding them.
- Ask for support and help from your family, friends, church or other community resources. Join or develop support groups.
- Set small goals to tackle big problems. Take one thing at a time instead of trying to do everything at once.
- Eat healthy food and take time to walk, stretch, exercise and relax, even if just for a few minutes at a time.
- Make sure you get enough rest and sleep. People often need more sleep than usual when they are very stressed.
- Do something that just feels good to you, like taking a warm bath, taking a walk, sitting in the sun, or petting your cat or dog.
- If you are trying to do too much, try to cut back by putting off or giving up a few things that are not absolutely necessary.
- Find something positive you can do. Give blood. Donate money to help victims of the attack. Join efforts in your community to respond to this tragedy.
- Get away from the stress of the event sometimes. Turn off the television news reports and distract yourself by doing something you enjoy.

What can adults do to help children cope?

- Let them know you understand their feelings. Provide extra reassurance and emotional support.
- Create a safe environment so that they feel they really are safe. A familiar environment and keeping to your usual routines is best. Children prefer things to be consistent and familiar.

- Keep them from seeing too many frightening pictures of the events.
- Be honest about what happened but make sure the information you provide is appropriate to their developmental level. Let them know they can ask questions.
- Be aware that children will take on the anxieties and other emotions of people around them, so try not to show to much anxiety or revengefulness and anger.
- Try to put the traumatic situation into perspective. Children need to know that an earthquake, terrorist act or house fire is likely to be a rare event.

The 'Serenity Prayer' of theologian Rheinhold Niebuhr, adopted by Alcoholics Anonymous, reflects the approach needed by those likely to meet stressful conditions:

> God, grant me the serenity to accept the things I cannot change;
> courage to change the things I can;
> and the wisdom to know the difference—
> living one day at a time;
> enjoying one moment at a time;
> accepting hardships as the pathway to peace.

Summary

The main points to remember about *Skill 10: Be prepared for the future* are:

- Learning to accept that the future is going to be very different from the present will help you prepare for the future.
- Planning for the future will make you better prepared for the stressful life events that are bound to occur in everybody's life now and in the coming years—a climate of rapid and, in some cases, very dramatic change.

By learning the skills in this book, you should have the confidence and strength to cope more effectively with possible adversity, and be adequately prepared to deal with the 'future shocks' that may occur in your life.

FINALE
Your contract for change

Introduction

By now you should be aware of what stress is, its sources, its effects and how to manage it. In developing a stress management plan, it is essential that you do not continue with a habitual response that may not be effective. One way of avoiding this is by having several alternative stress-reducing plans.

From among the various alternatives, it is necessary that at least one be selected for implementation. There are at least three criteria against which each alternative must be judged:

1. The desirable and undesirable short-term consequences that are likely to emerge if the alternative is selected.
2. The feasibility of each alternative. Feasibility takes into consideration your lifestyle, the likely degree of support from significant others and the likelihood of positive reinforcement from the societal elements with which you strongly identify.
3. The long-term probable effects of each alternative.

Different techniques will appeal to different people. Some jog away stress, others use muscle relaxation, some do breathing exercises while others seek a support group. The important thing is to experiment with each to see which one most readily suits the kind of person you are.

Inappropriate ways of managing stress

As long as a strategy for managing stress does not itself cause stress, it will be appropriate. Inappropriate strategies could have long-term side-effects that might have more harmful effects than the original problem. For example, prescribed medication such as sleeping pills, self-administered drugs such as cigarettes and alcohol, over-eating, aggression and anger, and obsessional behaviour are all inappropriate ways of managing stress.

Reminder for new actions and attitudes

The following table is a short summary to pin up in a conspicuous spot for you to refer to daily. It will act as a reminder for new attitudes and actions. Underline those that you find valuable.

Appropriate ways of managing stress and minimising worry

Actions to take	Attitudes to adopt
Talk it out	Share it with someone else. Others will welcome your trust.
Write it out	It is easier to see it in perspective when it is on paper.
Shrug it off	Raise your shoulders, then drop them. Relax your body.
Breathe it away	Inhale deeply and exhale heavily a few times. Calm your thoughts.
Sort it out	List practical options, weigh, decide and then act.
Delay it	Set aside 15 minutes for a worry session, and leave it until then.
Work it off	Do something physical. Clear your head, divert your energy.
Reverse it	Consider taking an opposite approach, explore alternatives.
Laugh it off	Lighten it with humour. Be generous with smiles.
Distance it	Imagine yourself a few years from now. How much will it matter then?
Balance it	Consider the good consequences and feel glad about them.
Cancel it	Think positively, don't let the negative pull you down.
Exaggerate it	Picture the worst that could *really* happen. Is it likely?
Win through it	Imagine yourself being successful and feel good about it
Hold it	Say 'stop', pause and then think. Now take a fresh look.
Escape it	Notice something enjoyable around you. Get into the present.

ACTIVITY **F.1**

Review your Stress Diary

1. Review your Stress Diary, identifying the activities and events that most commonly create stress in your life, and noting the behaviours you typically adopt to respond to them.
2. Recall all the ways for minimising stress that you have learnt
3. What activities and events seem to keep coming up as stressors? Do you notice, for example, that every time you meet the union representative an argument develops, or that when you do work on a particular subject you get a headache?
4. How do you typically feel when this stressor comes up? How does your body react?
5. What do you usually do when confronted with your most common stressors? What change in attitude or behaviour in response to your stressors have you noticed since you started doing the activities and practising the skills taught in this book?
6. What behaviours or attitudes seem to work best for you? What responses do not seem to work? Do your coping techniques support and promote your physical and mental health?

ACTIVITY **F.2**

Your contract for change

Prepare a contract for change. For example, 'My goal is to be less anxious about my job', or 'to be more assertive when someone asks me to do something I don't want to do'. It should relate to an issue that occurs in your Stress Diary, and which you have not managed successfully, but would like to change. Using your knowledge of the 10 skills for reducing stress, fill in the contract.

My contract for change
1. My goal is to _____
2. I will _____ from _____ (date) _____ to _____ and I will record my progress in a log _____
3. My support person will be _____
4. My support person will help me by _____
5. Along the way I will reward myself by _____
6. My end reward will be _____
Date _____ Signature _____

Assessment and review

After you feel you have achieved your contract with yourself, fill in the work activity analysis questionnaire (Activity I.1, page 20) again to see if there are any major differences in the levels of stress and tension or the numbers of stressed behaviours you are experiencing. If your score is higher than before, you are now likely to be:

- more proactive
- managing your job responsibilities more efficiently
- coping better with the pressure of work
- anticipating fires
- more in control of your job.

These improvements should also be flowing into your personal life, and you probably 'feel happier'.

Summary and conclusion

Remember stress by itself is not bad for you; it is your way of dealing with stress that may be harmful. Recognise those stress signs in yourself, and put some or all of the 10 skills to work for you. That is what this book has been about.

Let us leave the last word to von Bertalanffy (1971):

The principle of stress so often invoked in psychology, psychiatry and psychosomatics needs some re-evaluation. As in everything in this world stress too is an ambivalent thing. Stress is not only a danger to life to be controlled and neutralised by adaptive mechanisms; it also creates higher life. If life after disturbance from outside had simply returned to the so-called homeostatic equilibrium it would never have progressed beyond the amoeba which after all is the best adapted creature in the world—it has survived billions of years from the primeval ocean to the present day. Michelangelo implementing the precepts of psychology should have followed his father's request and gone into the wool trade thus sparing himself life-long anguish although leaving the Sistine Chapel unadorned.

References

Introduction

Cobb, S. and Rose, R.H. (1973) Hypertension, peptic ulcer and diabetes among air traffic controllers. *Journal of the Australian Medical Association* 224: 489–92.

Cooper, C. L., Davidson, M, and Robinson, P. (1982) Stress in the police service. *Journal of Occupational Medicine* 24: 30–6.

Cooper, C.L. and Melhuish A. (1980) Occupational stress and managers. *Journal of Occupational Medicine* 22: 588–92.

Cooper, C. L., Mallinger, M. and Kahn, R. (1978). Occupational stress among dentists. *Journal of Occupational Psychology* 51: 227–34.

Crump, J., Cooper, C.L. and Maxwell, V.B. (1981) Stress among air traffic controllers. *Journal of Occupational Behaviour* 2: 293–303.

Darley, M. and Latane, B. (1970). *The Unresponsive Bystander.* New York: Appleton: Century Croft.

Davidson, M. and Cooper, C.L. (1983). *Stress and the Woman Manager.* Oxford: Martin Robertson.

Erickson, J., Pugh, W. and Gunderson, K. (1972) Status congruency as a prediction of job satisfaction and life stress. *Journal of Applied Psychology* 45: 523–25.

European Agency for Safety and Health at Work, Dec. 2001. Report: *Stress at Work.*

Health and Safety Executive (HSE) (2000). Bristol Stress and Health at Work Study.

Kelly, M. and Cooper, C.L. (1981) Stress among blue collar workers. *Employee Relations* 3: 6–9.

Lazarus, R. (1966). *Psychological Stress and the Coping Process.* New York: McGraw-Hill.

MORI poll on work stress (2001).

O'Brien, G. and Kabanoff, B. (1978) Work, health and leisure. Working paper No. 28, Flinders University National Institute of Labour Studies, SA.

Otway, H.J. and Misenta, R. (1980) The determinants of operator preparedness for emergency situations in nuclear power plants. International Workshop, Austria.

Russell, R.W. (1978) Environmental stress and the quality of life. *Australian Psychologist* 13: 143–59.

Seligman, M. (1975) *Helplessness.* San Francisco: Freeman.

Tertiary Education Union (2002) July. Survey of Australian Academics.

Toffler, A. (1980) *Future Shock.* London: Bodley Head Press.

TUC (1996) Survey of Safety Representatives.

TUC (2000) Survey of Safety Representatives.

VAR International survey (2001) for National Stress Awareness Day.

Skill 1

Atkinson, R.L. et al. (1996). *Introduction to Psychology* (Ch. 2). New York: Harcourt.

Freidman, M. and Rosenman, R. (1974). *Type A Behaviour and Your Heart.* Greenwich: Fawcett Press.

Gross, R. and McIlveen, R. (1998). *Psychology—A New Introduction* (Ch. 5). London: Hodder and Stoughton.

Kelly, H.H. (1950). The warm-cold variable in first impressions. *Journal of Personality* 18: 431–38.

Kiecolt-Glaser, J.K., Marucha, P.T., Malarkey, W.B., Mercado, A.M., Glaser, R. (1995). Slowing of wound healing by psychological stress. *Lancet* 346: 1194–6.

Kiecolt-Glaser, J.K., Glaser R., Gravenstein, S., Malarkey, W.B., Sheridan, J. (1996). Chronic stress alters the immune response to influenza virus vaccine in older adults. *Proc. Natl. Acad. Sci.* 93: 3043–7.

Leshan, L. (1964). The world of the patient. *Journal of Chronic Diseases* 17: 119–26.

Leuba, C. and Lucas, C. (1949). The effects of attitudes on descriptions of pictures. *Journal of Experimental Psychology* 35: 517–24.

Marucha, P.T., Kiecolt-Glaser, J.K., Mucosal, F.M. (1998). Wound healing is impaired by examination stress. *Psychosom. Med.* 60: 3625.

Powell, L. (1987). Issues in the management of Type A behaviour. In Vasl, S. and Cooper, C. (eds), *Stress and Health.* London: Wiley.

Redman, B. (1988) *The Process of Patient Education.* Washington: Mosby.

Seligman, M. E. (1975). *Helplessness.* San Francisco: Freeman.

Selye, H. (1956). *The Stress of Life.* New York: McGraw-Hill.

Stoney, C.M., Bausserman, L., Niaura, R., Marcus, B., Flynn, M. (1999). Lipid reactivity to stress: II. Biological and behavioral influences. *Health Psychology* 18: 241–51.

Taylor, S. et al (2000). Bio-behavioural responses to stress in females. *Psychological Review* 107: 411–29.

Skill 3

Benson, H. (1976). *The Relaxation Response.* New York: Avon Books.

Jacobson, E. (1938). *Progressive Relaxation.* Chicago: University of Chicago Press.

Skill 5

Berne, E. (1972). *What Do You Say After You Say Hello?*. London: Corgi.

Skill 6

Ellis, A. (1977). 'Rational emotive therapy', *Cognitive Psychology*. 7: 2–12.
Glasser, W. (1976). *Positive Addiction*. New York: Harper & Row.

Skill 10

ABS (Australian Bureau of Statistics) (2000). Australia Now—Employment. Canberra: Australian Government Publishing Services.
ABS (2002). Australian Social Trends 2001: Work–Paid work. Reported on ABC NewsOnline, 13 September 2002.
Barnet, R. and Cavanah, J. (1994). *Global Dreams*. Simon & Schuster: New York.
BBC (British Broadcasting Corporation) (2002a). Reported on BBC NewsOnline, 29 March.
BBC (2002b). Report of study by Emmerik, A., University of Amsterdam, BBC NewsOnline, 5 September.
Ellyard, P. (2000). Preparing for Thrival in a Planetist Future. Paper to Community Services and Health Industry Conference, Melbourne.
Greider, W. (1997). *One World—Ready or Not*. Simon & Schuster: New York.
Pfefferbaum, B., Seale, T. and McDonald, N. (2000). Post-traumatic stress two years after the Oklahoma City bombing. *Psychiatry: Interpersonal and Biological Processes* 63(4): 224–35.
Raphael, B. (2000). *Disaster Mental Health Response Handbook*. NSW Health Department: Sydney.
Schlenger, W.E. et al (2002). Psychological reactions to terrorist attacks: Findings from a national study of American reaction to Sept 11. *Journal of the American Medical Association* 288(5): 581–88.
Smith, D., Vincent, R. and Hann, N. (1999). Population effects of the bombing of Oklahoma City. *Journal of Oklahoma State Medical Association* 92: 193–8.
Toffler, A. (1980). *Future Shock*. London: Bodley Head Press.
Vlahov, D. et al (2002). Increased use of cigarettes, alcohol and marijuana among Manhattan residents after September 11 terrorist attacks. *American Journal of Epidemiology* 155(11): 988—96.

Finale

von Bertalanffy, J. (1971). *General System Theory*, 2nd edn. Hammondsworth: Penguin, p. 61.